# RED SAINT, PINK DAUGHTER

SILVIA RODGERS

# Red Saint,

# Pink Daughter

*A Communist Childhood in Berlin and London*

ANDRE DEUTSCH

First published in 1996 by
André Deutsch Limited
106 Great Russell Street
London WC1B 3LJ

CIP data for this title is available
from the British Library

ISBN 0 233 98973 0

Printed in Great Britain by
St Edmundsbury Press, Bury St Edmunds, Suffolk

With love and affection for
Bill
Rachel, Lucy, Juliet,
Laura, Millie, Alexander, Thomas, Jacob, Isabel
and in memory of
Hélène.

# CONTENTS

# ACKNOWLEDGMENTS

As this is more or less an autobiography my greatest debt is to all those whose names appear in it, living and dead.

Details of my mother's life have been augmented by what she told my husband and our daughters in recorded conversations shortly before her death.

I am grateful for the access I had to the archives of the Wiener Library in London and the Institut für die Geschichte der Arbeiterbewegungen in Berlin. Their staff, and that of the Highgate Literary and Scientific Institution, were very helpful in checking certain factual details, as were a number of friends: Chris Basista, Ellen Dahrendorf, Ralf Dahrendorf, Tim Everard, Hugo Gryn, Yvonne Kapp, Betty Lewis, Ioan Lewis, Annegret O'Dwyer, and Renate Schussler.

I was glad that Wyn Borger was with me on my visit to postwar Poland. She and her son Julian Borger were a great comfort. Julian also provided practical help and valuable background material. Recent visits to Berlin, though in many ways difficult, were made enjoyable by Josiane Everard's and Andrea Loebell-Buch's kindness and understanding.

I am grateful to Anthony Lester for support for the idea of the book and to others who generously read the draft in whole or in part at different stages, among them Margot Finn, John Grigg, Patsy Grigg, Julia Neuberger, Eva Tucker, Ilse Yardley and Barbara Sand, who read certain chapters more than once.

I owe a particular debt to my agent Hilary Rubinstein for his wise professional advice and warm personal encouragement, and to Karen Lewis for her insight and editorial suggestions. Special thanks to my publisher Tom Rosenthal, who showed such enthusiasm, and to my editor David Wilson for his patience. He and Katherine Hockley, both at André Deutsch, have done so much to get the book ready for publication.

Rodney Needham, formerly Professor of Social Anthropology at

Oxford, may not realize how much I owe him. He taught me to write clear and concise English, not my first language.

My daughters were very keen that I should write this book. They read draft chapters with curiosity and delight mixed with pertinent criticism. As for my husband, he supported the venture from beginning to end, read the separate chapters and the whole book, including the proofs, and was rigorous and understanding in his many suggestions.

Silvia Rodgers

# PROLOGUE

I was born in the Berlin that Stephen Spender called 'the centre of the world', yet I was always off-centre. I was a Polish child in the German capital, a Communist child in a Fascist state, a Jewish child in a German school, an atheist child in a Jewish orthodox school, a refugee child in England, and later, when I was the wife of a British MP, Cabinet Minister, co-founder of a new party, peer of the realm, I may have looked an insider but that was misleading. Always, and from birth, I was on the periphery of politics.

I soon realised that I had never even been near the centre of my mother's world and that this story is as much about me and my mother as about my life as an outsider in other spheres. I wish it were otherwise because I hate to admit how powerful an influence or burden my mother, who died in 1979, still is within me. She is an immortal atheist.

I think of her as a saint not because I believe that's what she was, but it was how she liked to see herself – or rather she always said that was how others saw her. A red saint because she was revolutionary rather than sacred; her halo shone with the scarlet luminance of Marxism, and her idea of heaven was the Soviet Union. While my mother was a saint whose religion was global and mattered more to her than any one person, my father strove to be a despot or master in his own house. But he failed and is a much more shadowy figure in my life – my brother even more so.

I could divide my life into two phases: the first in Berlin when I lived under dictatorships – inside and outside the home where I saw everything through my mother's eyes and was a fervent Communist; the second in London, married to Bill Rodgers, when there was democracy within and without, when I was a Social Democrat and began to see at least some things through my own eyes. Of course, it is not as simple as that. There is an intermediate phase in London when the only dictatorship was inside the home, when even that came to an end and I had some time as an independent feminist without either mother or husband. But this book is essentially about me on a variety of private and social boundaries, edges and hedges during the first and intermediate phases. Plot the etymology of hedge or edge, and it will lead to *Hexe*, the German word for a witch. A witch is always an outsider.

# ONE

# Red Wedding and Blood

My slinky black dress is adorned for the occasion with huge cream satin sleeves. A tiara decorates my hair. 'You look like Josephine,' says my friend Helge, who writes about marriage and about chocolate. The occasion is the State Opening of Parliament in all its glittering pomp and circumstance. I feel as if I have intruded into an eighteenth-century painting. I sit on the floor of the House of Lords and all around are peers and some baronesses in robes of scarlet trimmed with ermine, and peeresses in glamorous and sparkling gowns and tiaras most of which – unlike mine – are heirlooms made of real diamonds. The Queen in crown jewels and satin, waits for the Commoners to come in. No one looking at me and not knowing me would regard me as anything other than belonging, and belonging to the centre of things. And yet my otherness won't lie down.

I was born on the Berlin Wall. Draw the course of the Wall and you draw across 44 Adalbertstrasse, the site of what was my home and where the Wall was put up thirty-three years after I had worked my way out of my mother's womb. At that precise moment she was lying in the Jewish Hospital in Wedding. Only in English does the name Wedding invoke a romantic rite of passage. Then as now, Wedding was the poorest district in Berlin. During the Weimar Republic, it was the hub of Communist activity and known as Der Rote Wedding.

My birth certificate is a small and indifferent scrap of paper except that it announces that I was born in the Weimar Republic. I am vain about being a child of Weimar, an exotic time and place, where Mr Norris caught his train, Marlene Dietrich doffed her top hat and crossed her silken legs and Dr Caligari went in and out of his Kabinett. Some of that political and artistic excitement and vivacity must surely have rubbed off on all its children.

I am well aware of the social realities hidden in all that effervescence, and as a child knew more about those miseries than the veneer of glamour. It was possible to be a child in Weimar Berlin without being aware of political mayhem, unemployment, hunger and disease and prostitution. If one's parents were German, even German Jewish and comfortably middle-class, one could lead a sheltered life in a bourgeois house in Grunewald, that most superior of suburbs. Daisy Meyer, my best friend when I was ten, lived there in cushioned ignorance at least until 1933. The only sorrow she might have been aware of was a paucity of male relatives because of the 1914–18 war, the only fear, economic slump. Her family's interests would have extended no further than musical evenings with friends, concerts on Sunday mornings in Schinkel's elegant Schauspielhaus and evenings at the Opera. The only political names she dimly knew were those of ex-Kaiser Wilhelm, the late President von Hindenburg, and Hitler.

But I was born to parents who were active card-carrying members of the German Communist Party – the KPD – who did not live in a safe suburb, who were Polish, not German Jews, and who brought me up to worship the names of Lenin, Luxemburg and Liebknecht. Political strife and demonstrations were part of everyday life.

On film, in eye-witness accounts in Communist newspapers and books by foreign and native authors who were there, people brawl and march. It's what they're doing in Isherwood's novels and in Erich Kästner's novel *Fabian*. Kästner published *Emil und die Detektive* in 1928, the year I was born. He wrote *Fabian* in the first couple of years of my life but, unlike *Emil*, this is no book for children. It is despairingly prophetic about what was to come and describes vividly the pervading sexual and political violence. When in a pub, a Nazi scrawls a swastika on the table at which a Communist sits and drinks, both draw guns and shoot it out. No policeman bothers to intervene and Fabian, the onlooker, takes the wounded pair to the nearest hospital. The doctor smiles: 'You've brought me two politicians? . . . Altogether, we've had nine cases brought in tonight . . . These political brawls are indistinguishable from dance hall scraps.'

I have no conscious memory of marches or fighting in the streets but my mother used to boast how her little girl always waved to Communist marchers, though one day she waved to the wrong lot.

I had stood at the open window and called out, 'Come, Mummy, look: *Proletarier!*' and waved enthusiastically. My mother hauled me indoors. 'They are not *Proletarier*. They are Nazis. They are bad men!' But I was still under five and forgiven for not recognising the difference.

As my birth certificate shows, I was born when the Republic was nine years old, nine years after the assassination of Rosa Luxemburg and Karl Liebknecht, five years after inflation of surreal proportions had panicked everyone but a few speculators, after several governments of various moderate hues had been in and out, after several putsches of the left and of the right had been attempted and repelled. Art was still flourishing but Nazism was on the rise and the worst was still to come.

Not only my childhood was permeated by these social and political upheavals. Politics had entered my circulation at conception and during gestation. And like a drug, politics was good for me as well as bad. During her pregnancy, my mother neither smoked nor drank but she did continue to indulge in politics. She may not have carried banners or made speeches in the later stages, but she wrote leaflets, distributed them and attended cell meetings until contractions finally diverted her. But even a fanatical Communist like her, caught up in the turmoil of Weimar and the work of the KPD, could still be tormented by nothing more political than the colour of my hair when I was born.

Never mind that it was 1928, the year when elections brought in for the first time a government with a Social Democratic leader, that Hitler's Brownshirts were stepping up their street fights, that unemployment stood at two million and rising fast, that outside Berlin 60,000 metal workers had been locked out, and that George Grosz, a member of my mother's party, was being prosecuted for obscene drawings. In the midst of all that frenzy, what bothered my mother was that I was born with red hair. In a way I am glad, as it shows her to be more human than the single-minded Communist Party activist.

My mother hated the colour of my hair and accused the nurses of a mix-up. Wasn't her own hair black, and her husband's, too? The problem for my mother was that her father had red hair and she despised him. *'Er war ein gutmütiger Mann'*, but it was this good-naturedness that she could not abide. I don't know why she used to tell me so often how she rejected me at birth because my hair was the wrong colour, nor why she told me so early on. It was as if she could hardly wait to tell me. Her dislike of my gingery hair is something I have grown up with. In spite of this, I like the colour of my hair. It is an essential part of my identity. As Samson depended on the length of his hair, I depend on the colour of mine.

I grew up with another story about my birth but in this one red was the colour of my mother's blood, not my hair. More dramatic and more gory, this story tells of how my mother nearly died. The placenta which had fed me for nine months had not been completely expelled, and back in her own bed my mother began to haemorrhage so profusely that the blood dripped through the mattress. The prognosis was hopeless, the doctors gave up.

But my mother, a passionate atheist, was nursed by a nun from a nearby convent. Sister Beatrix, wringing her hands at the fate of *'Die arme junge Mutter'*, begged her to try her own special remedy. From an apothecary in a small town not too far away she ordered what sounds like a stone. Several times a day and night, she ground this stone up for my mother to swallow neat. 'It was horrible and disgusting. Like eating debris from a building site,' shuddered my mother. But swallow she did, and she got better and she lived. While grinding the stone and feeding it to my mother, Sister Beatrix had been praying to God to save her patient. My parents laughed at the very idea that God could have replenished my mother's red corpuscles. Just as they laughed at the idea that He could have put them there in the first place.

When my mother's convalescence was over, she asked Sister Beatrix how she could repay her. 'Frau Szulman, christen your baby a Catholic, I beg you.' Of course, to my freethinking parents, this was the very request they could not possibly fulfil. How, in fact, did they repay her? Being my parents they had to challenge her life, her faith, and advocate their own convictions and dogma. 'Have you ever *seen* God?' they kept asking her, and as she was no St Bernadette or St Joan and not given to visions, she had no adequate reply. My mother, even as she languished near death, must have been very forceful and my father too could be quite persuasive. But in this case their Marxist proselytising never seemed very successful: they couldn't even persuade her to sleep in our flat. She often stayed the whole night but only to watch over my mother. To have slept anywhere else but in her cell would have contravened the Order.

Some time after Sister Beatrix had stopped coming, the convent telephoned to enquire of her whereabouts. She had jumped over the wall.

Was her leap all that surprising? There must have been other factors that pushed her, but I imagine that in any crisis of faith she heard my parents' comments echo in her cell. No missionaries were ever more zealous.

Jumping over the wall was a drastic step but at that time confined to nuns and monks. It is ironic that the house whose occupants might have provoked Sister Beatrix to jump was the site where, thirty-three years on, a wall was built in actual concrete. This wall protected the dogma that had been preached by my parents and was far more drastic to cross than the convent wall. The transition was not only from one ideology to another but, in 150 cases, from life to death.

In 1928, the idea of the Berlin Wall was unbelievable. A fortune-teller seeing the Wall in her crystal ball would have shut up shop and pleaded a nervous breakdown. But in fact we were already living along a boundary. The Weimar Republic itself was a boundary – not spatial like the Wall, but temporal and ideological. The Berlin Wall separated Eastern European Communism from Western Democratic Capitalism; the Weimar Republic was the democratic wedge between the Imperial reign of Kaiser Wilhelm II and Nazism. Whereas, apart from graffiti on its western side, the Wall was dead and barren, the Republic sizzled with elements opposed to both the regimes it separated.

The lifetime of the Weimar Republic was half that of the Wall, but its fourteen years were so exuberant, so crammed full of innovations, as if the collective unconscious understood time was short. I am gratified to be one of the offsprings of the Republic. I am even proud of the decadence it is famous for, proud too, though with a post-dated sense of doom, of its political events and reforms. They make up a staggering list for so brief a time: a revolution, an abdication, the replacement of the Imperial reign by a democracy which involved a brand-new constitution, a new government consisting of parties of the centre, a Social Democrat as first Reichskanzler, and new elections based on proportional representation, which brought more women into the Reichstag. Censorship was abolished and ideas of pacifism and internationalism and atheism allowed to be disseminated. Artistic achievements in all categories were dazzling. I grew up believing that all innovative artists, and even the more conventional ones like Max Liebermann, were politically committed to the Left – in Weimar's Berlin that was how it seemed. Many were members of the KPD: like Grosz, Piscator, Weill, and Herzfeld, who changed his name to Heartfield.

I could have been born into an unfolding Utopia but instead it was a cauldron that bubbled with as much misery as creativity. By the time I was born censorship was again on the increase, but during that push and pull of creativity and repression much enduring and progressive art was still being produced. When Hitler crushed the Weimar Republic in 1933 he did his best to destroy the art he despised as a *Trümmerhaufen*, a heap of rubble. In the end it was Hitler's legacy that was reduced to a heap of rubble, in reality and metaphorically. After the destruction of much of Berlin in 1945, the women who scavenged and rummaged in the rubble to keep their families alive were dubbed *Trümmerfrauen* or rubble women.

The outlawed art and architecture survived to be influential, though not in the Third Reich. The Bauhaus has asserted itself in America in public buildings as well as lesser artefacts. And even as I wander into our nearest Habitat, I see familiar objects – chairs, storage jars, units, lamps. All have integrated – rather better than I – into the British environment.

Were I to design a series of stamps to commemorate Weimar, I would have to depict deprivation and destruction as well as creative achievements. I would start with the assassination of Rosa Luxemburg, and finish with the rise of Hitler set against the burning

Reichstag. For the stamps in between I would pick out brawls between the Nazi Brownshirts and the KPD; Marlene Dietrich decadent in the top hat and cane outfit she wears in *Der blaue Engel*; a still from *Das Kabinett des Dr Caligari* by Wiener side by side with one from *Kameradschaft* by Pabst; a drawing by Grosz or Kollwitz, of the deprivation of the working class; a painting by Dix of a prostitute with a soldier hideously disfigured by a war wound; a Bauhaus building – either by Gropius or Mies van der Rohe – and a Breuer chair.

I would leave out a portrait of Hindenburg – he already has a stamp to himself – but I would be wrong because he signifies the old values of Germany which resisted any changes in politics and art but were nevertheless part of Weimar. For a seventh stamp I might add billion mark notes of the Great Inflation.

With any luck, the issue of my stamps would provoke a stream of letters to the German equivalents of *The Times*: How could I possibly have left out the theatre of Piscator, Toller and Reinhart, of Brecht with and without Weill, the films of Lang (*M* and *Metropolis*), the actors Lorre and Jannings, the literature of Erich Maria Remarque, Thomas Mann, Hermann Hesse and Erich Kästner? And what about the music of Hindemith and of Berg, the conducting of Klemperer, and the art of Kandinsky, Hannah Hoch, Schwitters, Beckmann, Moholy-Nagy?

The list is long and could decorate several years' supply of those tiny prints sold over Post Office counters. But of special relevance for me are Remarque and Piscator. Remarque because he was about to publish *Im Westen, Nichts Neues* (All Quiet on the Western Front), Piscator because a couple of days before I was born he had opened his second theatre in Berlin on the Nollendorf Platz where cast and audience had burst into song with the *Internationale*. This event was reported in the entertainments page of *Die Deutsche Allgemeine* on 3 March 1928, the day I was born. These pages also tell those in the capital who had not just given birth or been born but were ready for an evening out that they could listen to Mahler's Eighth Symphony, or watch Stravinsky's *Petrushka* conducted by Otto Klemperer. If they fancied an evening in the cinema, there was Emil Jannings in *The Way of all Flesh* and Harold Lloyd in *Um*

*Himmels Willen* (For Heaven's Sake). During the day one could hunt for bargains in carpets and cashmeres and gentlemen's hats in the sale at N. Israel, the Jewish-owned department store, founded in 1815, and to be destroyed by Hitler in the pogrom of 1938.

Nothing momentous was reported to have occurred on or around the day of my birth. Weimar turbulence had become the norm and in any case was always played down by the *Deutsche Allgemeine*. The 3 March issue has nothing else to feature on its front page than a very minor assassination attempt. A small, elderly and respectable looking man had got into the office of an official who dealt with compensations. He drew a pistol, waved it at the official and demanded 112,000 Marks for the farm he had lost in the Cameroons. He fired but missed, he tried to run but was caught. This pathetic episode, as well as making the headlines, was featured in a leader as yet more evidence of the desperation wrought on the German nation by the Treaty of Versailles.

A small paragraph of an inside page announces Mussolini's *Italianisierung* of the South Tyrol. Nothing at all about his future partner-in-crime, who was still confined to Germany where he was stepping up intimidation and street fights with the Communists. Not a whisper of this in the *Deutsche Allgemeine*, but it was these conflicts rather than carpet and cashmere sales that were part of my parents' life.

*Die Rote Fahne*, founded by Karl Liebknecht and Rosa Luxemburg, filled the gaps left by the *Deutsche Allgemeine*. My parents took both papers but it was *Die Rote Fahne*'s convictions and causes that were wholly in keeping with theirs: calls for strikes, for the release of political prisoners, for equal pay and rights for women, the role of Britain as the exploiter of black and brown people, and the *Klassenkampf* (class war). Above all and whenever possible, the paper vilifies the German Social Democratic Party, the SPD, whose politics were moderate. The issue of 3 March 1928 barely mentions the wretched farmer from the Cameroons. It concentrates on the plight of political prisoners, and castigates the SPD as sabotaging the campaign to free them.

If 'the SPD is our enemy' was the Party line the paper constantly drummed into their readers, it was also drummed into me by my mother when other children learnt about Little Red Riding Hood and the big bad wolf. The SPD was the big bad wolf quite as much as the National Socialists. For the week of my birthday, the paper celebrated *Frauenwoche* (women's week) and praised women for having fought *Schulter an Schulter* (shoulder to shoulder) with the men. As the increasing employment of women threatened the wages of the whole of the Berlin workforce, the paper called for equal pay: 'The greater the move to employ women, the greater the need to fight for equal pay.' Good stuff for 1928.

*Die Rote Fahne* was the essential notice-board for cell meetings, rallies, marches, demonstrations. Most of these outings provided more patients for the hospitals and bodies for the morgue. Most of the marches started in Rote Wedding; all of them upset respectable citizens as the marches passed through their districts. The paper gloated when in the middle of March 1928 (just after I was born) a motor cavalcade of Communist Youth, with banners and music, drove 'the petit bourgeoisie terrified to their windows and the doors of the cafés'. They would have been even more alarmed had they followed the procession to its destination on the Helmholtz Platz, where the speakers' platform was crowned with a bust of Lenin and where the crowd of over a thousand sang the *Internationale* and pledged themselves to vote Communist. Around the same time, a band of two hundred fascists beat up the group of musicians who had parted from the main body of a similar procession.

My birth certificate does not announce my birth into any cauldron of political activity and doesn't mention the Communist Party. Instead it announces my birth into the Jewish community. This bureaucratic and mistaken assumption was based on the place of my delivery, the Jewish Hospital in Wedding, Rote Wedding. The colour of the district suited my parents rather better than the denomination of the hospital. My parents had come from orthodox Jewish homes in Poland but apart from using the Jewish Hospital for my birth and later, in the time of Hitler, sending me to Jewish schools, they had completely cut themselves off from any Jewish community. My mother had left Poland as a wanted revolutionary Marxist, and converted my father, a Polish Jewish tailor who had fled to Berlin from Polish conscription. For them, as Marxists and therefore atheists and internationalists, Judaism and Zionism were irrelevant as were any other ethnic identities.

For my parents, being marginals or outsiders was always less of an issue than it is for me. Each had grown up safely tucked inside a tight Jewish community, albeit in a hostile country, then they had become members of the KPD, though at the same time accepting the fundamentalist principle of Internationalism.

I have been forced by political circumstance to face up to all sorts of betwixts and betweens. Being born a Jew and a woman and a foreigner, I was marginal from the start. I like the coincidence that I was born in the Weimar Republic and on the site of the Berlin Wall. A coincidence no doubt, but could it have been an omen? As if a mischievous fairy had placed me there to avenge the atheism and rationality of my secular mother who denied fairies as she denied God. Whereas God punishes the son, mischievous fairies punish the daughter, and always at birth and with a gift. Red hair was one such gift, symbols of marginality another.

In Nazi Germany, this marginality was highly dangerous. But in England I have come to glory in it as a gift. It is my permit to flout convention, to rebel, and I am permanently in two minds whether to use it, or whether to conform. The word *Gift* in German means poison and the two concepts have an etymological link. My friend Daisy stumbled on this unwittingly when she started in her English school in 1939. She lent her pencil to another girl who began to lick the point. Daisy was a kind girl who knew the lead was poisonous but who knew no English. So she said: '*Gift, Gift! Das ist Gift!*' The other girl was very happy.

# An Absolute Woman

My mother was a revolutionary by vocation and my father was a tailor. My mother had no interest in my father's work and little respect for it. Revolutionary politics and Russian literature were what fired her. When they met, my father was ignorant of both.

My mother and my father were Jews from Orthodox households. Both spoke Yiddish, both had heavy Polish/Russian accents, neither had German citizenship. Otherwise, they had little in common. My mother's family, the Bidermans, though poor, were higher up the social ladder – rabbis in the family, one of them well known, and lots of education, whereas my father was almost illiterate. Both had crossed the border illegally but for very different reasons and with very different ambitions. Yet they had met in Adalbertstrasse.

I know why each of them had fled from Poland, but I know far more about the circumstances of my mother's flight. She had fled from the Polish secret police and was proud of it. Her journey to 44 Adalbertstrasse began in the small *shtetl* of Lubartov in either 1898 or 1900. Throughout her life, she insisted that she was two years younger than my father and born in 1900 though her passport said 1898. She had a perfectly sound explanation. Though the eldest of five children, she was not the first-born. The first child, also a girl, was born to my grandparents in 1898 and had died as a baby. My mother was born two years later. After she had illegally crossed the border in 1921 she deceived the Polish Embassy in Berlin into issuing a passport for the dead sister born in 1898 and not for the living and wanted sister born in 1900. Using the identity of a dead person is a trick still used by passport forgers. In the muddle in Central and Eastern Europe after the First World War it was easy to confuse the bureaucrats, and though the dead baby's name was Ethel, my mother managed to retain her own name, Frida Maria.

When my mother was dying she asked me to make sure that on her tombstone her date of birth would read 24 August 1898. She liked to think she had reached eighty but I don't think she had. I don't know at what age she liked to be thought of as older rather than younger. A switch of vanity.

Lubartov was a typical *shtetl* in an area that had experienced several changes of nationality. *Shtetl* is Yiddish for a small town and has come to mean a small town or village in Eastern Europe, with a sizeable Jewish community. Now bereft of Jews – apart from those in the miraculously unspoiled cemetery – Lubartov is no longer a *shtetl*, just a small town inside Poland and twenty miles from the Russian border. But between 1872 and 1918 Lubartov was under Russian rule. A Russian Orthodox church stood at one end of town, a Roman Catholic church at the other end; the synagogue stood halfway between, in a poorer part of town. The six thousand inhabitants consisted of Jews and Poles. 'Jews and Poles' is how my mother put it. The Lubartov Jews were mostly very poor. The Poles were not much better off, but they had their pieces of land which provided enough to eat even in times of wartime shortages.

My uncle-in-law, Paul Gradstein, also from Lubartov and married to my mother's sister Regina until she died in Auschwitz, told me that when he was little he often went hungry, not starving but hungry, a difference he learnt in a German concentration camp. And as he talked he absent-mindedly pressed his stomach as he might have done when he suffered from hunger. We had this conversation in a plush London hotel full of guests whose only dietary problem was overeating. The change of material fortune for Paul from hunger in Lubartov, horrors in a concentration camp, to his present luxurious lifestyle is only apparently a happy ending.

My mother had one brother and three sisters. Their Yiddish names had Polish, Russian, German or French equivalents and they were born in this order: Frida (my mother), Szya or Charles, Rivale or Regina, Mira or Mania or Mireille, and Sarah or Sonia. This family of seven were reduced to living in a tiny dwelling. Several of them slept in one room, but in spite of the cramped space various cousins from Lublin often came and stayed overnight. Mania talked about this when I visited her in Paris in 1987. Sitting at the long table in her flat in the Rue des Filles du Calvaire, she shook her head and laughed. 'It's only nowadays that we never have enough room,' and she waved her hand round the four-roomed flat in which she now lives alone. Her smallest room, which really is small, is the size of both rooms in Lubartov.

A few chickens ran around outside my grandparents' house providing eggs and the occasional weekend meal of chicken and noodle soup, but the family's livelihood depended on the shop. The exact nature of this shop varies in the telling. Shortly before she died, my mother told my children that her father had inherited a large and thriving tobacconists. He was the youngest son but my great-grandfather had regarded him as the most capable. The eldest son was furious and at least as envious as Esau when Isaac stole his birthright, and his wife was demented with envy. She would rush into the shop and, in front of customers, shriek that my grandfather was a thief: 'You stole from your own brother!' This wore my grandparents down and they took a smaller shop. My mother didn't explain whether this was to give the jealous brother money from the sale or another shop. According to Paul Gradstein, the larger shop wasn't a tobacconist's at all, but a less prestigious hardware store. They did sell tobacco but only under the counter as they did not have a licence.

I don't in any case believe a word of this story as told by my mother to my children. Whenever she talked to me about it, the loss of that large shop was wholly her father's fault. He was hopeless, inefficient, and got deeper and deeper into debt. I never knew what she despised more – his good-naturedness or his inefficiency. She certainly resented the hardship caused by their reduced circumstances, but as the eldest daughter she must have borne the brunt.

Nor did she like coming down in the world. She may have been a Marxist but she always felt strongly that her mother should have made a 'better' marriage, with 'better' having nothing to do with love or character. Ironically, she was to repeat her mother's 'mistake' and regret it.

Once the Poles took over the country, life was much harder for them, as it was for all Jews. The Poles were even worse to the Jews than the Russians had been. To the end of his life, my father constantly reminded me how the Poles, once they had won their freedom from Russia after the Revolution, felt free to express their anti-semitism in every way. Felt free to continue with pogroms, and to start levying higher taxes from Jews than from Poles. Some Poles even felt free to take over Jewish businesses by force. It was then that my maternal grandparents became really poor, though not as poor as families who could not afford to buy bread and had to live on cabbages and potatoes. My mother claimed that the Bidermanns did eat meat every day, even if the portions were not large. 'We were healthy and fit and my sisters were beautiful.' They were, and so was my mother. I have photographs to prove it.

But what counted even more than health and looks was that the Bidermann siblings were educated and they owed that to the efforts of Malle, their mother, a formidable woman. When my mother was born, Lubartov had no school for its Jewish children. The churches had some facilities for teaching the alphabet and religion, though most of the Christian Poles were as illiterate as some of the Jews.

My grandparents, who could speak, write and read both Russian and Polish fluently, formed a group with other parents to establish a school for their children. If most Jews lived in poverty, a few were well off enough to own and let houses, so there was some money to spare for a school. As my grandparents were literate, the pressure group met in their house. My grandmother was the leading force and the group could not have picked a better fighter. She had fervour, she was resourceful and an impressive letter writer. Above all, she had an important contact. Her home *shtetl* of Konskayavola was unusual in that it had a school. It had been founded by Chil Naiden, a teacher from nearby Alexandrov, a town with a High School and University. She wrote and persuaded Naiden to uproot himself and his family and settle in Lubartov.

His own children, all graduates, taught at the school. One daughter taught Russian language and literature, the other the reading and reciting of poetry, which was fashionable at the time. His son opened the first book shop in Lubartov. Polish was also taught, not by a member of the family but by Federbusch, an ex-pupil of Naiden's who had come straight from university. To teach Polish was very courageous as it was banned by the Russian authorities, who wanted to impress on the people that they were no longer Poles.

My mother was six years old and spoke Yiddish and Russian when Naiden's school opened; she was one of the first pupils. In Berlin and later in London, and until the week she died, she talked about the man who took such risks in teaching them Polish, the forbidden language. She talked rapturously of the young Joseph Federbusch, an inspiring teacher, who cut a dashing figure in his blazer bound with petersham, and fine leather belt: 'He looked like life itself and we were all in love with him!' And to judge by the sound of her voice she still was, even at the age of seventy-eight or eighty.

The school only took pupils up to the age of twelve. The lucky ones went on to the High School in a nearby town and though Naiden and Federbusch begged my grandparents to let my mother go too, they would not hear of it. The whole Jewish community would be outraged at the idea of sending a young girl away from home! There was also the question of cost. But they did allow Federbusch to give her lessons. He would not take any money but for years he came to the house twice a week.

My mother's devotion to this man, her admiration, the sexual and romantic emotion still evoked by his memory when she was more or less eighty and on her deathbed, leaves me ever more puzzled at her adamant resistance to visit Federbusch after the war. Federbusch and his wife Mathilda had survived the war by fleeing to Russia. But when they came back to Poland they found that their son had been shot in a massacre by a trench grave, and that their daughters had perished in a concentration camp. Mrs Federbusch went mad and never fully recovered, but she and her husband emigrated to Tel Aviv. They were housed in a block of flats reserved for survivors and that was where I went to see them in 1963. He was almost blind, very ill with diabetes, and he yearned to see my mother before he died. 'I left Poland because I want to see her again,' he told me. He thought it more likely that she would visit him in Israel. But she kept making excuses until the year after Federbusch died. Then she went. Perhaps she shrank from seeing him old and ill, not long out of a camp and far removed from the dashing young man in the blazer and the leather belt. Conversely, she might not have wanted him to see her, even though he was nearly blind, since of course she was no longer a young girl. Perhaps she didn't want to face up to her own feelings for him. She always ran away from emotions.

I wonder exactly what and how much he had meant to her. As her first guru he had certainly taught her to be receptive to new ideas. Without this, without him, she might not have accepted an ideology that in the context of her family and the *shtetl* was cataclysmic and was to change her life.

My mother's family, though not belonging to any extreme orthodox sect, were strict enough. Throughout the sabbath no shoes were cleaned, no fires made up, no Russian and later no Polish books were read. On my visit to Paris in 1987, my aunt Mania had just made me a cup of tea when she was reminded how in her parents' home, a jug for milk had to be washed separately and kept separate and that 'to bring ham or bacon into the house was suicide'. Until she was sixteen my mother was a good orthodox Jewish girl. She abhored pork, she went to synagogue not only on Yom Kippur and Rosh Hashanah, and on Yom Kippur she fasted all day: 'It made me feel heroic and virtuous,' she remembered on her deathbed. But then she began to read literature. I am not sure how these books created doubt. Possibly the case they made for heaven and God was full of holes. What is clear is that the Russian Revolution which coincided with her seventeenth or nineteenth birthday introduced her to different ways and thoughts and, by the time she was eighteen (or twenty) 'I was agnostic, absolutely agnostic.' The absolute agnostic soon became an absolute atheist. When my mother used the word 'absolute' to talk about herself, she meant 'committed, determined, absolutely certain'. When I use it about her I mean all that, but also despotic.

She was always an absolute woman, and by her eighteenth birthday she had also become an absolute Communist and a member of the Communist Youth. Many Jews had sided with the revolution, and small wonder when Jews all over Russia had repeatedly to endure pogroms instigated by the Tsarist regime. But my grandmother, along with so many Jews, passionately opposed atheism.

The Bolsheviks closed churches and synagogues the moment they took over and any priest who resisted was beaten up, put in prison or shot. My mother recalled how she scorned their fine words of freedom: 'What about freedom for religion?' But she herself had been convinced by Marx and Engels that religion was the opium of the people. Apart from one unconscious lapse in 1969, when my father was killed and a funeral had to be arranged, she remained an atheist.

There could have been no more rebellious act in that family than to give up God and Judaism. Her father cut short any talk of religion and I am sure her mother did, too. 'God simply is', and there was no more to be said. Yet my mother converted all her siblings to the new and godless creed. The four sisters managed to keep the peace with their parents by being considerate and diplomatic. My mother recalled that 'If one of us fancied a bit of bacon, we ate it outside.' Not so their brother Charles, also an apostate, who modified neither his words nor his actions and antagonised and hurt his parents. But then they had wanted him to be a rabbi and so he had to shout much louder in case they were left with any hope. My grandmother may have been fairly progressive, but she came from a family of rabbis. Her father was a rabbi from Biala and an uncle, of whom she was particularly proud, was Rabbi Schleume of Konskayavola. My Marxist mother was also proud of him, but not until the end of her life.

Charles started to read mathematics at the University of Lublin but he was expelled because he spoke his political mind. To even reveal an interest in Communism, let alone sympathise, and on top of that to be a Jew, was madness in Poland between the wars. But Charles could never keep his counsel about anything, political or personal. He always expressed his views starkly, and could be totally crushing. Like my mother, he fled into the Weimar Republic. For a brief while – and to my father's annoyance – he stayed with my parents in Berlin while he continued at the university there before going on to Paris and the Sorbonne. While he was still in Germany his political activities got him into trouble with the police. But the Communist Party obtained a false Czech passport for him and he travelled as Francisco Bruno.

My uncle Charles was very much one of the men in my mother's life. My grandfather was not her type at all, and I am not sure about my father. But Charles was dashing, careless of his own safety, certain of his opinions, with a touch of madness and great sexual charm. My mother was five years older than Charles but 'we were not just brother and sister. We had the same ideals.' There was perhaps more than that. While they both still lived in Lubartov, she would keep the samovar going to supply him with tea as he played chess through the night. It was her most subordinate and nurturing role ever but she reminisced about it with an almost sensual pleasure and she kept boasting about his irresistibility to women. She adored him uncritically and always took his side against her parents, though not to their face. The relationship between Charles and his parents was severed for ever. But even though all the daughters had also rejected their parents' traditions, my grandparents lived for the frequent letters from them.

While my mother still lived at home, her atheism may have been taboo but her parents did talk and worry about her member-ship of the Party. The Communist Party was not only proscribed, it was anathema to the authorities, or 'a red bull' as my mother said. Prison without trial was the usual consequence for simply being a member. The government was scared stiff by the example of the Revolution across the border. It was mainly the Russian Revolution that propelled my mother from one orthodoxy to another. As it shook the world its waves, like any earthquake, were strongest near the epicentre. Lubartov was pretty near and so was Lublin. But not many Jews from my mother's background, even if they abandoned Orthodox Judaism, turned to Marxism and athe-ism, and with such passion.

My mother, that absolute woman, was passionate in whatever she did and this passion was fanned by a charismatic young man called Benny Biderman. He played upon her doubts which had been triggered off by the Revolution, but he also awakened aspects of her non-political self. (I don't know how much Federbusch had brought to life.) Benny, who lived in Lublin, was her first cousin – her father's brother's son – and the eldest of six children all of whom were Communists. She may have ended up a Communist without him, but Benny, an intellectual and a revolutionary, drew her into the movement just as he had drawn in all his siblings, and inspired her not only with Marxism but also with Russian literature. He showed her what to read – Marx and Marxist literature of course, but also non-political authors like Tolstoy, Turgenev and Dostoyevsky. Benny may not have fathered her children but he did father her ideas and set the climate I was brought up in. 'Benny was my prophet, he was Karl Marx to me.' She adored him, she was in love with him. He may have been the only man she was ever in love with. His photograph shows a slim young man, with considerable composure. The hair which is brushed back from his intelligent face may have been groomed for the photograph but he needed to look respectable as a cover for his underground activities. He was a romantic-looking figure even in his sober suit.

Benny and my mother had first become close not in Poland but in Vienna in the winter of 1916–17. As the eldest daughter my mother had gone to Vienna with her mother, who needed a gallstone operation. Polish medicine was rather basic, whereas Viennese medicine and doctors were famous, and not only for psychology. Benny was in Budapest at the time. My mother never knew exactly what he was doing, but 'it had something to do with the war and the Party' and he was working 'day and night, night and day'. He nevertheless found time to visit Vienna and call on my mother and my grandmother. Back in Poland he and my mother began to see each other frequently.

It was not only Benny's siblings and my mother who had been swept into the Party by Benny's magnetism. He was surrounded and adulated by a host of young intellectuals, all sworn to the Communist cause. One young woman had been born in a Tsarist prison where her parents, as Social Democrats (the name of the pre-revolutionary Communist Party), had spent many years. My mother revelled in this milieu: the social bustle and intellectual excitement, the presence of the adored Benny, but most of all the idealism and the danger. They were ready to risk their freedom and even their life.

Benny's political work and adventures were the stuff of spy stories. His clandestine missions took him to Vienna and into Russia as well as to locations in Poland and forced him to hide in some remote and inhospitable places. The winter before my mother had to flee Poland was particularly severe and Benny had to hide in a disintegrating shed for several days and nights. By the time he got home to Lublin he had pleurisy. My mother went to see him every week and he organised the business of the Party cell from his bedside. He must have been a compelling figure as he gave instructions to the comrades. I imagine him with eyes and cheeks burning with fever but a manner that is cool and indifferent to his condition. Though this bout of illness did not turn out to be his deathbed, his lungs never recovered and he died a few years later – in bed, but as a result of another dangerous mission.

Early in the summer of 1922, very soon after she had become a full member of the Communist Party, my mother noticed she was being followed. Being a member of the Communist Party in Poland meant clandestine activities: attending illegal gatherings, distributing prohibited literature, drafting and printing propaganda, subversive talk, recruiting members – and all under an alias. 'Wherever I went, there was this same man.' It's easy to spot a stranger in a small place where everybody, including the local policeman, knows everybody else. The stranger could only be a government spy. She told her alarmed parents and quickly left for Lublin. She stayed with her aunt and uncle, Benny's parents, and got work in a factory that made knitted cardigans. This factory employed lots of young people whom my mother began to organise for the Party. She never wasted time.

One day, the same wretch who had followed her in Lubartov was lurking round her uncle's house. 'It was high time I got out.' The prison sentences given to Communists were severe: five years merely for distributing the Communist Party newspaper, the 'Red Banner' (*Czerwony Sztandard*), five years for 'throwing a red flag', their term for just leaving that paper lying around as they used to do in the factories. Five years which either killed you or left you with TB, and she was doing rather more than 'flag-throwing'. So she fled to Warsaw and stayed with her mother's sister, Channala. A few days later, a couple of plainclothes men knocked at the door and asked for Frida Biderman. Luckily she was out and they went away. But she had to flee again and there was no time and no point in packing anything; the smallest bag would have alerted her pursuers. She went a couple of blocks down the road to the flat of Mania, a comrade. Her friend was very agitated. Two men, obviously on my mother's trail, were in the porter's lodge. It looked as if they had caught her.

She couldn't stay and she couldn't go – at least not as she had come. Even had she been wearing something less conspicuous than a red dress, that pair in the porter's cabin would pounce. A disguise was essential, but was there time? Mania was very tall but nevertheless my mother donned her huge black suit over her own red dress, hitched up the skirt, tied it on, and topped the ridiculous outfit with an enormous black hat. In this weird get-up, my mother walked slowly down the stairs, and past the danger zone – the porter's lodge. The secret policemen barely looked at her; clearly the porter was an entertaining fellow.

She walked, calmly, towards the home of Sara, also a Party member. There she found another comrade on the run, Jacov Goldman, a student. He had been organising students for the Party and had come under surveillance at the University. The three made plans to flee across the border into Soviet Russia. In the evening before they were due to leave, yet another old friend and comrade called round. My mother and Sara had known him well in Lublin. He had been in the army at the time and at great risk had distributed Communist Party literature among the soldiers. They told him their plans to cross into Russia. The frontier police had been bribed and a password arranged. The crossing was to be made the next day.

The next morning, just as the three were on the point of leaving, a beggar came to the door and handed them a note addressed to my mother and Jacov Goldman. It read: 'Don't go to the frontier. Nothing is now safe. You will be arrested by the Poles. Please believe me. Don't do it.' It was initialled by their old comrade from Lublin in whom they had confided. He had betrayed them but his conscience was tormenting him. The three comrades faced a dreadful dilemna. My mother and Jacov couldn't go home and Sara couldn't stay home. What could they do but take a train in the opposite direction and into the Weimar Republic? Sara suggested they should leave straightaway and take the next train to Berlin; her brother Leo lived and worked there. Once the three were there and safe they could decide on the next step. They went to the station in the evening at nine o'clock, and to avoid drawing attention they took nothing with them, not even a jacket. They couldn't travel directly from Warsaw to Berlin and all the borders were closely watched. Their first stop was at a little town near Katowitze called Bydgosz, to meet the contact who had been alerted. This contact turned out to be a Jewish woman and her husband, not a Jew but experienced at taking people over the border. He did just that and accompanied them all the way to Berlin. They took several detours and travelled the whole night. 'I was so cold' – my mother shivers at the thought – 'that the man who smuggled us took off his coat and put it over my shoulders.' She was still wearing her red dress.

Bydgosz had been used for illegal crossings for some time, and it was there that, in 1889, Rosa Luxemburg crossed from the Russian part of Poland into the German part. She had escaped by hiding under a bundle of straw in a peasant's cart. Although less comfortable, she must at least have been warmer than my mother shivering in her red dress.

My mother and her friends arrived in Berlin on 24 August 1922, my mother's twentieth birthday. It was a time for a new beginning, but without a birthday party. The three went straight to Sara's brother. Leo lived in one room in a boarding house, and for a couple of days he rented another room for his sister and her friends. Then he sent them to one of the leaders of the Jewish community, who would advise them on a place to live, how to obtain a residential permit and how to get work. But this man was so hostile to their politics that he took immense pleasure in refusing them any help. He had no sympathy for Communists, for the Third International in particular, and 'none at all for you!' The three refugees had to spend two nights in the bare, squalid dormitories of an *Asyl*, a hostel for down-and-outs. They had no baggage, no change of clothes, probably no toothbrush, and no money, but they did have a few addresses. One significant address was Jacobsohn's. He was a Lubliner who worked in a shoe factory and he sent my mother to a friend of his, Hersz, whom he had known from childhood. Hersz was a tailor who had his own workshop in Adalbertstrasse and employed several people. Jacobsohn thought Hersz, who was known as Heini, was sure to help. Perhaps my mother could learn to sew.

'And so he brought me to my husband. I worked with Heini for some time and then he thought he fell in love with me, and after a few years, in 1925, we married.' This is all on tape and my children are quite shocked at the cold, indifferent tone of her voice.

I have no idea what work my mother ever did in my father's workshop. She never learnt to sew and they did not live happily ever after.

# THREE

# A Family of Weimar

My parents lived through difficult and sometimes horrendous times. Their married life had begun in the restless atmosphere of Weimar, in the year of the Great Inflation and while Germany was suffering ever more from the effects of the unfortunate Treaty of Versailles. It continued through six years of Nazi persecution, and as refugees in wartime London. They did not separate until they had lived for some years in the calmer atmosphere of England – calmer even in wartime.

While my mother and her comrades were spending a night in cold trains, crossing illegally from Poland into Germany, staying in one abode more miserable than the last, two gentlemen were heading for Berlin, but in the public gaze and staying in comfort and splendour, to negotiate with the Weimar government. Sir John Bradbury from Britain and M. Mauclere from France went to Berlin on 23 August to discuss the reparations the Germans still owed after the Treaty of Versailles – the Treaty that was crippling the Weimar economy and doing worse to the German character. The British government and press were even more concerned with the falling Mark. In August 1922 inflation had not yet reached its nadir, but the thunder of its avalanche was ominous. In July 1919 there had been 14.2 Marks to the dollar. In July 1922 there were 493.2 Marks to the dollar. By November 1923 it took 4,200,000,000,000 Marks to buy a single dollar.

I don't know how my father managed to survive the Great Inflation. Small enterprises like his were the most vulnerable and yet his business thrived. My parents, like all those who witnessed it, had their favourite stories about the inflation. Their best was the cautionary tale that if you had a cup of coffee in a restaurant it was wise to pay when you ordered. By the time you had drunk your coffee it would cost ten times as much and more.

By the time I was three, my father had lived and worked in Adalbertstrasse for several years and made enough money and name for himself to afford not only a workshop but a salon where he could see individual clients, though much of his work still went out to large firms. He specialised in *Damenmoden*, designing and making suits and coats for ladies. In 1931 he graduated to much bigger and slightly smarter premises in the Köpenicker Strasse a few minutes walk away. Before we left Adalbertstrasse, I was just tall enough for my eyes to skim the top of our one and only large table.

My parents' marriage progressed less well, though it creaked along for decades. The main problem was not so much all the things that divided them, but the one personality trait they shared: both were autocrats, both needed to be on top. My father was brought up to be a patriarch in the Old Testament manner. My mother was as autocratic as any patriarch but also a rebel who had absorbed feminism along with Marxism.

My father had a strong personality but next to my mother's it was blurred. I find it difficult to draw a portrait of him without constant cross-reference to my mother. I am glad to have photographs to remind me of how he and my mother looked when they were young. My father was handsome – he might well have been cast as a Central or Eastern European matinée idol – with black-brown hair and brown eyes and good cheekbones, a curved forehead, full well-shaped lips and splendid teeth. His skin tanned easily.

My mother was rather beautiful, with dark hair and fair skin that turned red in the sun and flushed on her neck when she was excited. But she never blushed. When she was embarrassed she just looked cross and sour and her eyes would focus into the distance. My mother's forehead was straight rather than curved, her mouth was wide and her nostrils flared when she was annoyed. Neither parent had a stereotypical Jewish nose; my mother's, if anything, tilted up at the end.

My father was barely 5 feet 6 inches, my mother 5 feet 2 inches; short for England but not short for Eastern Europe. It is difficult to believe that my mother was a bare half-inch taller than me. Not only my children but everyone else always thought of her as tall. Her back was as straight as any guardsman's, with that same touch of lordosis or slight concave curvature of the spine. Berliners call it

*Potsdamer Rücken*. But it was her confidence and the clarity and forcefulness of her speech that gave her such a commanding presence.

Both slim in their youth, my mother filled out into a full-bosomed magisterial matron; my father came to look like any of those squat men with receding hairlines up on the podium taking the parades on Red Square, Gorbachev in particular – the same facial bone structure: pronounced jaw and cheekbones, a domed skull.

Apart from her looks, my mother had intelligence and a compelling personality. She was a talented speaker who carried an audience with her. I used to think it was lucky that she was so charismatic because it mattered desperately to her that she was admired and followed. Now, having been quite close to various charismatic figures, I am sure the desperate need to be admired predates the charisma. Her voice was always loud but never more so than later in England, where people speak more quietly. She was better at speeches than at conversations, which she always sought to dominate. She tended to hold forth rather than to converse, and she preferred to dispute rather than to discuss. Having made the leap from Orthodox Judaism to Marxism, she defended her new dogma with spirit and intolerance. She was utterly inflexible. Her voice would rise, though never to an unpleasant pitch, and her neck and throat flush. She was quick to bring in quotations and examples from literature and history and always with a triumphant flourish, like a card player throwing down the winning ace. And when she had won the argument, which was every time, she would sit back and say, 'You see!' and her eyes would flash in exultation. I envy her confidence – I am such a ditherer – but I also deplore it since she was no more flexible when it came to personal issues.

This formidable woman talked in exclamation marks and never – but never – admitted to being in the wrong. When she was angry with me, her anger was coated with the ice of exclusion, and I shivered as she withdrew any semblance of warmth and liking. Then almost imperceptibly she would give a hint that I might be back in favour. When she was angry with my father she was not in the least icy but shouted as fiercely as he did as they fought back and forth over current and old grievances. What I feared more than her icy anger was her sulking when she withdrew even more and without explanation. Equally disorienting, if not more so, was her ability to swear hand on heart – she really would put her hand on her heart – and with innocent and self-righteous indignation that she had never ever said something was black, but that it was white. When I hear Petruchio in *The Taming of the Shrew* insist that the moon is the sun – or the other way round – I think of my mother, though he resorts to neither innocence nor indignation.

I must be wrong but I can't remember that she ever hugged me, though she is doing so in a photograph when I am a tiny baby. When I was an adult and a mother myself she was quite keen to embrace me, but then I shrunk from her. There was too much envy and jealousy in our relationship when I was grown up. She envied my being close to politics when she was excluded, my good marriage when hers had been bad, and my third child when she only had two.

For my part, I did and do admire as well as envy her. But I never told her. I admire her guts as an underground political activist, her independence – despite the occasional guru – and her self-confidence. I admire and envy her for her ability to make speeches, to be so articulate, to be so erudite in Russian literature and political history and theory and to have garnered so much without going to university. And she had so much vitality. When I was child, my admiration was more like adulation and it was boundless. She was wonderful, she was a superior being, she knew everything about everything, personal as well as political, and knew better than anyone else. I was not at ease with her but always in awe and never doubted anything she said, not for a minute. I now despise myself for that, and though I still admire her I also hate her. It irks me that although she died in 1979 she is still within me to influence and irritate. I wince when I look in the mirror and catch a glimpse of her. It gets worse as I get older with even my wrinkles now copying hers. I hate it when I hear myself being strident and intolerant in argument and not listening – especially not listening.

Yet I miss her. But love? As a child I must have loved her; I certainly longed for her warmth and approval. But my love was unrequited. She was my focus and round her I circled like a wan moon which hardly ever catches the light of the sun. Being so peripheral to my mother must have infinitely increased my feelings of marginality.

I still don't know if she felt any warmth for me at all, or was completely indifferent. I have got so used to blaming her indifference for all sorts of problems within me that I cannot let it go now. I blame her indifference for my depressions, my need for reassurance, my lack of confidence, my indecisiveness, my need to be first and my inability to be so, oscillating between showing off and shrinking, my resistance to push any of my talents to their limit and therefore never to excel even though I am desperate to. They are all part of the same syndrome, even the fact that while I blame her I really blame myself. At the same time, I cannot bear indifference from other people. I even prefer their disapproval.

She had enormous charm and I admire that too, but there is one gift she lacked utterly: she could not tell a joke. She did occasionally repeat one, but it was excruciating. She never realised how flat those jokes fell, and when there were some laughs how forced these sounded. For as well as having no talent for telling jokes, she lacked a sense of humour. It was part of her unshakable belief in her own goodness and nobleness. She used to go on and on about her sainthood: how everyone saw her as saint – her sisters, her comrades, even the doctors at the prestigious Charitée hospital in Berlin. I, too, was mesmerised into believing that she was every bit as wonderful, as charismatic as Rosa Luxemburg, her own saint, and as glamorous and turbulent as Joan of Arc. Every one of her pronouncements was gospel to me. This gave me a certainty and a belief in myself, or rather a belief in her creed of Communism and in me as my mother's satellite or disciple, which isolated me. I can't say when I began to abhor the straitjacket of the mind and soul that accompanies sainthood, or to fear the risks of her saintly self-sacrifice and to resent the impossibility of standing up to a saint.

My father had more of a sense of humour but otherwise he was no match for my mother. He was very intelligent and could be quite effective in a political argument. But he was uneducated and had neither her knowledge nor her conviction. Nor was his psychological need to impose his view quite so extreme. All he wanted was to be *Herr des Hauses*, master of his home and family.

I do remember his hugs; he was altogether more demonstrative and physical than my mother and took pleasure in physical things. As soon as he could afford it, he used to go off to Czechoslovakia for a couple of weeks skiing, leaving my mother wild with resentment at being left to look after me and the household. At our New Year's Eve parties, as soon as I could walk, he danced the old-fashioned waltz and polka with me with great gusto. Not that the waltz was known as old-fashioned; it was just 'the waltz' and the only one we knew until we moved to England, where we came across a very tedious dance called the slow waltz.

If only life with my father had been one lovely lilting waltz after the other! But he had a grim temper and his despotism, when it could not subdue my mother and it rarely could, was directed at me. It was not too irksome, until I was in my teens and we were in England, except for one small thing, absurdly small but it recurred daily. I liked to drink lemon juice with water and sugar with my meal, but my father decreed I had to abstain from all drink until I had finished eating. He said it was bad for my health, but it sounded more like a moral sin. I would sit at the white table-clothed table and look longingly at the cloudy drink and beg for 'just two gulps'. But the despot's face would contort as he yelled at me to eat up first. I still order *citron pressé* in France and *limone naturale* in the square in Siena. I don't hear him shouting any more and I think of him far more often in connection with oranges than with lemons. When I peel an orange, and I do so every day, I see my father cutting the peel into a certain arrangement of segments and lifting them off so that the pith adheres and the orange comes out in a perfect state each time.

I know why my father went to Berlin, even if I do not know exactly how and when. He didn't talk about it because the circumstances of his journey were more commonplace than my mother's. Like so many young Jewish men he fled into Weimar to avoid service in the Polish Army, where relentless anti-semitism was a daily routine. I don't know where he crossed the border, but he may well have crossed at Bydgosz, the place my mother and her friends had used. The penalties for what counted as desertion were at least as crushing as for political fugitives. The worst consequence my father had to suffer, like all refugees, was loss of citizenship. He had no passport, no embassy to look after his interests in a foreign country, no rights in his own country. All he could expect there was prison. He had a bundle of loose-leaf stateless papers, plain and unadorned by any crest. At least my mother had the dignity of a proper passport, even if she got it by using her dead baby sister.

Avoiding conscription, however good your reason and however many others do it, is nothing to brag about. When my parents first explained to me why my father had fled across the border, they spun me a tale of his selfless pacifism. Killing people is wrong, they told me, to be a Communist is to be a pacifist. But that story soon collapsed. It clearly did not apply to my father's *Landsmänner* (friends from one's home region) who had fled the border at the same time. No group could have been more apolitical: there was not one comrade among them.

My father's home town was Lublin, which was Benny's home town, too, and bigger and better known than little Lubartov. But his home was poorer than my mother's at its poorest. My father was the eldest; next came Josse or Joseph, then Paula or Pesse, and finally Hella. Their mother had died in 1914 when Hella, who now lives in Aylesbury, was a tiny baby. Hella hates me with a passion that took root in Berlin, where she lived with us when I was small. My father ruled the family in Lublin with an iron fist. His own father was a simple man who spent all his time in prayer – at least that is what my mother used to say with great contempt. Sadly, after my father had left for Berlin, his brother for army service, and Paula for Warsaw, Hella was taken into an orphanage.

My father had not been inducted into the Communist Party or any other political organisation, but was apprenticed to a tailor and had learnt his trade inside out before he fled to Berlin. He never talked about the flight into Weimar and very little about Poland. He never discussed the extreme poverty in his home. All I know about his apprenticeship is the trick played by the apprentices on the tailor's wife who made gloves in her spare time. The boys were always made to sit on the gloves to iron them out, but one day, when her back was turned, they threw them out of the window. My father thought this hilarious and laughed uproariously every time he told this story, which he did often. He also told a story about a hard winter when he was a very small boy and he and his uncle had come close to fatal frostbite when the train they had taken was stopped by a huge wall of snow.

He told only one political story from his years in Poland. Pogroms were so common, they barely warranted special mention. But one incident did. A Polish – not a Russian – horseman rushed again and again at a slight man, a Jew in a long black coat who had snatched his small son up in his arms and clutched him close to his body. The horse reared up, his front legs towering over the man and his child. The rider lashed out with his whip. The man was my grandfather, the child my father. The memory of this terror made him detest Poles to the end of his life.

My father crossed into Weimar around 1920 together with, or around the same time as, his friends from Lublin. Each had a trade and was a tailor, a furrier or a shoemaker. I have group photographs of them in Berlin wearing stylish winter clothes: well-cut 1920s suits and coats with fur collars and soft trilby hats. Holiday snaps of 1921 and 1922 by the seaside reveal my father as the most vital and handsome man of a very merry and mixed crowd. Later pictures of him with my mother and friends are much more solemn.

For my father, escaping to Berlin meant freedom from cultural and family constraints. The progressive and decadent climate of Weimar was just right, and when he met my mother he was having the best time of his life. For my mother, escaping to Berlin meant the freedom to work flat out and unhindered for the Communist Party and to convert as many souls or minds as possible.

My mother married the boss but what he was boss of was not enough for her. She was always vexed – to the day he died and almost to the day *she* died – that she had married beneath her. She was never aware that she had repeated the mistake her mother had made. That this vexation contradicted her Marxism never struck her either. The inequality between my mother and father was mainly evident in education. She had gone to school, and was widely read in politics and literature. He had attended religious classes at the local synagogue which only made him proficient in prayers that he abandoned anyway. No Benny or Federbusch equivalents had helped him. That he was a skilled and trained tailor, a talented designer and expert cutter of patterns, impressed her not at all. She had no respect for *schmattes* – her derogatory Yiddish word for clothes, that made them sound like jumble-sale rags – even though we prospered, even though her second baby was born in a private clinic, even though private medicine became the norm, and we came to live in an expensive part of Berlin. She enjoyed material comforts but squared this with her Marxism by never being impressed by them.

For my mother, life was the Party. The conversion of my father was her first political act in Berlin. In the idiom of the party, she 'enlightened' him. This meant membership of the KPD, and complete dedication to it. Before 1933 this entailed a life with some danger. After 1933 the danger increased.

With Communism went not only atheism but cultural conversion. Culture with a capital K for *Kultur*. My mother introduced my father to literature, philosophy and above all politics. He may never have read or completed *Das Kapital* but he did persevere with my mother's books on philosophy and sociology, starting with Rousseau, Müller-Lyre, Feuerbach – I was enchanted by their lilting names – and later, much later, ending up with Russell. Reading for him cannot have been easy. His handwriting betrayed how unpractised – I can hardly bring myself to say barely literate – he was.

Before my father's conversion, he had liked popular music and shows. He ended up with a passion for classical music which far exceeded my mother's, and when I was old enough to switch on the radio he banned any other music. My mother was the censor of ideas, but he had become the censor of taste and culture. I used to listen to jazz with the volume low and one ear listening out for his footsteps. Opera was his true love and he loved to sing arias around the house with gusto and feeling. His voice was strong and very good. But my mother mocked his efforts. Did he think he was going to be discovered like Caruso, by someone accidentally hearing him sing! And wasn't it she who had introduced him to opera!

When they met, he had only liked *Quatsch*, rubbish. Weimar gave him lots of opportunity to indulge his passion, with no less than three opera houses in Berlin alone. And after Weimar, there remained the records – those heavy one-sided plates, one of which lies unbroken but unplayed in a safe in my house in London like some Sleeping Beauty. It is Caruso who dozes in the metal coffin.

My father's faith in Communism was less immutable than my mother's and more wobbly from the beginning. He had never sought it out, nor had it hit him on any road to Damascus. Its prophet was my mother. It might have been better for both had it been the other way round. For all her feminism, for all her need to be in control, my mother, I now suspect, needed to look up to a man, needed a guru. Like Federbusch when she was six, like Benny when she was sixteen, and like Hermann Mendelsohn, another Communist Party activist, whom she met in Berlin.

The feminist component of Marxism irked and undermined my father. My mother's powerful personality and her superior education were threatening enough. But not only did my mother put the Party first, and certainly before him, she also justified this with articles of her faith. In left-wing circles of Weimar much was made of the equality of women. This was in great contrast to traditional German and Orthodox Jewish mores that were even more reactionary than in contemporaneous England. Emancipated from orthodoxy in many ways, my father still believed that women had a place to which they should be restricted.

There is a popular and mistaken assumption that Jewish society is matriarchal. It is no such thing! There is no matriarchal society anywhere and never has been. Jewish society is matrilineal as far as the principle of being Jewish is concerned, patrilineal in everything else, and wholly and totally patriarchal. Women may look after hearth and home but men are dominant. A traditional Jewish woman's place was, and is, certainly not in politics. Especially not for a woman with a husband and child.

My father's typically Jewish attitude to women conformed to that of most Germans who never shared the liberal stance of Weimar intellectuals, and wouldn't be seen dead carrying their wives' shopping basket. That in 1919 – and for the whole of the

Weimar period – women made up 8 per cent of the Reichstag's members, when Westminster's first and only woman MP had not even taken her seat, is misleading: it came about from the Republic's system of Proportional Representation. Only the Nazis were in tune with populist leanings and never fielded a single woman candidate. Women in Weimar had got the vote and seats in Parliament without a suffragette movement. Had such a turbulent movement existed, my mother would no doubt have taken a forceful part. Instead, she became a leading member of the women's section of the KPD.

Though initially attracted by my mother's good looks, my father must also have been drawn to her forceful personality, and excited by her radical ideas and involvement in politics. He could never have expected, or should never have expected, to subdue her into domesticity; he kept trying, though all he achieved was noisy and miserable scenes. She was the more effective and forceful proselytiser and started on me when I was still a toddler. But I was intimidated by my father's temper, which could even upset my mother. She used to tell me – when I barely understood what it meant as I knew more about Marx than sex – that he forced first me and then, nine years later, André, my brother, on her. I don't really believe that now. If my mother did not want to do something, she wouldn't. She may have wanted sex and not motherhood, and it is true that our births did interrupt her political activities, if only briefly. She told me that she left my father in 1927, discovered to her dismay that she was pregnant, and had to go back. So she objected to more than just the colour of my hair.

One way my father kept control of my mother was to keep her short of money. On Friday evenings, when good Jewish families sit down to celebrate the sabbath in warmth, harmony and candlelight, my parents did the weekly budget and rowed. I would creep out of my bedroom and watch and listen with a sinking heart. My mother sat at the desk lit by that traditional green-glass shaded lamp, and my father would bully her as she accounted for every penny spent during the week. She was inefficient, she was a spendthrift and a good-for-nothing; while he worked his fingers to the bone. She sat and wept. It was the lowest point of her week.

While the Party was legal, things were not too bad, even though they quarrelled a lot. After 1933 rows were more frequent, and more serious. Added to her neglect of domestic duties, her superior literacy, her contempt for his work, was the danger that now faced her political activity. They were constantly anxious in case there was that knock on the door at midnight or midday. But still the marriage lasted. Refugeehood was far more destructive. It ended her political activities, and nothing ever mattered more to her.

# Barricades

My mother could not pick up her political life immediately she had crossed the border because her German was not good enough. Hers was the common enough experience that she had learnt a language, but when she came to the country she couldn't understand the first policeman on the street. When she showed this *Schupo* (bobby) an address and he told her '*Gehen Sie Links, gehen Sie rechts*' (turn left, turn right) and so on, she wished she had never asked him.

Consequently, she threw herself into learning German. She had a powerful incentive – what was life without political activity – and she joined the Party the moment she was sure she could make herself understood. She would have had to be pretty fluent: for her there would be no point in being understood if she could not persuade. Lack of fluency, however, would not have stopped her from engaging in political activity. She joined marches, carried banners through the streets of Berlin and shouted slogans. The first man she met in the Party was Hermann Mendelsohn. Hermann was my mother's lover; luckily only for a short while because later he contracted syphilis. A puritan would say that it served him right for practising the free love that was the ethos of Weimar and the Party. Hermann died before I was born and I remember his name mainly because he had a younger brother, Jaques, who kept turning up in my life in England – first in 1939 as a penniless refugee and then much later as a Labour MP.

Hermann introduced my mother to other members, very few of them Jews because there were so few Jews in the KPD, far fewer than in the Polish Communist Party for obvious reasons. In Poland the Jews formed ten per cent of the population and with few exceptions were poor and working-class. In Germany, the Jews were a tiny 0.9 per cent of the population, mostly middle-class, well educated, and not barred from any of the professions. But the essential difference between the Party in Poland and the Party in Germany, and one my mother rejoiced in, was not the proportion of Jews but the fact that the KPD was legal and its activities out in the open. No more looking over your shoulder, no more listening for footsteps or the peremptory knock at the door. Like Communist Parties everywhere, the KPD was organised into cells, but whereas my mother's and Benny Bidermann's cell had sometimes met in shacks, in the woods or in the hills outside the town, in Berlin no hiding place was necessary. Not until 1933.

'Cell' sounds exotic but a cell is no more exotic than a ward. However, I hardly think a cell in Lublin, in Weimar or in Hitler's Germany ever organised a jumble sale, or a tombola, or played musical chairs at Christmas like the Labour Party wards I came to know so well in Stockton-on-Tees in the Sixties, Seventies and Eighties. And the women members of the KPD certainly did not bake cakes that had their weights guessed and were raffled. Together with the men, they concentrated on printing leaflets. Each cell was in charge of its own propaganda, which was always up to date. Organisation was efficient. 'Typically German,' says my mother on her deathbed in her small terraced house in Willesden in 1979. She could still see the rooms in Berlin where, before 1933, they used to meet once a week, sometimes once a fortnight. This is where she came into her own as a dominant figure. Her command of German was by then near-perfect, and apart from helping to formulate propaganda she was soon in demand as a charismatic speaker and took a prominent role in the women's section which gave her a public outlet for her feminism. The Party was unequivocal in its campaign for female emancipation, a campaign supported by *Die Rote Fahne* and not only during its women's week in March 1928. When the paper challenged workers everywhere to lay down their chains, it called on the women in particular: *'Frauen, legt ab Eure Ketten!'* (Women, lay down your chains!)

What did my mother and her comrades hope to achieve, and how? Fifty years later, when she talked about this with Bill, my Social Democratic husband, she maintained that revolution was a last resort. It was far better to win through elections. 'We had six million people voting Communist at one time! This gave us hope of achieving our aims through the ballot box.' This is not a conclusion she came to after forty years in England, nor was she being tactful because of Bill's politics. The Communist Party was certainly not democratic, the power they sought was not democratic, and they, as well as the National Socialists, tried coup after coup to seize power. But neither of the extreme Parties was averse to using democratic elections as a means of achieving their undemocratic ends. Elections were, after all, the stepping stones that led Hitler to his dictatorship.

But revolution through elections didn't really suit my mother's style. She was never a democrat, either at heart or at home or in politics. Yet being able to fight an election was nevertheless bliss and joy to her. She looked back on it as coming 'from hell into heaven!' Heaven was that she could take part in demonstrations, of which there were many, some of them involving thousands of people, 'And I could just walk with them! I, who couldn't walk on the street in Poland, could walk freely in Germany!' She could take part in elections, she could stand outside election halls carrying political sandwich boards which told the voters *'Wählt Kommunistische Partei!'* (Vote Communist!), and no one stopped her. She recalls that 'Everything was free, the cells were free' (she means legal) and that 'it was like paradise' – especially as the adrenalin of danger on which my mother thrived was never absent in Weimar. Furthermore, although she was a foreigner with a strong foreign accent, she was much in demand to address large public meetings, and how exhilarating that was! If there was a police presence, and there usually was, it was there for everyone's safety, including hers. The guardian angel in my mother's heaven would be a policeman on duty during the first ten years of the Weimar Republic.

But paradise soon started to slip away and hell caught up with her early in 1933. The Party was banned and my mother was back underground. As early as six years before Hitler came to power, the atmosphere began to change. 'The atmosphere of his coming' is how my mother described it. The phrase has a messianic ring. It is easy to understand how the Left hated the Right and the Republicans hated the Imperialists and vice versa; but it is less easy to accept that the Social Democratic centre and the Communists could not combine to fight the extreme Right.

My mother put all the blame on the Social Democrats: they were scared to death by the Revolution in Russia and the attempts at something similar in Berlin in the November Revolution of 1919. Rosa Luxemburg was right to despise the Social Democrats and regard Ebert, the Social Democratic Chancellor, as the enemy. Ebert had made use of the *Freikorps*, those paramilitary anti-democracy units, to quell the November Revolution. And when the *Freikorps* murdered Luxemburg and Liebknecht, Ebert left them virtually unpunished. She never tired of telling me how Ernst Toller, the Communist playwright, was imprisoned for five years for his part in the November Revolution in 1919, whereas Hitler served three months for leading the Bierhalle putsch in Munich in 1923. The SPD bias against the KPD continued even as the National Socialists stepped up their streeet fights and intimidation.

But it is the incident on May Day 1929 that rankles in my mother's recollections of Social Democratic sins. On her deathbed, she relived the event and spilled out her fury at a villain called Zorgiebel. The KPD had organised rallies in various parts of Berlin to celebrate May Day. It contravened the orders of Zorgiebel, who was the Berlin police chief, but 'It was our right', my mother insisted. She described the rally on the Bülow Platz. Huge crowds had gathered, but there were also huge numbers of police, and without warning they charged into the crowd with rubber truncheons, fire-arms, on horseback or in armoured cars. The workers erected barricades but the battle was uneven and many were wounded, some fatally. My mother never forgot that 'this vicious cavalry was sent in by Zorgiebel', and that his boss was the SPD President, Ebert.

Reports of the atrocities in *Die Rote Fahne* and the *Arbeiter Illustrierte Zeitung* give convincing details. A vast crowd had assembled when the police were ordered to advance. As soon as the first wave of workers had been beaten back, the next wave assembled. A red flag was unfurled, and the *Internationale* roared out across the square. The police called for reinforcements but their way was blocked by makeshift barricades. One barricade consisted of vehicles, shelves, planks, building materials, and another was constructed out of crates and balls of tar. This was the signal to the police to shoot indiscriminately into the crowds. One of the victims was shot in the stomach, not once but four times, and as he lay dying they trod on his feet. They fired into the windows of the Karl Liebknecht Haus, into an innocent bicycle shop, and when two little children appeared at the windows of a fourth-floor flat — a worker's flat of course — they fired there as well.

The guilt of the 'Social Democratic Fascists' is emphasised throughout the accounts. As I read the reports and comments in the archives, my skin tingles with recognition. This is the tale my mother told me of battles and barricades, a magic word for me to this day; this was the language of my childhood indoctrination. Just listen:

> German Social Democracy . . . its hands sticky with the blood of Karl Liebknecht and Rosa Luxemburg and the Spartacists.
>
> Zorgiebel and the Social Democratic agents of the bourgeoisie have declared war on the workers of Berlin.
>
> Down with Social Democracy!
>
> Long live the struggle for the proletarian dictatorship of Germany!

It is five months after the fall of the Berlin Wall and I am reading this in the library of the Institut für die Geschichte der Arbeiterbewegungen (Institute for the History of Workers' Movements) at 1 Wilhelm Pieck Strasse in what was East Berlin. The librarian has just introduced me to the director of the Institute as 'Frau Rodgers, ihre Eltern waren im Widerstand'. I've never thought of it in this heroic way, but he is quite right of course: my parents were in the Resistance and my blood begins to throb with pride. I must be the first non-Communist ever to have crossed the threshold of that Stalinist building. The moment I entered the foyer, I felt excited and reproached by familiar quotations of Marx and Engels that covered the walls in huge gold letters. Engels' 'Unsere Theorie ist kein Dogma. Theorien entwickeln sich.' ('Our theory is no dogma. Theories are developing.') and Marx's 'Die Theorie wird zur materiellen Gewalt sobald sie die Massen ergreift' ('The theory becomes concrete power as soon as the masses have grasped it.') flanked 'Proletarier *aller Länder vereinigt euch!'* ('Workers of the world unite!'). But I am now a passionate Social Democrat, I tell these accusing walls, and surely this can't only be because of the need to rebel against my mother – to be moderate in contrast to her extremism.

My mother recalled the Zorgiebel affair and others like it as being exciting, as well as sad. It was all part of the atmosphere of 'his coming' in which the Party had to be increasingly vigilant as the Brownshirts scented victory and provoked more and more confrontations. The continuing helplessness of the government provided that milieu of unrest and uncertainty in which messianic movements always flourish. I wonder how far my mother closed her mind to the fact that the Right was bound to win with its powerful messiah whose promised land was just what the German people wanted. Rosa Luxemburg, the Left's messiah, was no more and their Utopia, as epitomised by the *Internationale*, encompassed the whole world whereas all the Germans cared about was Germany.

At the age of fourteen months I had no views on messiahs, nor could I have witnessed the turmoil of 1 May 1929. As usual I was being looked after by my sixteen-year-old aunt Hella while my mother was risking life and freedom. I might well have been left motherless and in the charge of the unloving Hella for ever. But my mother never gave this a thought. The Party meant more to her than people. The event on the Bülow Platz simply infused her with yet more passion, yet more ammunition and loathing against the SPD.

In 1981, my husband, Bill Rodgers, was one of the 'Gang of Four' that founded the Social Democratic Party in Britain. My passion in support of this venture equalled my mother's passion against the Social Democrats of Weimar. A fraction of my fervour was probably based on having triumphed over the indoctrination against Social Democracy from an age when, according to the Jesuits, it should have stuck.

# FIVE

# Scapegoats and Playgrounds

Much of what I learnt about barricades, the righteousness of Marxism, the iniquities of Social Democracy, capitalism and imperialism, especially British, came from listening to conversations between my parents and the comrades. To make quite sure I was learning the creed, my mother would occasionally, though mostly in passing, take trouble to explain things to me. But most of her time was devoted to the Party. Neither my birth nor my babyhood nor my childhood interrupted my mother's political activities to any serious extent. As soon as she had recovered from her post-partum anaemia she was back at work, even though financially and ideologically she was barred from employing any living-in help, let alone a nanny. Instead she left all the housework and most of the childminding to her utterly dependent sister-in-law.

My mother might have thanked heaven – had she believed in it – for sending this young girl all the way from Lublin to Adalbertstrasse and so releasing her from domestic chores to work for her beloved Party. But not so. Nor did she have any warmth or compassion for Hella, who was still a child herself and a victim of famine. My parents had only just married when my father sent for her. Hella was fourteen, and in an orphanage in Lublin. She had starved during the First World War while her bones were forming and she is the only case of rickets I have ever seen. She has bow legs, a pigeon chest, and is very short. She is a reminder now, at the end of the century, of the dire conditions in Poland early in the century.

Newly married, living in cramped rooms that were part of the workshop, and without domestic help, my father was nevertheless morally right to bring Hella to Berlin. His virtue, however, was quickly tarnished because the moment she arrived she became my parents' full-time, unpaid skivvy, and instead of thanking her they made her the centre of dreadful and daily rows. I am not saying she was an angel; I am convinced she wasn't. But neither was she the witch they made her out to be by blaming her for every little mishap. Ironically, poor Hella, the vulnerable outsider, was our scapegoat just as the Jews came to be scapegoats of the Nazis.

She was blamed for everything that went wrong in our home, from spilt milk to marital strife. Every lunchtime my father would scold and shout at her till she wept. One day he brandished a heavy wooden spoon as she stood weeping against the wall of the kitchen where we ate. For once she really had been the cause of an accident: she had just finished scrubbing the kitchen floor and had left the bucket of dirty water standing around, and I had tripped over it. The water had flooded the floor and I had hurt myself, though etched in my mind is not the gash above my eye but Hella sobbing against the wall and my father threatening her with the spoon.

But it was my mother who really hated her and whom she hated. 'I was a young woman, I had only just got married,' my mother used to complain, even years later in England, 'and I was lumbered with this filthy, flea-ridden, lice-infested, sticky-eyed, deformed child, and it was me who had to take her to the Charitée (public hospital), me whom the doctors scolded for neglecting her so shamefully. But I told them the facts, and then they apologised and said, "Frau Szulman, you are a saint!".' To have this view of herself authenticated by the medical establishment made up for much of the irritation that Hella caused her. For an atheist, saints and heaven featured large in her vocabulary.

If she could not regard Hella as a godsend, she might at least have tolerated her. If not for Hella, my mother would have been stuck at home washing nappies instead of marching shoulder to shoulder with the *Genossen* (comrades) and inspiring the *Proletariat*. It was Hella who, when my mother came home from the Jewish Hospital after my birth, had noticed the blood dripping through the mattress and on to the floor. It was Hella who sounded the alarm and who was left to look after me and feed me while my mother was ill – far too ill to breast-feed – as well as to do all the housework. Later, when my mother was rushing around speaking for the Party, drafting and typing their propaganda, raising her fist on demonstrations, shouting against Zorgiebel and Social Democrats, Hella continued with the household chores and looked after me as well, though not with much loving kindness.

Hella remembers to this day how she was exploited. 'A slave I was, and your mother calling herself a Communist!' How right she is. My mother, who fought so passionately against exploitation of the workers, exploited Hella without mercy. Hella never blames her brother, only my mother, and her loathing is unbounded and frightening. 'You look exactly like her,' she growls as her fist tightens round the breadknife. I shudder. My mother often told me that Hella hated me because she was jealous of me. But now there is more to it: she not only associates but confuses me with my mother. I know circumstances for her were miserable, and I can just about forgive if not forget how she mercilessly left me to cry when my parents went out at night.

Despite the political turbulence at home and outside, some of my earliest memories are as ordinary as anyone else's and as painful. Hella is central to my earliest one. I remember being about eighteen months or two years old, just old enough to talk, standing up in my cot in the middle of a dark room, screaming and crying until I was beside myself. My parents had gone out. They had left sixteen-year-old Hella to look after me. She had shut herself up in her tiny room that led off from the narrow gallery. My cries must have been keeping her awake, the flat was so small. I screamed and screamed and promised to be good – *'Wieder gut sein, wieder gut sein'* – but not a soul came. I looked at the closed door, but it never opened and it stayed dark. Had she too slipped out? I held on to the rails of my cot: I was alone in the world, they had left me. If only they could hear that I wanted to be good, that I promised I'd be good . . . Hours later my parents came back, and with them some relief but more misery because they were angry with me. I had wet myself and the bed and Hella swore she had not heard me, so I couldn't have been crying for long, could I? Just this once they chose to believe her.

As an adult – and one in whom compassion and understanding

for the underdog were instilled as part of Communism – I can find excuses for her; or at least extenuating circumstances. Her mother died shortly after she was born, she was deprived of love, kept so short of food that her body was permanently dwarfed and bent by starvation, she was cruelly treated by her elder sister, who packed her off to an orphanage as soon as possible. Then her brother sent for her and allowed my mother to exploit her. 'Your mother was a beautiful woman,' she tells me some sixty years later, with venom rather than generosity, 'but she was useless in the house. I had to do everything, everything.' We are sitting in her overfurnished front room in Aylesbury, in a small house on a meanly built housing estate, and outside it is drizzling.

After a few years of servitude with my parents, she told them she was going to live with her friend Erika and get work elsewhere. 'We'll denounce you to the police,' they threatened. Her permit allowed her to live only with them. I just hope it was the Weimar and not the Nazi police they threatened her with. She did leave eventually, though contact was never broken and she came to England just after us. The sore between her and my mother never healed, but she has transplanted it on to me. My mother still haunts both of us.

Another early and non-political memory, with pain of a different sort, has nothing to do with Hella, only with my parents and a doctor. This time my parents had not left me to cry my heart out, but were selflessly trying to do what was best for me. I was born with a small birthmark under my left breast: a red splash approximately 3cm long and irregular in outline. It upset my mother less than my father, who feared it would make it difficult for me to get a husband, but it was my mother who took me to the doctor to excise the blemish. He saw me a few times afterwards to check the healing process. All the visits were terrifying for me but the journeys themselves must have been nightmarish for my mother, though for once she was saintly indeed. Each time we set out, no matter which way we took, even if we set off in the opposite direction, I knew exactly where we were heading. My mother would try every roundabout way through Berlin – different trams, different buses, tram, bus and underground combined, different streets – but I would cry and scream and, as we got nearer, behave like an angry mule and refuse to take another step. She had to pull and push me through the door of the house and into the lift that took us up to the surgery. I have forgotten the pain but I can still experience the terror and helplessness as the doctor picked me up, as he held me close to his chest, as well as the fear as we approached his house and were ineluctably carried up in the lift. I feel uneasy in lifts and have never liked being picked up, especially from behind. The excision left a pale scar which disappeared in my early twenties. A later scar on my neck caused much greater concern for my father and bothered me too, but for different reasons.

Another early memory is about the destruction of something I loved, and it was all my fault. My *Glockenkleid*, or bell-dress, was my favourite dress of all time, and judging from photographs I couldn't have been more than about a year and a half when I wore it. It was made of grey-beige satin cut on the cross with a bow on each shoulder. Simple, elegant and, from my perspective now, a good colour for my reddish hair. Then, I liked the way it shone, the way it flowed round me when I moved and lay in waves when I sat, and above all how it felt when I ran my hands along it. And yet I destroyed it in a fearsome tantrum.

Like typical Berliners, my parents and I had spent a summer Sunday on one of the Berlin lakes. When we got back home, I refused to be undressed. They sat me on the sofa, I punched, I kicked, I arched my back and I screamed and screamed and screamed. They were not going to take my dress off me! Futile, of course. In spite of all my efforts and willpower, they won and the dress tore – not merely along the seams but the very weave was laid bare and pulled out of shape. To the wildness of my fury was added the loss of my beloved dress, which has never been replaced.

Photographs and memories vaguer than the demolition of my *Glockenkleid* tell me of other outings to Erkner, Grunau, Mügelsee. One lake had particularly dark and slimy mud which clung to my toes. In Erkner someone photographed me feeding the chickens with my father crouching down and helping. There is sunshine and rural tranquillity and we are clearly very happy with each other. A tantrum is unthinkable. I am not wearing a pretty dress but short dungarees, much cuter. In other photographs of similar outings, I am alone and naked. I am young enough – two or three – not to mind. Unlike a later outing, when I was six or seven or eight, and had a grim fight with my father because I wanted to wear more than bathing trunks. My chest was as flat as a boy's but I was desperate to cover it. Trunks were quite enough, my father insisted: 'You are wicked and stupid to want to cover your body. It's unhealthy and bourgeois.' Apart from any Freudian motives which I am not aware of, and the need to bully me, a need which grew in my father as I got older, this was a hangover from Weimar and its cult of nudity.

Whether they had a babysitter or not, my parents often used to go out in the evenings, mostly to political meetings, sometimes to restaurants with comrades and friends, and during Weimar often to left-wing plays and films, cabarets, and occasionally to gymnastic displays with some performances in the nude. Everyone's body was a thing of beauty not to be hidden, they explained, and to be ashamed of nakedness was a bourgeois failing. As I never went to any of these performances, all I have is my fantasy of what they watched, a fantasy that is deadly dull and not at all erotic. I imagined people like mine and everyone else's parents with bodies a bit lumpy, thighs a bit pitted, stomachs slightly pouched and breasts slightly sagging, parading up and down on a small stage or clumsily performing gymnastics. Why would anyone want to watch or take part in such an unlovely and boring show?

My parents may even have gone to the occasional boxing match. That bellicose sport was much admired by Weimar pacifists, progressives and intellectuals, and Grosz did at least one drawing of Max Schmeling. Schmeling became German heavyweight champion in the year I was born, and when I was two he won the world title. My parents thought he was great, though later they thought Joe Louis was even greater. They pointed out to me that he was black, that 'all his ancestors were slaves, but look at him now!'

Gymnastics were part of the Weimar cult of the body and I liked it so long as I was a participant. Participation began at home when my parents bought me a set of rings and a bar suspended by two strong ropes from a door. I swung and rotated there for hours. I

was about five, and when I was older still, about eight, I took a bus
– all by myself – once a week in the early evening in winter, to a
*Turnverein*, where groups of children did gymnastics.

I was never an angelic child and outings with me when I was
two and three years old could be a trial. For apparently no reason
at all I would start to scream right in the middle of a walk, often
with Hella, and nothing and no one could stop me. My screams
filled my head and the street around me so that everything was
almost excluded in a haze of intoxication. Passers-by stopped to
stare as I screamed. They shook their bourgeois heads, made
disapproving noises and faces, and either accused whoever was with
me of ill-treating me, or – and this happened more often –
suggested I should be given a good slap.

I can't just have been getting my own back at Hella for leaving
me to scream at night. I did it to my father too. One of his
treasures was a photograph of me screaming while he bent down,
held my hand and pointed, laughing at the photographer. He had
it framed and kept it on a little chest of drawers in his bedroom,
first in Berlin, then in Haverstock Hill in London and finally in
Ealing.

But it was not all howling and kicking when I was little. As
well as sundrenched days paddling in lakes and in rural Erkner
feeding the chickens, there were calm summer days and winter days
spent on the Michaelkirch Platz. This was our neighbourhood
playground, with large grassy areas overlooked by the eponymous
church. It had swings that often, though not always, made me feel
dizzy. It was and still is halfway between Adalbertstrasse and
Köpenicker Strasse, where we moved when I was three years old,
and which also came to run into the Berlin Wall.

It took me twenty-seven years to go back to Berlin – it was
1966, a few years after the Wall had been erected – and then I
could not face going raw and unprotected but took care to take
with me the cushion of my life as the 'wife of'. I had then been
married to Bill Rodgers for eight years and, as the wife of a member
of the Government, I was taken under the wing of Peter Hayman,
'our' Minister in Berlin, a genial man who later achieved notoriety
as a member of a pederast ring. He took me to the garden party of

the British garrison in Berlin where the band played tunes from *My Fair Lady* and the colonel wore a black eye-patch. The next day, Hayman's diplomatic limousine drove me to some of the sights of the city where I was born. I stood on that platform, contemplated the Reichstag and nearby, but on the other side of the Wall, the Brandenburger Tor and the Unter den Linden, and felt like an ancient Mesopotamian resurrected to look at dead and silent monuments where in my lifetime there had been the bustle of people and buses and cars. I walked up to the flame that burns for the Unknown Soldier, and turned round at the very moment when the guard was marching up in their ritual goosestep. Mrs Hayman sat in the car and watched in fright as I stood transfixed. It seemed inevitable that the boots of these programmed automatons would demolish my face. It was crazy of me to stand still but I thought: 'You kicked me out once, I am not going to move for you lot now!' My face was spared by inches.

Neal Ascherson, then *Guardian* correspondent in Berlin, showed me landmarks less formal but important to me and my childhood: Michaelkirch Platz, the bathing station on the Mügelsee, the dead and eerie Potsdamer Platz. Later, when I stayed in the ambassador's residence in East Berlin with our friends the Everards, who had been posted there, I was well cushioned.

On my visit in 1966, I kept my feelings well reined in. Neal told me years later that I fell into complete silence. Even when I walked in the Michaelkirch Platz which is *the* monument in Berlin for me, the most emotive monument of, or to, my childhood, where I was allowed to be an ordinary and non-political child, I resorted to the British stiff upper lip, so unlike me. Perhaps I didn't want to give 'them' the satisfaction of seeing that they had succeeded in hurting and harming me. The second time I returned, in 1986, I ran weeping from one end of the square to the other and round and round the broken church. I was with Josiane Everard, who is the daughter of a Greek father, a French mother, was born in Egypt, and had understanding and sympathy for my feelings. On my third visit, in 1988, I was no less devastated but more in control. The church was still in the ruins it had incurred at the end of the war, and still looked in pain at the Berlin Wall a hundred yards away.

On my fourth visit in 1990, I asked a mother with a daughter the same age as I had been when I played in the Michaelkirch Platz, where the Wall had stood.

When I hear children of that age speak in German, I ache deeply for my childhood, I grieve for the dreadful loss of home. Michaelkirch Platz feels like my place, but I know it isn't my place because they who owned it threw me out and forced me to play in other playgrounds and speak a strange language. The feeling of not belonging to either there or here was reinforced by the presence, and later the ghost, of the Wall. It was also reinforced by a simple problem of language on my first visit in 1966, when I went into a pharmacy. In fluent German I asked for 'some pink sticky material that I can put over a cut on my hand'. The puzzled assistant said, 'Elastoplast'. Then I asked for 'handkerchiefs made out of paper'. 'Kleenex!' she snapped, and was no longer puzzled but hostile. But I was neither mad nor trying to make a fool of her.

Michaelkirch Platz was where the local children played when they were not at school. A German school day is from 8 a.m. till 1 p.m. and most children took, and I dare say still take, a mid-morning snack. We carried ours in a special basket slung across the shoulders on a leather strap. In season and when I was in luck, my mother would pack the basket with strawberry sandwiches: scrumptious, because by the eleven o'clock break juice from the soft sweet fruit had impregnated the bread. No doubt such a sandwich was the origin of the English summer pudding, which I came across decades later.

In summer, when we got home from school, we would rush through lunch and then our mothers – or Aunt Hella equivalents – would take us to Michaelkirch Platz. Mothers and child-minders and, until the mid-1930s, the unemployed, would sit on those park benches made of curved wooden planks on an iron base and ubiquitous in London as well as Berlin parks. In an area sheltered from the sun was a semicircular bench of stone. There on one very hot afternoon a large, flabby and clearly abnormal boy in his early teens peeled off all his clothes. A perfectly sensible thing to do in the heat, but against convention and therefore shocking and mad.

The boy stood there in his huge, white, baby-shaped, hairless body trimmed with small, innocent genitals. He was strong enough to fight off any mother who tried to keep him covered up. In the end he was carried off but I do not know how and by whom. I doubt that he was allowed to survive into the 1940s. The master race did not tolerate such flaws.

The public lavatories were looked after by a middle-aged and very grumpy woman in a dingy apron. She would grudgingly hand out torn pieces of newspaper and as we sat on the lavatory she mumbled aloud to herself '*Ja, Undank ist der Welten Lohn.*' (Ingratitude is the wages of the world.) I'm sure she made a splendid member of the master race.

Most of the children I played with on the Michaelkirch Platz were local. But occasionally Mia would come to play. Mia was the daughter of Polish friends of my parents. She was a sunny girl who pulled funny faces and had short frizzy light brown hair. And the lucky girl had a doll's pram! In a photograph the two of us are grinning and laughing as she holds on to her lovely doll's pram made of wickerwork. A quilt lies across it but it is not possible to see what it covers. Mia and her parents left Germany in 1937 before Polish Jews were forcefully shoved across the border, and before the *Kristallnacht*. They went home to Krakow, and died either in Auschwitz or on the way there.

In the winter a skating rink appeared near the Michaelkirch Platz, on the Engelbecken, a small pond on which I learnt to skate when I was only two and a half. By the time Hitler came to power I was quite proficient, except on the first day of the season when I wobbled for the first half hour or so before my feet remembered those gliding movements. On the first day of the winter of 1933, some big girls came to my aid as I hobbled and wobbled, and took me round the Engelbecken rink. One girl on either side of me, calling out 'right, left, right, left', skated in rhythmic unison with me in the middle. 'She's adorable,' they told my mother when they returned me to her, and I was very pleased with myself. My mother kept telling her comrades how I had been taken up by Hitler Youth girls, who never realised that I was not the Aryan child I seemed. She was delighted that the girls had been taken in, but I suspect she was also rather glad that I didn't look Jewish and that she didn't either.

In winter, when the temperature falls below zero, a number of tennis courts in Berlin are flooded – I used to imagine a man with a watering can going back and forth along each court – and transformed into skating rinks. When I was older, seven or eight, I used to go to one or other of these on my own. They were much safer than the ponds or lakes – so many tales of children falling through the ice – and I still had that same exhilarating sense of sailing or flying through the air and landscape that only skating at speed out of doors gives. Intoxicating especially at that age when I felt no physical fear. The only drawback was that my toes got numb with cold. But there was help for that and compensation: a cosy hut by the side of the rink was warmed by an oven that glowed red-hot and thawed out my toes. The woman behind the wooden counter sold hot drinks and snacks and sweets. I would pull out some small coins stuffed inside my gloves and buy a bar of delicious nougat. By the time I had crunched it to dissolution, my toes had thawed out. I have tried in vain over the last fifty years to find nougat as delicious.

When I was tiny and before I could skate properly, my mother often took me tobogganing in the Tiergarten. The slopes were true nursery slopes with no danger at all. My mother enjoyed it at least as much as I did, though she enjoyed steeper and more exhilarating slopes even more. She wore her long coat with its fur collar, and I a blue and white striped woollen outfit: long-sleeved top, leggings that ended in spats, hat with a pompom and mittens. Even at that age I usually carried a muff suspended round my neck. My muffs were made of fur, lined with slippery satin with a pocket closed by a zip. Pretty, frivolous things and not at all the correct style for little 'Comsomols', or young Communists.

By the summer of 1934, we had moved to Bayreutherstrasse off the Wittenberg Platz in the smart West End of the city. From then on the more formal and much larger Tiergarten became a favourite park. As well as its monuments to German *Kultur* and triumphs, it had lakes and huge trees, some of them chestnuts that were the homes of beautiful, deep auburn squirrels with huge bushy tails. The grey squirrels in England are quite beguiling but only like the poor relatives in Victorian novels. Though, like the workers in a revolution, they have largely supplanted the aristocrats.

When twilight set in and I was on my own in the Tiergarten, I began to fancy that I saw strange and sinister men lurking behind the trees. I ran out of the park and home as fast as I could. Those grand trees have gone. They were victims of the war — not of the bombs but of Berliners who felled them for fuel. The new trees were planted in 1949 and have nothing to do with me.

All the years in London, it was only thoughts of red squirrels as well as crunchy snow that evoked *Sehnsucht* (a pining for things past) in me for Berlin and my childhood. Once the Wall was open, I suffered *Sehnsucht* for other things, including my schooldays.

# Food and Birthdays

Places and landscapes are effective triggers for memories. Locations like the Michaelkirch Platz, the Tiergarten, the Wittenberg Platz evoke specific incidents for me. Lakes and birch trees and evergreens and wild purple flowers and heathland anywhere take me back to my childhood less specifically. When I walk through the Faccombe estate on the Hampshire/Wiltshire borders near our weekend cottage, I am back in the countryside within reach of Berlin as well as in the dark forests of Grimm's fairy tales.

But food is just as effective at pulling the past into my consciousness. It often combines with places and landscapes, and occasionally with political episodes. And, except for garlic, it is the taste of food rather than its smell which evokes memories. Unsurprisingly, the chronicle of my eating habits reflects my ethnic background, the extent of our assimilation, the political climate, as well as my parents' attitudes to celebrations, to religion and what was good for me.

They regarded yolk of egg as the food-of-foods, the essence of all that was wholesome, the source of growth, bodily and mental. The white was superfluous. But the white was the only bit I liked; the yellow was disgusting and impossible to swallow. So twice a week in the kitchen in Bayreutherstrasse, my mother force-fed me with a hard-boiled egg. What a pity she had never been a suffragette. She might then have realised that to me this dry stuff being pushed into my mouth was nearly as repugnant as having a tube forced down my throat.

The kitchen led to the backstairs via a big iron-clad door with innumerable bolts and plates. I studied this metal work in minute detail to take my mind off the yellow muck my mother shoved into me. How can one yolk be so large and one metal door so fascinating! Not till I saw Donatelli's door of the *duomo* in Florence years later was I so mesmerised by a door.

I can't imagine why she forced me to eat the yolk – unless she thought it was egg in its purest form – because I had a weekly meal of scrambled eggs. They formed the basis of our Sunday breakfast fish, which was delicious. Chopped onions sautéd in butter were heated up together with beaten eggs. This recipe was imported from Poland and prepared, not by my mother, but by my father and it was the only way I would eat onions. The dish was a treat in itself and with it went the Sunday morning ritual of my going into my parents' bedroom, clambering onto their bed and lying on the *Besuchsritze*. German marital beds are usually constructed so that a narrow unupholstered section separates the two mattresses. This is nicknamed the *Besuchsritze*, or visitor's gap. Lying on the bare strip of wood was quite uncomfortable but very satisfying as it was between my mother and father. I really felt I belonged. My father brought everything in on a tray and we ate in bed. Whether they made this breakfast once we were in London I cannot remember. By then I was too old to get into their bed and I was no longer the only child.

Sometimes these mornings would be marred, but only briefly, by the smell of garlic. There was none in the breakfast but it exuded from the pores and breath of my parents and permeated the bedroom. As garlic stays on the breath for twenty-four hours and as my father could hardly breathe it over his clients, they saved it for Saturday nights. Then they had a feast of it. Much as I like garlic now, I could not bear it as a child, either the taste of it or the smell.

Food was not always the idiom of harmony in our house. Veal schnitzel was a favourite but my father used to suspect my mother of using pork, which was cheaper than veal. '*Schweinefleisch*,' he grumbled as he toyed with the egg-and-breadcrumbed slice, 'Do you want to make me ill?' He sounded like the giant when he smells Jack after he has climbed up the beanstalk. But my father was less easy to pacify than the giant. He had shed his Judaism and with it the dietary taboos, but the edict that forbids the eating of pork remained with him to the end of his life. It was masked by the usual rationalisation that it harboured tapeworm. He shared the common mistake that tapeworms are only killed at very high temperatures, though in fact they perish at 58° C and anyway were unknown at the time the Bible was written. When in 1936 or 1937 my father went into hospital – a private room in a private clinic – I was sure they were ridding him of a tapeworm by a series of enemas. This was a fantasy but one I cherished for years until I learnt he had been treated for a gastric or duodenal ulcer.

He did eat pork but only in the disguised form of bacon or ham. Perhaps he believed that the dreaded and mythological worm had been smoked out or maybe the disguise was effective. Ham and bacon do not look like pig, or like pork, and moreover the German words are different: *Schinken* and *Speck* instead of *Schweinefleisch*. In German the euphemism pork for pig does not exist. *Schwein* is *Schwein* in the sty and on the table. Ham and bacon might also fit Lévi-Strauss' theory that the same meat can have different connotations and values according to the way it is served: raw, boiled, roasted, smoked. Smoked is the most prestigious. There was one Jewish and meatless dish, a *shtetl* dish, which my father enjoyed without fuss: matzos broken into onion soup – a truly soggy concoction.

Along with German words, my mother learnt something about German food, especially the *Eintopfgericht*: meat, potatoes and beans all stewed in one pot. It was the loyal duty of every housewife in Hitler's Germany to feed her family on this dish at least once a week. The money saved went to that phony charity, the *Winterhilfe*, which purported to help the poor in winter but, as my mother knew, went into the Party coffers. Not that Party functionaries came to peer into each *Hausfrau*'s cooking pots to check she was ladling out the patriotic dish, but I am told that collectors in the Brownshirt uniform called at every house for the weekly donation.

What my mother excelled at was a couple of Polish and Russian dishes based on red or white cabbage and beetroot. Carp, the Polish dish for high days and holy days, we reserved for New Year's Eve. I preferred it on New Year's Day, when the juice had set to jelly. Another of her Polish recipes was a highly alcoholic concoction. Into an enormous glass bottle covered by a wicker basket she stuffed plums and morello cherries, sugar and heaven knows what else. The bottle was left out on the balcony till winter, when the contents were wildly intoxicating and delicious. I now concoct a hybrid version, not in wicker-covered bottles on the balcony but in jars in the fridge.

I also learnt from my mother that fresh fruit was good and virtuous but that sweets and chocolate were harmful, almost sinful. I could have turned into a sweet-eating fiend, but food never was my focus for rebellion and I became addicted to fruit, in particular soft summer fruit.

Twice a week throughout the year a van filled with smoked fish from the North Sea called at Bayreutherstrasse. Smoked eel was my favourite but I also liked the eggs from the female buckling. And *Gansegrieben*! What would I not give for one of those crunchy chunks of goose crackling, and yet when I went back to Berlin in the Sixties and again in the Eighties I made no attempt to find any. Despite their sublime taste, they stir up a memory of violence and persecution. We used to buy them from the Jewish-owned Café Adler on the Wittenberg Platz at the bottom of our street. This smart restaurant sold some of its produce over the counter and the most delicious, apart from the *Gansegrieben*, were goose-liver sausage and cherry cake. Real cherries, not the simulated glacé type I found in England, were rolled up in the lightest of pastries and the whole cake powdered with fine sugar. During the *Kristallnacht* all that exquisite food was strewn over the pavement to be trodden on and peed over by Aryan dogs whose equally Aryan owners pulled them away before they could eat that 'Jew food'. And that is why I cannot and will not buy and eat that food in the very place where it was desecrated.

There is something else I avoid eating in the Wittenberg Platz because the delicacies of the Café Adler are not the only food memory intertwined with persecution. One of my favourite foods has always been *Wiener Würstchen* or Viennas. Twice a week there was a market on the Wittenberg Platz and I would be treated to a pair of these *Würstchen* with a dollop of German mustard – not the powdered English sort that brings tears to my eyes – and a *Knüppel*, a crisp roll shaped like a small truncheon.

The KaDeWe, *Das Kaufhaus des Westen* (The Store of the West), the Harrods of Berlin, overlooks the Wittenberg Platz from the opposite side of the square to the Café Adler. On occasions, my mother took me up to the restaurant on the top floor, and I would eat *Würstchen* with potato salad instead of the *Knüppel*, and in grown-up style and comfort. Then some time before the *Kristall-nacht* in 1938, in the middle of dipping my second sausage into the mustard, I caught sight of the notice on the wall which told me that '*Juden sind hier unerwünscht*' (Jews are not wanted here). I couldn't eat any more and we left. My mother had hoped I would not see it, at least until I had finished eating. She could be kind.

I did not go to that store again until 1966. It was my first trip to Berlin since we left and on that visit to the KaDeWe my only indulgence was a row with the assistant in the toy department on a lower floor. Not for another twenty or so years did I walk into that top floor that had wanted me out. In 1986 there were no hostile notices but it was repellent in a different way. A huge area was given over to selling food and was crammed full with the most ostentatious display I have ever seen. It boasted not just one counter with several types of salami, but several counters with several types of salamis: several counters heaped with profusions of ham, with smoked fish, with fresh fish, with poultry, with game, with expert cuts of meats. No less than three counters were laden with marzipan in plain and fancy shapes, and the choice of chocolates was dazzling. And looking at the range of exotic fruits you might mistake West Berlin for the capital of a vast Empire.

The display was the incarnation of the *Schlaraffenland* (like the land of Cockaigne it flows with milk and honey and more) in the picture books of my childhood, only exaggerated. It made the food halls of Harrods and Fortnum and Mason look like OXFAM stalls and its main purpose was to taunt the citizens of East Berlin. The effect of this bragging and shameless temptation to consume was to take away my appetite and rouse my latent Communism. I did, however, buy some marzipan for Bill – greed is catching and I bought two types. Josiane Everard, who had taken me up to this shameless exhibition, bought some smoked eel for our supper. I can never resist smoked eel.

Before we left that outrageous cornucopia of cornucopias, a woman carrying a tray of bits of *Lebkuchen* approached and I picked up a morsel of the honey cake with my fingers. She did not hit me over the knuckles but scolded me: '*Das macht man nicht!*' ('One doesn't do that!'). So I started again and picked up the piece with a plastic toothpick. I would have liked to have shoved the tray at her and had Josiane, whose role as wife of the British Ambassador inhibited me just a little, not been with me, I don't know what I might have done. As it was, I felt cross and small. I comforted myself by thinking, 'This could never happen in a London store', but what I really thought in my anger was, 'What can one expect of a German!' This woman had almost spoiled a memory for me. The KaDeWe always had numerous stalls which offered sweet and savoury titbits, including sips of Maggi soup. I used to sample everything, even if I knew I did not like it.

Eating from stalls and in restaurants were treats and so were picnics on summer Sunday outings. Most of these outings were spent by the Wannsee and the woods above, usually with our friends and comrades, the Danielsohns. We would all catch a train to the Grunewald and then walk past silver birches, low bushes and wild purple flowers, which I now see on walks through the English countryside. The flora is the same, only the proportions are different; I have never seen more silver birches than around Berlin. They are still my favourite trees despite my recent visit to Birkenau, the concentration camp named after its many birch trees – *Birke* means birch, *Au* means meadow.

We never took sausages but we always had one large thermos of potato salad and another filled with cold sweet lemon tea. We carried our picnic in bags – no Ascot or Glyndebourne baskets that need the boot of a smart car – to a clearing in the wood above the lake. The blankets were spread, avoiding pine needles as much as possible. The sun was hot and we stripped down to our bathing suits. We didn't start lunch till we heard the chant '*Saure Gurken, saure Gurken*' and a youngish man appeared in the clearing selling cucumbers pickled in salt and dill. He carried them in two buckets which he swung back and forth without a drop of liquid spilling over. We bought at least two each.

An hour or so after lunch we would go down to the overcrowded beach. After games on the sand and in the water, we sat on the beach and feasted on plum tart. But one fine afternoon my mother screamed out as she and a wasp bit into the same piece of tart simultaneously. Her lip immediately swelled to grotesque proportions. They rushed her to the First Aid station. She was always allergic to insect bites but she lived and we continued to spend our summer Sundays in Wannsee.

Plum tart on the beach, a rare piece of cherry cake from Café Adler – apart from that we hardly ever ate cake. Cake is thoroughly bad for you, almost as bad as chocolate, insisted my mother, and anyway she did not know how to bake. To bake a cake was not after all part of the requirement for a good Communist Party member. Moreover, baking a cake was a particularly telling symbol of the traditional restriction of women to the kitchen. *Kuchen* (cake) must linguistically be very close to *Küche*, one of the corners of the *Kinder, Küche, Kirche*, (children, kitchen, church) triangle which imprisoned German women, and others too.

Nevertheless, on my birthday I was not deprived of cake. On the contrary, the day before my birthday was wholly given over to cake-making and was one of the delights of my childhood. The fairy godmother who was the source of this delight was a friend of my mother's, and I loved her. Käte Schädlinski was tall and large and her long blonde hair was plaited round her head. Her teenage daughter, also Käte, was tall and slim and her blonde hair was bobbed. Both were Communists, and known as *Die grosse und die kleine Käte*.

*Die grosse Käte* was every bit as good a comrade as my mother but less inhibited about domesticity. The day before my birthday, both Kätes turned up at the apartment and baked a host of cakes for me. This event became a celebration in itself and lasted into the evening and past my usual bedtime. My mother mostly stood around and I licked the sweet cloying dough off all the paraphernalia. I felt so important, especially as the Kätes were so large that they and their cakes filled out the kitchen and beyond. All this excitement, this activity and chaos, just for me!

They made *Apfelkuchen* and *Marmorkuchen* and a third concoction of walnuts and hazelnuts which was their *pièce de résistance*. I took one cake of each sort to school. I was then at the school in the

Fasanenstrasse where it was the custom for each girl to bring in cake to pass round the class on her birthday. Holiday and weekend birthdays were celebrated retrospectively, and so during the year we ate cakes on more than twenty days.

The ritual baking of the cakes was not the only joy of the night before my birthday. Just as Christmas Eve and New Year's Eve are each the best part of their respective festivals, so this night was more dramatic and richer in pleasure and fuss than my birthday itself. By around nine or ten o'clock all the cakes were cooling off, and the smell throughout the whole flat, in Adalbert, Köpenicker or Bayreutherstrasse, seductively mouth-watering. But tasting was not allowed. 'Fresh cake gives you stomach ache,' *Die grosse Käte* warned, and my mother said it really was time for me to go to bed. I went. I knew the sooner I was in bed and feigned sleep, the sooner the next ritual would start. In this ritual, my father was the only officiant. He would tiptoe into my bedroom and start to festoon the room. He left the door ajar so that he could see what he was doing. When all was done, and the door firmly shut, I opened my eyes. My room had been transformed into a magical cave. Streamers and shiny paper shapes stretched across the ceiling and trailed over furniture. Japanese lanterns of painted paper hung from the lamps. All for me and surely a sign of my father's affection – dare I say love? It made me feel warm and unique and this feeling lasted the whole of the next day. The birthday parties themselves are blurred, the presents left behind less so. I loved the many books, I abhorred any new Meccano pieces. There was, of course, never a single doll.

The birthday of Christ was not celebrated in our home – no presents, no tree, no special food. But I did not feel deprived because Christmas was centred on the church and the church-going family. Not till we came to England did we find a Christmas that was more secular then religious, and extending into the day after Christmas with endless gargantuan feasting, revelling and exaggerated present-giving.

The Nazis, in their attempt to turn Christmas into an essentially Germanic and Nazi festival, turned the Virgin Mary into an Aryan maid and gave St Nicholas a rival, a doughty Aryan lad called Knecht Ruprecht. They circulated pictures of Christmas trees surrounded by images of Hitler and swastika flags instead of nativity scenes. As a child I was completely unaware of this manipulation of symbols, though I watched how the Christmas tree on the Wittenberg Platz was surrounded by SA men rattling collection boxes for the *Winterhilfe*. Some German Jewish families, so my mother used to tell me, had a Christmas tree 'as a gesture'. But a gesture of what? Of assimilation? Integration? Tolerance? A plea for acceptance? My mother told me that even some Soviet families had a tree, not at Christmas but on New Year's Eve when they called it a Soviet Tree. We had neither one nor the other.

But there was something special leading up to Christmas for me, too. Every year my parents and a couple of *Genossen*, comrades, took me to the *Weihnachtsmarkt*, the Christmas Fair that was spread out across the square of the Lustgarten. The Lustgarten (a garden of pleasure rather than of lust) is in the centre of Berlin. It began as a botanical garden, was converted into a parade ground for ceremonial pomp by Friedrich Wilhelm I, renamed Karl Marx Platz in 1948 by Ulbricht but reverted to Lustgarten after 1989.

I avoided the swings and roundabouts in the fair as they made me feel sick, and my parents avoided and despised the *Schiessbuden* (shooting ranges). I peeped at them surreptitiously to watch the clay figures rise and fall and coveted the prizes of outsize and garish soft toys; mostly rag dolls with flat faces. Christmassy things were there in profusion: tinsel, baubles, and – despite Nazi efforts – Sankt Nikolaus and nativity scenes of carved and painted wood. But the adults walked past all those stalls, as well as others full of rows and rows of yet more well-stuffed rag dolls. If they were ignored by my parents and their comrades, and apparently ignored by me, too, they were not forgotten. I never owned up, not even to myself, how much I hankered after one of those vulgar dolls with rosy cheeks, long eyelashes and everlasting smiles. Just one of them would have made me a happy child.

We did stop and buy a few modest items at stalls laden with spiced honey cakes in fairy-tale motifs of Hansels and Gretels and witches' cottages. At other stalls, I was allowed not one but two pairs of Viennas. My Christmas treat.

The barrel-organ music from the roundabouts faded out towards the edge of the market. There a large space was turned into *Liliputenland* made up of small bungalows or large doll's houses full of dwarfs. We paid to wander round the enclosure and peep into the houses to watch the small people simulate family life. I can still see – too often and too clearly for comfort – a group of child-sized and oddly proportioned men and women with lined faces, sitting and standing round in a living room furnished with small armchairs and sofas. They talked to each other as we peered in at them through the little windows. What were my parents and their comrades thinking of in tolerating this human zoo? I can't claim that it bothered me much either. I only remember wondering what it felt like to be stared at by strangers. Would it make me behave differently?

At Christmas 1986, I went back to East Berlin in search of that market. On the credit side there was no sign of *Liliputenland*, though I pondered on the fate that must have been meted out by the Nazis to those dwarfs. But in the main I felt hugely disappointed: the Lustgarten was still not restored and the new site could not have been bleaker and draughtier. The East German economy was unable to provide my favourite sausages, the never-forgotten dolls, or anything else in the least desirable; each stall was shabbier than the last and the queues were endless for the little that was on sale.

It was a dismal scene and I began to feel very low, when Josiane, whom I had dragged along, spotted something incongruous and colourful. Right in the middle of this dingy campus sat a jovial Father Christmas in traditional garb – white beard, red face, red gown, red sack. On his lap he bounced a little girl. I could hardly believe my eyes. Father Christmas in the capital of the Communist DDR? It cheered me up no end. But when I got back to London I was sure I had imagined it all. How could Father Christmas have appeared in a central role in East Berlin, ruled as it was by despots who shared my mother's fundamentalist contempt for the iconography of mythology and religion? So I looked through the photographs I had taken in that drab market, and there indeed sits the white-bearded, red-gowned old man, surrounded by children. This Communist child was never visited by him, but he is not to blame because at that time I was sure Father Christmas did not exist. When my own children expected him, he came and then I was as entranced as they were.

As for *Chanukkah*, so important to Jewish children, for me it was irrelevant. To my parents *Chanukkah* and Christmas were both religious festivals and as such superstitious nonsense and nothing to do with us. But while we did not rejoice over the birth of Christ, or the victory of Judas Maccabeus, we fêted the birth of the New Year and in style. Each year the pagan *Silvester*, or New Year's Eve, was celebrated with a delirious party. The flat was cleaned and tables covered with white damask cloths and Rosenthal china. My mother cooked the carp. Käte Schädlinski brought cakes and puddings. I was dressed in whatever was my best dress, and I knew I would be allowed to stay up till the New Year had been brought in. Such bliss!

All my parents' friends and comrades were invited. Comrades outnumbered non-political friends and included the Danielsohns, the Lederers, Dr Baer, our small, hunchbacked family doctor, and, before he fled to Russia, Hugo, a tall and handsome man who was a spy.

Was there music from the gramophone or radio? There was certainly lively dancing and boisterous singing and it got noisier and more ecstatic as the evening progressed. The New Year was rung in on the radio, toasted with *Sekt* and marked by the sound of those paper trumpets (traditionally found in Christmas crackers in Britain) that unroll as you blow them and the throwing of streamers until everything and everyone was covered in coloured tagliatelli-like paper. We all went wild. *Brüderschaft* was drunk by any two people who were still calling each other *Sie*. They intertwined arms, drank each other's health and called each other *Du*. I was given a sip of the champagne-like *Sekt* and then it was bedtime. I fell asleep immediately, though the celebrations continued till morning.

The *Silvester* parties were highlights during the Weimar period and after. It was only in 1938 that New Year's Eve became nothing but a wake, and once we were in England it was quiet and sad and such a letdown. I have searched all these years for another party to equal that frenzy of Berlin but guests at English New Year parties become so self-conscious around midnight that it can be embarrassing.

I still dream of those *Silvesters* and of my birthdays. I miss the excitement, as well as the food: the walnut cake and the baked carp. Altogether the food of my childhood was rather good. If only my parents had not quarrelled quite so often at meal times, if only my father had not made such a fuss about me drinking while eating, I could look back on my childhood meals with some pleasure. Not that I escaped being forced to eat up. All those starving children that are brought in to coerce little children everywhere were brought in for me too. Though in my case the children lived not only in Africa but also in Weimar Berlin. But I was never forced to eat anything I really loathed, like asparagus, mushrooms, spinach, most fish, all onions, damp matzos, and anything flavoured with garlic. Apart from the yolk of egg.

# SEVEN

# Saints Begin with 'L'

My meals were varied and cosmopolitan. But what about my spiritual, political and moral diet? No one ever asks their children whether they would like a portion of Catholicism, Judaism, Islam, Marxism or Conservatism, and no one asked me. I absorbed the basic precepts of Marxism with my mother's milk. Of her milk I had little, since almost immediately after my birth she hovered near death. But the diet of Marxism never dried up and, until I left home, I was sure that it was the most satisfying and the only health-giving and toxin-free diet. No doubt my mind was closed, no doubt I was indoctrinated, but no more so than any child born into a religious family.

As for morality, the ideology of Communism — as opposed to its practice — has no less strong a moral basis than Christianity. I learnt about good and bad, and about caring — caring is more realistic than loving — for my neighbours, especially if they were *Proleten* and underprivileged. As there was no God, and no one was going to reward me in heaven or earth for good deeds and selflessness, any love and duty shown to my neighbours had a purer motive — the nearest I shall ever get to altruism.

Marxism affected aspects of life other than the strictly ideological: clothes, hairstyles, choice of toys, to bake or not to bake, crime and punishment and compassion. In this, it was no different from other beliefs, sacred and secular. Little Hindus don't eat beef, Sikh boys don't cut their hair, children of Jehovah's Witnesses get no presents, little Muslim girls cover their hair and don't eat pork, and nor do Jewish children. I did not discover much else about the routine of a religious Jewish child until I was seven and went to a Jewish school. The trouble with my creed was the extent to which it exacerbated my marginality. We did not, after all, live in the Soviet Union, and once the Weimar Republic had fallen Communism shrank to a tiny minority faith and a forbidden one. Furthermore, by denying God, the significance of ethnic identity, and the morality of private property, it kept me on the periphery of the Jewish community, the minority group into which I would have otherwise fitted.

I grew into a little *klassenbewusst* (class-conscious) Communist who despite this class consciousness knew that everyone was equal, that ethnic differences were unimportant, and Zionism an irrelevant and mistaken movement. I knew that Jews already in Palestine would live in harmony with the Arabs if only the British imperialists would cease stirring up trouble between them. I knew that men (and women) are basically good, but that this natural goodness is spoiled by Capitalism, including Imperialism. I knew that the workers were exploited by the bourgeoisie and the upper classes, that the only valid struggle was the *Klassenkampf*, the class struggle, and that the World War had only been possible because the workers had been duped by their rulers. I knew that those in power never suffered from the wars they instigated. They prospered from the sales of arms and lounged on the beaches and in the casinos of the Riviera, sipping cocktails while the workers were killed and mutilated on the battlefields. With barely suppressed sobs my mother would talk about the shock and disillusionment when in 1914 ordinary working men had rushed to volunteer to fight their working brothers of another country. They were swept up by patriotism, and patriotism is a false sentiment.

The only hope for mankind was Internationalism, which meant a world united under Communism where everything would be run for the common good and never for profit. Everyone would get what they needed – whether they cleaned the streets, taught in Universities, removed tonsils, dug the fields or scanned the skies for distant planets. This would do away with envy and therefore with wars and we would all live happily ever after. True Communism, however, could only exist when the whole world was Communist. Before the promised era, some wars and rearming were inevitable. My parents would remind me how after the Great War the White Russians were helped by the British and the French in their fight against the Revolution. Even so, the Soviet Union was paradise on earth, as far as this was possible with enemies staked out around the whole perimeter. But we couldn't go and live in the land where people were equal and free because it was our duty as Communists to work to establish Communism here in Germany.

I knew, because my mother said so, that as God could not be seen he did not exist and that religion was the opium of the workers, and of the peasants. It kept them in their lowly places, while the rich and powerful were secure in their lofty luxury. A persuasive thesis, which I swallowed whole and which led me into sterile conflicts. As I progressed, I learned other tenets of the creed. The role of the trade unions was one, the role of the charities another. The unions were heroes in the fight for the rights of the working class, and the word *Gewerkschaften* still has noble connotations for me despite later encounters with British trades unions. Trades unions, I learned, are always undermined by industrialists, some of whom masquerade as do-gooders. Henry Ford, for example, provided hospitals and convalescent homes for his workers but the patients had to do compulsory home work for the firm while they convalesced. But I never understood what this was. How could anything you make sitting up in bed help towards the manufacture of a car?

As for charities, they sound well-intentioned but do not be misled. They may ameliorate intolerable conditions, but that only prolongs the misery of the status quo and delays the uprising of the proletariat. Therefore, according to Communism, one should not give to charities: a merciless doctrine, but luckily my mother, who always knew exactly what was right and what was wrong, could also be inconsistent. She was quick to notice the plight of poor people – there were plenty in Berlin – and she never passed a beggar without giving him something. Whenever we approached one, she dug in her handbag to give me coins to drop into his cap. Once when I took a box of matches from the tray the beggar was carrying on his chest, my mother sent me straight back with the admonition, 'You don't do that'. So I walked back and wedged them into his tray. I felt inept as well as mean and wondered if my mother knew him; she seemed to know so much about beggars.

When my mother or Hella took me to the park, Michaelkirch Platz or Treptow, there were always many young people sitting on the benches. A few had children, none had jobs. My mother knew some of them and that their future looked hopeless. She explained to me as I got older that they would sit there for hours playing cards but only in the afternoons. They had no money for heating and none for breakfast and so they stayed in bed till midday and in the park till night.

When I was two, unemployment in Germany stood at three million; when I was two and a half, at four million; when I was three, there were five million unemployed. Relief began in 1933 when I was five, through Hitler's programme of rearmament. Even before he took over, he put unemployed men into uniforms and how both men and women loved that. Pacifism was not universal in Weimar Germany.

But Hitler was the devil and the saints in my pantheon all had names that began with L. They were Lenin, Luxemburg, Liebknecht. Marx was God and Trotsky was a puzzle and a problem. As for the saints, it was less their ideas my mother talked about than their heroic exploits. They all espoused pacifism but their lives had been one dramatic fight after another. Lenin was the hero of the Revolution: he fought Kerensky's as well as the Tsar's troops, was wounded by an assassin, but ran the country in spite of this wound which led to his premature death. His real name was Ulyanov, and he was a glorious saint. More glorious even than Lenin was Rosa Luxemburg, whose martyrdom had elevated her prematurely to sainthood. His martyrdom did the same for Karl Liebknecht, but Rosa Luxemburg became a more luminary saint. To have achieved power in the man's world of politics was more than enough for my mother to worship her. But she also identified with her more personally. Luxemburg, like my mother, had come from a Jewish household in Poland, like my mother she had rebelled, and like my mother she had fled across the frontier – and at the same crossing. Luxemburg came to lead the Party in Germany and to be elected to the Reichstag. Before Hitler took over, my mother had hopes of emulating that. She certainly shared Luxemburg's views and especially her distaste for the SPD. She even shared her taste in poets and artists: Heinrich Heine and Max Liebermann. What she did not have in common with her heroine was a deep compassion for animals. Could my mother ever have read that moving letter from prison, when Rosa Luxemburg describes how she meets the eyes of a draught animal dimmed with suffering and near death? If she had, she would have dismissed it as quaintly eccentric, or forgotten it at once. My mother's attitude was much like the Christian dogma that denies animals a soul, whereas Luxemburg included them in the downtrodden of the earth.

In all else Luxemburg was her model and mine, and I still admire Luxemburg for her feminism, her strength and love of animals. But as for her contempt of Social Democrats, a view that my mother forced into me time and again, that is the very focus of my rebellion, though it did not surface till I married Bill. I have never felt the need to conform with his views, but I am committed to Social Democracy. Yet the depth of my Communist self reveals itself now and again, a Communist self that has no kinship at all with the British Communist Party but feels utterly European in the continental sense.

It is impossible to plot the course of my childhood indoctrination. By the time I started school I was a steadfast little Communist and the saints in my pantheon included my mother. I was also a pacifist. Pacifism was part of our Marxism and one of its codicils forbade parents from corporal punishment of their children. So in spite of his temper and inclination my father never hit me until I was in my teens. Once, when I was around eight, he very nearly did. It was evening, I was in bed and my parents were dressed and ready to go out. I had promised earlier to 'be good', but when it came to the point I did not want to be left on my own. My father raised a coat-hanger to beat me but put it down again quickly; he had remembered the Party line just in time. So they simply ignored my protests and went out. I did not scream as I did in my cot when I was eighteen months old, I did not even wimper or weep, there was less terror in my dread of abandonment, but it was as intense and as deep. I felt it, not in the proverbial pit of my stomach, but behind my breastbone. I did not yet know the terms 'depression' and 'anxiety'. There was a theory around at the time that it was good for a child to be left on its own – not a Party theory but convenient.

I myself was so imbued with the Party line of 'you shall not hit children' that whenever in some playground I saw another child being slapped, I would get enraged enough to run up to the culprits and shout: 'Stop hitting her! She is smaller than you!' The adults would indeed stop, and stare, through sheer amazement. I was very small and still under school age.

Although I was never hit, I experienced another form of punishment which I now call 'shaming' but which my parents called 'reasoning' and 'teaching responsibility'. The principle was that if one reasoned with the miscreant and underlined the anti-social nature of the misdeed, she (or he) would see the error of her ways and mend them. I would be scolded by both parents, in sorrow as well as anger, and in the Communist idiom which placed my misdeeds within the context of the common good. (In a different household it might have been the all-seeing God.) I would confess that I had done wrong, they would order me to stay in the sitting room, the scene of the proceedings, and I would promise not to leave until they said so. The door was not locked, the key not turned, but I was quite unable to run out. They had put me on my honour as a true Communist. I have no idea what the ultimate sanction would have been had I ever broken out. Luis Buñuel's *The Exterminating Angel* stirred some recognition when the elegant guests at a dinner party in a grand house are unable to leave the dining room. I don't know what intangible power prevents that smart dinner party from crossing the threshold back into their world, nor what restrained that wretched child in Berlin. But in my case a great part of it must have been 'shame' and the wrath of parents who were even more godlike than parents in a religious family.

The shame I feel now is that I obeyed and stayed put. I wish they had turned the key and saved my face. But then I still believed that they were the best parents I could have, that any child could have. They told me this good news repeatedly, just as in Samuel Butler's *The Way of All Flesh* Mr and Mrs Pontifex convince their son that he is exceptionally lucky to have them as parents. Just as I believed in the righteousness of Marx, Luxemburg and Lenin, I believed in the virtue of my parents. I have not the slightest idea when I began to doubt their infallibility and all-encompassing goodness.

One particularly shaming incident happened on a Sunday visit to some comrades. We had by then moved to Bayreutherstrasse, whereas they lived in a poor part of Berlin. They had a daughter of my own age called Helga who, unlike her parents, had whitish blonde hair that was much longer than my own very short, pale gingery hair. I was fascinated by her hair but our friendship was fostered by my parents, who made more of it than it actually ever was. And it was my mother who used to go on and on about Helga's hair. Helga's presence may have made visits there more fun, but so did their music machine. Whereas my parents had a proper gramophone with proper His Masters Voice records, at Helga's they fed perforated bands of metal through the roller and fascinating sounds of a different timbre rolled out. But that Sunday all fun was wiped out. Another family was there with a daughter around the same age, seven I think, and the three of us went for a walk.

The day was bleak and the streets empty. We walked and talked and I noticed a stain on the front of the other girl's dress. I thought she might want to remove it and pointed it out to her. She didn't mind but it was Helga who flew at me in a fury: 'It's not her fault! She doesn't have any other dresses. Not like you! You, with your cupboards full! You just shut up!' She put her arms round her friend and the rest of the walk was conducted in silence. The moment we got back to the adults, the girl with the stain on her dress burst into tears and Helga told them: 'It's all Silvia's fault. Her dress wasn't good enough for her!' Now the adults raged at me: how could I, as a Communist, look down on her dress when they were too poor to buy another one? The tirade went on and on and was led by my parents, my mother as always the most articulate and abrasive and doing her best to shame me. But what I felt far more acutely than shame was the hopelessness of being so misunderstood. No one would listen to me: all assembled were virtuous Communists, I alone was not. I felt isolated, hurt, puzzled and indignant. Looking back, I am outraged and incredulous at how my own parents could have led the drive to push me out of the group. I also wonder how I could have got myself into that position. What made it all worse was that the father of the girl with the stain on her frock was still unemployed. Though help was at hand. It was after 1933.

As well as a Communist and pacifist, I was also a steadfast feminist. The two chief catechisms of feminism as preached by my mother were: a woman is as good as a man; a woman's place is not – definitely not – in the home. It followed that I was not allowed – not just discouraged but not allowed – to play with dolls, and was never taught domestic skills. I was allowed to watch Fräulein Pelz, my mother's *Putzfrau*, do the weekly wash; not to learn but to keep out of my mother's way while she worked for the Party.

My mother met my father when she was down and out and he was looking for a seamstress for his expanding workshop. She must have bewitched him the moment she walked into his workshop. How else could she have got the job? She was no seamstress and always claimed she did not know how to sew. She certainly never sewed a single stitch. Perhaps she wanted to escape having to help out in the workshop. If she could sew she hid it well – it was the last thing she wanted to spend her time doing. Her ideology despised domestic activity of any kind but she could not avoid it completely. She would have needed to marry a far richer man and one uniquely tolerant.

What she did do in the domestic sphere and what she did not was full of inconsistencies. Though she neither sewed nor knitted anything for me, she occasionally crocheted; and then not warm scarves and sweaters, but lacy blouses and jaunty hats with frilly rims in angora wool and delicate colours – the only frills I ever wore. She never baked a cake but she did cook meals that were syntheses of Jewish, Polish, Russian and German cooking. She was good with cabbage, as one would expect from her background, but her puddings were limited to stewed fruit. She did not dress it up in pastry or pie, and that was good as there was nothing for me to leave by the side of my plate. My mother's inconsistency regarding the avoidance of as much domesticity as possible stretched to making pasta, which takes a huge amount of time and trouble and surface area. Sheets of pasta would be draped over every surface in the flat. She also made chicken soup – that quintessential Jewish dish – for the pasta to float in.

It was my mother's inconsistencies that made not only food but life tolerable. Inconsistencies, aided by her not taking the trouble to check upon me, allowed me to read *Struwwelpeter* and Grimm's fairy tales – too horrific for left-wing children – and Max and Moritz. These two naughty boys and their antics were dreamt up by Busch and peppered with a fair amount of anti-semitism which I never noticed; nor did my mother, who never looked at them.

I loved books and became addicted. But I was also sentenced to Meccano sets, which were consistent with her non-sexist views. And it was a sentence. I loathed those primary-coloured inflexible metal discs and bars and rods and screws. I never made a single structure myself. Various friends of my parents did it for me, especially on my birthday, and I watched pulleys pull, wheels turn, pistons move, and felt as inadequate as any girl brought up in a non-feminist household. Only more so as I had failed in what was expected of me. It was a good thing I did not know that Meccano was a British invention. It would have been another black mark against the British, on top of all their political misdeeds.

A pity my mother's inconsistencies did not extend to dolls. My deprivation of dolls was a cruel consequence of my mother's feminist fundamentalism. If I had had dolls to play with, Meccano might not have seemed so bad. It would also have brought me closer to other girls including Communist girls with less fanatic mothers, but in this respect my mother was an unrelenting fundamentalist. She may have cheated when she rolled out the pasta, stewed the *Eintopf*, boiled the chicken, but she was not going to bring up her little girl in the bourgeois ethos of *Kinder and Küche*, never mind *Kirche*. Deep down I longed for dolls and I have never forgiven my mother. But the only conscious feeling I allowed myself as a child was to be righteous and smug that I had no dolls. Real pets were never even thought of, nor was the welfare of animals. With so much human misery, how could we afford to worry about animals? My mother's response to donkeys beaten and exploited by Arabs was: 'You just think of the wretched owners of the animals and their miserable lives! When we have changed all that, then we can turn to animals!' I did not then know of Rosa Luxemburg's compassion for animals, and my mother's indifference to them soon inhabited my thoroughly washed brain cells. So no animals for me, no soft ones after the age of eight and three-quarters, and real ones – never if it could be helped. When we were refugees in London, a mouse came to my aid and we got a cat. But I never came to own a doll. Only cold Meccano sets and, thank God, heaps of books, even some unsound ones.

I was not dressed in trousers – too extreme for the time – but frills and lace were banned unless crocheted by my mother, and my hair was cut as near a boy's as was decent. A centimetre of my earlobes had to show, which turned my face into the roundest moon. I dreamt of plaits, waist-long if possible. My mother despised this as being 'like Gretchen' (she who was seduced by Faust) and *kleinbürgerlich*, petit bourgeois. I didn't care. And didn't *Die grosse Käte* wear her hair in plaits wound round her head? I fought for long hair all through my childhood, and lost. To be fair to my mother, many of the girls I went to school with had short hair, if not quite so short or severe, and perhaps I only imagined they had a choice. They certainly had dolls and these always had long hair in plaits.

Consistent with my mother's brand of feminism was her attitude to clothes and make-up, which is not too far from some of my daughters' generation's feminism. Powder, lipstick and nail varnish were banned, the redder the more sinful, as were perfume, long hair, and shoes that were high-heeled, sling-backed or open-toed. My mother's hair was cropped – she would never have called it an Eton crop – long after it was the fashion; her suits, her shirts were masculine, sometimes embellished by a tie and always described as tailored and sporty. She liked to be described as '*sportlich*' and was quite vain about it. She would stand in front of her mirror in a new suit and ask me, 'How do I look?' Mirror, mirror on the wall, who is the sportiest of them all?

My mother's and Weimar's feminism did little for female self-confidence but bolstered the primacy of maleness and masculine manners. She and her comrades wanted to be better than any man, not different. They would have denied furiously and indignantly that they suffered from penis envy. Nevertheless, they did aspire to and envy everything that the possession of that organ symbolised: male power and a masculine style – which is what penis envy really means. Women members of the Reichstag had a tough time because they were not aggressive enough and their voices were too easily drowned out by the men. This would not have bothered my mother had she only had the chance to show them how it was done. Her voice was louder and stronger than many a man's, her manner assertive, to put it gently, and she looked very dashing in her shirt and tie and Eton crop. But she never looked masculine and remained a feminine woman, which she may have liked but might not have admitted.

On an outing when I was about six, to one of the shops in the Tauntzienstrasse, she tried on a huge brimmed hat and looked ravishing. I pleaded with her to buy it but she wouldn't. When could she possibly have worn it? Party meetings? Party rallies? She couldn't even have worn it to restaurants – her friends and comrades would have thought she had gone mad and certainly disapproved of it as heresy. She did own a cream silk blouse with red spots which was very elegant and suited her. The spots were a rare decoration, but then their colour complimented her religion.

She was given to wearing winter coats with fur collars and had one in her cupboard in Willesden in London when she died, though this was not half as becoming and stylish as the ones she wore in Berlin when she was slimmer. In accordance with her Marxist principles – and it had nothing whatsoever to do with animal rights – it was all right to have fur trimmings. What mattered was their extent and the kind of fur. One comrade was all but ostracised for having a coat completely lined with mink. Nothing showed on the outside, but as her coat hung on a hook during a Party meeting some nosy and suspicious comrade peeped inside and beheld the luxurious lining of mink. The owner was ideologically unsound for ever more.

I have always been fascinated by clothes. A fascination stimulated by my father's craft, and by my mother's rigid ideas on the subject. And I loved buying shoes. Children sang a ditty about the shoe shops in Berlin: '*Immer Leiser, immer Stiller, schlägt das Salamanders*

*Herz'* (Ever more quietly, ever more still, beats the salamander's heart). Walking through West Berlin's shopping centre in December 1986, I murmured this ditty to myself as I passed Leiser, Stiller, Salamander. Rather too symbolically, Herz has disappeared. It had probably been a Jewish heart.

Sensible clothes, short hair, Meccano sets instead of dolls — Communist Fundamentalism sounds bleak but it wasn't that bad. Quite apart from school, there was skating and tobogganing in the winter, outings to lakes in the summer, visits to the cinema, museums, concerts, and at home I took up gymnastics and played games.

Games require partners and mine were too rarely my peers. It was usually one or two of the comrades who threw dice or moved the pieces with me when they needed a break from politics — a bit like licking a choc ice in the interval in the theatre. And even my mother found time to play games, especially the more combative ones.

Dominoes, Halma and draughts were gentle games, with well-designed pieces and boards. The wildest game and the one I played most frequently with my mother who enjoyed it more than I did, was *Mensch Ärgere Dich Nicht*. This board game with gaudy pictures was a version of snakes and ladders: the excitement depended on being pushed back to the start the moment you think you're winning. *Mensch Ärgere Dich Nicht*, the injunction not to get vexed, only incites the very opposite with lots of shouting and thumping of fists on table. Much of this was because of the way my mother played. She would flush with fury or triumph, her throat would be covered in pink blotches, her face transfigured in exultation — as if at a political rally. She flourished in battle and this was a battle on the dining table. She willed those dice to turn up sixes for her. Incidentally no one ever played cards in our house. My father had become a keen and proficient card player but my mother banned 'this bourgeois pastime'.

What a good thing she did not despise the cinema. She had taken her cue from comrades who before 1933 had flocked to films made in the Soviet Union and the Weimar Republic. By the time I was old enough to go to the cinema, the films shown were made either in Hollywood or in Nazi Germany, but she enjoyed these too. So did I. Films have always been important to me. I need them as I need to dream, as I need to escape, and often a film has jolted me into an insight about myself as well as about others. Going to the cinema was the light relief of my childhood; not the art films, Weimar's speciality, with their often expressionist and surrealistic representation of social and psychological reality; nor those that disseminated the political message. I did not see *Das Kabinett des Dr Caligari, Kameradschaft, Der blaue Engel, Metropolis* or *M* until I was an adult and in England.

It was *Dick und Dof*, or Fat and Simple as Laurel and Hardy were called, and Shirley Temple that were my escape to fun and optimism on grey wintry Sunday afternoons when my parents would deposit me in a cinema turned over to performances for children. Best of all was Shirley Temple. Her hair was in ringlets and covered the lobes of her ears, her trials and miseries always ended happily, the goodies and baddies always got their deserts, and how I revelled in those songs of hers. Not that I ever heard her own voice. This was dubbed by an Austrian child actress whose first name was Trudl and who turned 'Animal crackers in my soup' into '*Auf meinem Teller allzusamm*'. I enjoyed everything that happened on the screen except for kissing scenes, which made me shut my eyes. Bill assures me that English parents used to send their children off to Sunday school so that they could make love undisturbed. But I have always been sure that while I sat there in the dark yearning for Shirley Temple's ringlets, my parents went to Party meetings. I used to feel they had dumped me.

When I was older, my mother sometimes took me to more adult films. Instead of Shirley Temple, we watched Zarah Leander with her auburn hair, Lilian Harvey with her blonde corkscrew curls (films were black and white but publicity was colour-conscious), and Emil Jannings, who was memorable for his acting and not his hairstyle. All three were friends of the Nazi leaders. Some films were memorable for their nail-biting qualities rather than their stars. In *Die weisse Hölle von Piz Palü*, heroes and heroine are in constant danger of falling down snow-covered Alpine ravines and two of them eventually do just that. By far the most horrible scene I remember is from another film in which the baddie, and very nearly the goodie too, is sucked into a quagmire, centimetre by centimetre until the quicksand closes over the top of his head and air bubbles gurgle on the surface. I trembled in my seat. I covered my eyes and ears. 'Don't be silly,' my mother told me, 'It's not real. It's only a film.' But I have never been consoled by that thought.

On a few Sunday mornings in winter while my mother, in rare conventional moments, was preparing lunch, my father took me to a concert or a museum. The ethnographic collections in the museum for *Völkerkunde* were arranged as they used to be in the British Museum before they were pared down into those elegant designer displays in the Museum of Mankind with most of the artefacts hidden from public view. But the Berlin showcases were never as rich in artefacts as those bygone British ones because the German Empire never rivalled the British Empire in size and wealth. The Pergamon altar, however, outshines every treasure in any British museum. It is dedicated to Zeus and Athena and is incomparably more numinous than the Elgin Marbles. As a small child I clambered up the altar's white marble steps in awe and excitement, and only slightly afraid, though the steps were steep, the marble slippery, and the altar immensely high. When I returned in 1966, so much bigger and older, the steps were as steep, the altar as high and the marble as incandescent. I could not test the slipperiness as it was *verboten* to climb up.

In 1986, when I went back to Berlin, I was forcibly estranged even from that childhood memory. I had gone to the museum with Tim Everard and was taking a photograph of the altar steps when a nasty little guard literally took me by the collar, snatched my camera, barked that it was *verboten* to use a flash and to take any photographs without a licence. He was about to frog march me to some office, but I pretended to know no German and called Tim Everard, who in conciliatory tones persuaded the small-minded functionaries to let me off with an instant fine. I felt pretty small for having resorted to the help of the British Ambassador. Immediately after this episode, Tim introduced me to a rather more

remarkable photographer who was looking round the Museum —
Cartier-Bresson. He mistook me for Tim's wife, began to talk
French and I felt reduced to nothing.

When my father and I did not go to museums we went to
concerts, usually in the Schauspielhaus, but the music was often
unfamiliar and difficult. I have always been intrigued by unfamiliar
visual art and artefacts, but I could only sit through the hours of
new music by painstakingly counting the people in the audience.

When I went back to the Schauspielhaus in 1988 with Bill, I
did not count the whole audience but I counted the Soviet Army
officers sitting right next to and near me. I could hardly believe
that here was I, sitting with Soviet Army officers with red stars on
their shoulders. This was my mother's wildest dream come true
and one concert she would not have missed.

# EIGHT

# Words Sacred and Profane

My mother never bothered with concerts and museums. The serious part of life had to be linked to politics and that included my out-of-school and before-school curriculum. For my Marxist education to be effective I had to learn to read as soon as possible. School did not start before the age of six but my mother began to teach me when I was five, though only sporadically. Her Party work always came first. But she had already begun to teach me Russian, her holy tongue, as part of everyday life. When she gave me an apple, it was a *yabloko*, the tea she drank was *chai*, a house was *dom*, a friend and comrade was a *tovarishch* and I would grow into a *comsomol* (a young Communist). When we went for walks, we would march to: *odin, dwa, tri, chetiri*. The first song she taught me was not Russian but Ukranian and non-political. I still sing it but I am sure the words are double-dutch to any Ukranian. All other songs I learnt from her were strictly political: like the *Internationale*, the Red Airforce Song, and '*Brüder zur Sonne zur Freiheit.*'

As soon as I had learnt the German alphabet, she added the Russian. All her life my mother boasted how when I was five or six I startled her by suddenly and fluently reading out a headline in a Russian newspaper and translating it. It must have been a paper for White Russians since by then anything printed in the Soviet Union was banned. She never taught me a word of Polish except basic survival phrases when in the summer of 1934 she took me to Poland. And Hebrew and Yiddish did not exist. My parents spoke only German in front of me. They needed the practice but above all it was to shield me from learning Yiddish, the language of exile, humiliation and their ghetto past. Yiddish and Hebrew were furthermore the languages of religious practice and Zionism, both outlawed by my parents' creed. Yiddish may be a kind of Esperanto in that it links Jews across the world, and my parents were all in favour of Esperanto but only one that was truly international. So they banned Yiddish just as the Russians had banned Polish. My father's compatriots tried hard not to lapse into the proscribed language in front of my mother. Her contempt was too crushing and soon frightened any Yiddish out of my aunt Hella, though not before Hella had coined one marvellous word which my mother mocked till she died. Apart from cleaning the living quarters of our flat Hella also had to clean up the work rooms. When she could not find the magnet to pick up the millions of pins, she would ask for the *Spilkechapper*. *Spilke* are pins and *chapper* is grabber but my mother did not appreciate this fine example of how a language develops. To her, Yiddish was not a language but a handicap.

I have grown up wincing at Yiddish. It sounds like broken and polluted German. But is that an objective and aesthetic judgement or prejudice instilled at home? I use the word 'polluted', and when that word is applied to anything other than sewage or oil spills, it usually reveals prejudice. People of another race, forbidden food like pork for Jews and Muslims, are all said to pollute by those who are bigoted.

My Communist picture book before I could read, and my 'reader' the moment I could, was a slim book of cartoons by Heinrich Zille. Zille was a Berlin cartoonist who preached the Marxist message. His cartoons concentrate on the *Lumpenproletariat* now called the underclass, with its poverty and sleaziness – and inevitably with a political joke slipped in. His most pungent cartoons deal with war and its aftermath: lost limbs, lost eyes, lost sons, lost jobs, suicide, prostitution, food and fuel shortages, destitution and homelessness. A mother and father, for example, dressed in rags, sit on a park bench. She is wiping her daughter's bare bottom, and he with his crutch and one leg sighs *'Ja, mein Kind, so ist das ganze Leben'* (Yes, my child, that's our whole life). Shit and shitting feature a lot in allusion and image and it is those cartoons that have lingered in my mind even if the symbolism was lost on me at the time. They linger together with still more mysterious ones about prostitutes standing on landings, their breasts hanging out of gowns as soldiers queue up. Mysterious because I was too young to grasp the needs of the soldiers.

The cartoons of Zille were pretty tame compared with some I

devoured in my childhood. I don't mean the anti-semitic Streicher obscenities which I shuddered at from the age of five, but others in my parents' propaganda books. One book, which I named *Allerlei* (allsorts), was fatter, had more text than Zille's but still more than enough pictures. Some of them were ferociously violent, as when the arm of a heavy machine comes down with full force on its operator and the sharpened steel blade transfixes him to the work-top through his bare neck. It puzzled and repelled me: how could he raise his head from his elongated, pierced and partly flattened neck and why were his eyes still open and expressive – albeit of horror? I saw it simply as an industrial accident and more proof that the owners of production did not care for the safety of their workers. Although I knew how exploited the workers were, I missed the symbolism.

After the exploitation of the workers came lessons about the exploitation of women, for after Zille came Ibsen. Ibsen's *Nora; or a Doll's House* was the nearest I ever got to a doll's house. It was my mother's text for feminism – and it was drummed into me even before I could read it myself. Especially the scene where Nora leaves husband and child. A shocking ending for the time, my mother told me, and when the original ending was booed by the first night audience – all solidly bourgeois – Ibsen had been forced to write an alternative one with Nora going back to her husband. My mother's copy of the play followed the original. She often told me that she herself had tried to do what Nora did but got caught in the alternative ending. She had walked out of the flat – it must have been Adalbertstrasse – down the stairs, but before she had left the front door my father had said to me, 'Look, Mutti is leaving you for ever', and I had run screaming and weeping down the stairs after her. 'Don't go, don't go, Mutti.' 'And so I gave in and stayed,' she told me. I was stunned. 'You should have gone in spite of me' is what I said. But is that what I really felt?

I was a toddler when it happened, less than ten when she told me. So indoctrinated was I into believing that she could do no wrong, and that a woman's duty was to herself rather than to her children, so anxious was I to please her, that I told her I admired her, for at least trying to throw off the yoke of my father. 'The yoke'. Such dreadful language. But even as I uttered those ingratiating words, my throat tightened, my eyes watered, I felt dazed. My mother had been ready to abandon me. But for the time being I pushed that awful rejection out of my mind. It was not until much later that I began to wonder what in fact had persuaded her to walk back upstairs. What had my father shouted out to her? Warnings? Promises?

I have only recently allowed myself to acknowledge that my mother was wickedly fond of rubbing in how much of an irritation and nuisance I was to her. She used three episodes to illustrate this: her pregnancy with me that sent her back to my father, my red hair that reminded her of her own and despised father, and my tears as a toddler that again chained her to my father. She might as well have told me simply that she did not want me.

Ibsen was her text for other issues besides feminism, especially those plays that show how the iniquity of bourgeois men results in spreading syphilis to their wives and their offsprings. The sins were the sins of the fathers all right, but the lesson was preached more convincingly than anywhere in the Bible. I experienced the consequences at close quarters because the little girl of a friend of my mother's had to go weekly for very painful treatment for congenital syphilis. Her eyes were being treated with an acid-like substance and she was very brave, my mother said. I used to try to imagine what it felt like to offer up your eyes to be etched.

Women other than the wives of the well-to-do were also victims of men and society. Syphilis goes with prostitution, and prostitution goes with capitalism, my mother constantly preached. The only way some women have to keep themselves and their children from starving was to sell their bodies. I got the political message long before I understood the carnal details.

I have never liked reading plays and A Doll's House is the only one I ever read more than once. But poetry was different and fortunately my mother shored up my Marxist education with Heinrich Heine. I became addicted to his poems not because they were forced on me but because they were puzzling, rhythmic, sometimes fun, often disturbing but never too much so. The poem I can still reel off is about two expatriate Poles, Krapülinski and

Waschlapski, who lived in Paris when they should have been fighting for the fatherland against the Russians. Krapülinski has the same allusion in German as Crapilinsky would have in English, and Waschlapski derives from *Waschlappen* or dishcloth and means a wimp, a jerk. These two jerks or heroes lived in the same room, slept in the same bed, scratched the same louse, and had their two shirts washed by the same Henrietta each Monday morning.

> *Wie Achilles und Patroklus,*
> *David und sein Jonathan,*

they adored each other and as neither could bear that the other pay for supper, neither paid. Above all, they felt that

> *Leben bleiben wie das sterben*
> *für das Vaterland ist süss.*

Or: to stay alive for the fatherland was every bit as sweet as dying for it. This good-natured satire with its rollicking rhythm was one of the unforgettable pop songs of my childhood.

Decades later in London when I met Leo Pliatsky, the lines of that poem started to dance in my brain. We were having dinner with friends. It was long before Leo became a Treasury Knight, not that that ever cramped his style. He was passionate, crisp and contradictory, the very opposite of those anti-heroes in the poem. It was his surname and the rhythm of his personality and style, which must owe something to his Jewish and Eastern European antecedents, that pushed that poem into my mind so that it wouldn't let go. Around midnight when Bill and I stepped out onto the pavement and no one else was around I started to hop and skip to the lines of

> *Krapülinski und Waschlapski*
> *Polen aus der Polakei*
> *Fochten tapfer und entkamen*
> *Moskowiter Tyrannei.*

At last I could sing out, even if not at the top of my voice.

Another poem about two heroes continues to puzzle me, and I can't imagine why Schumann used it for one of his Lieder. Two

French Grenadiers worship Napoleon to the exclusion of everything else. They are ready to die for him in battle and ready to commit suicide when he is captured. They are not in the least bothered that their wives and children would starve: let them go and beg! Our sole concern is for our emperor: *'Mein Kaiser, mein Kaiser gefangen!'* One more example of Heine's satire, explained my mother. He was poking fun at soldiers who put king and patriotism above even their own kith and kin. She never revealed that Heine had at one time admired this Emperor, and had welcomed his conquering of German territory where he replaced the feudal system with rights of citizenship. It was only later that Heine came to oppose capitalism as much as feudalism.

On the whole, Heine was tailor-made for my mother, just as he had been for Rosa Luxemburg. He lived in a time of war and political turmoil and was a poet but also a political activist. He was born a Jew but renounced Judaism. His mother had wanted him to be a rabbi but he had rebelled. Later, in order to get a job at the University, he converted to Christianity but was never a Christian in any other sense. He was a free thinker, my mother insisted. She did not tell me that he was torn between denying and believing in an afterlife.

Heine may or may not have known God, but he did know Karl Marx and to Marxists that was irresistible. Marx had inspired the *Zeitgedichte*, some of Heine's most anti-nationalist and anti-mon-archist poems. The one that likens a king to a donkey always made me laugh. I never reached his prose, but one day when I was eight or nine, and my mother and I were in the living room, both of us reading Heine, she read out a paragraph of his prose which clearly delighted her. It was Heine's idea of heaven which, unlike my mother's, was quite pastoral with not an election poster in sight. It featured a cottage, a garden, wholesome food, fresh butter and milk, flowers by the window and some beautiful trees. To complete the idyll and the poet's happiness, the good God has used those trees to hang half a dozen of Heine's enemies. The piece ends: 'Yes, I must forgive my enemies, but not before they have been hanged.'

I was shocked but my mother said, 'Isn't that clever of him?' as if she wished she had thought of it herself. I nodded but I felt the same unease, only more so, that had gripped me when I learnt how God drowned Pharaoh's soldiers and their horses by closing the divided sea. The irony of an atheist writing about God and heaven – and irony is Heine's hallmark which up to then I had liked – did not alleviate the gruesome imagery of this passage. I saw the poet relaxing in his garden with flower beds and flower borders, having his breakfast or morning coffee and glorying in the sunshine; and the dangling bodies with their swollen and familiar faces.

But his poetry never brims over with sweetness and light and even the romantic poems are full of foreboding, mythology, darkness, sardonic bite, and the occult. That only made them exciting for me to read at an age when I was ill at ease with overtly romantic writing. All his love poetry is set in rural idylls. But in and around these idylls, lovers and ghosts of lovers suffer and take revenge. The bride is forced to dance with the ghost of the lover she jilted, dead brothers duel nightly over the woman they both wanted, and from her rock the Lorelei lures every sailor who crosses her riverine path to his doom. The mischief in Heine's love poems is always wrought by women, but I missed that point and my mother never remarked on this anti-feminist trend. She may have missed it, too.

Heine's poems were for me what *Winnie the Pooh, The Wind in the Willows, Alice in Wonderland, Gulliver's Travels* are for English children, including mine. I wonder what was the effect on my inner self of poetry so full of pessimism, sarcasm, cynicism and with not a happy ending anywhere. The sarcasm and cynicism, though not the pessimism, matched my mother's style. But I am sure he has deepened my pleasure in landscape. It's scenery rather than people that Heine depicts as beautiful and inspiring.

Rousseau and Voltaire – though she couldn't read them in the original – meant almost as much to my mother as Heine and the Russian authors. Especially Voltaire. He had been expelled from his country, she told me, because he was a free thinker, did not believe in the absolute right of monarchs, was passionate about free speech and had stuck to his beliefs no matter what the consequences. How I admired this brave man! I was thrilled when we went to Sans Souci in Potsdam and saw Voltaire's room in Frederick the Great's castle. But something bothered me. How could a writer who is a free thinker and who believes that everyone is equal be friends with a king? Because, explained my mother, Frederick the Great was an unusual, enlightened king who liked to surround himself with thinkers who accepted new ideas, even those that threatened his divine right.

One of the non-palatial sights at Potsdam was the mill. Every child in Prussia knew the story of Frederick the Great and the miller. It showed just how enlightened the King was. The story goes that the King ordered the demolition of the windmill as it spoiled his view from his beloved Sans Souci. The miller fought him in court and won. The King gave in. This story still moves me, almost to tears, and I don't know why. The mill was destroyed in the war. A bomb proved to be more powerful than a king and a judge.

The King's castle still stands and painted gesso flowers still decorate the walls of Voltaire's room, but they look dingier, either due to time, neglect or my memory. I went back in December 1986 with Josiane Everard, and apart from the two of us the guided tour consisted of a group of Russians who only spoke Russian. Over our shoes we had to pull on the same soft slippers as on my first visit as a child. They may have been renewed but they looked the same.

From Rousseau, as distilled by my mother, I learnt that humanity is essentially good but corrupted by capitalism. It is the savages who are truly unspoilt and noble – I cannot remember whether they were more noble than the workers – and white colonisers sought to destroy this pure essence of humanity. None were more ruthless, of course, than the British Imperialists.

From Tolstoy, one of my mother's beloved Russian writers, I learnt something that is still relevant. Beware the goosepimples of patriotism, he warns; the tingle catches you unawares when they play the national anthem or perform a national ceremony, that tingle which turns into a frenzy that carries you away with the crowd and provokes even a pacifist to shout for war. People are constantly brainwashed that God is on 'our' side, a 'false public opinion' that is engendered by pomp and circumstance. This kind of patriotism, according to Tolstoy, is incitement to murder, and murder flouts Christianity. Murder and patriotism also contradicted the essence if not the practice of my mother's Communism, and that's why she passed on Tolstoy's lesson. She left out the bit about Christianity.

I have never become immune to the tingle itself, only its translation into blind patriotism. I experience that tingle quite often and against my will. I get furious with myself when actual or fictional state ceremonies and jingoistic crowd scenes and songs bring me out in goosepimples. But I am conscious and even self-conscious of it and resist the illusions that come with the thrill. I am suspicious of all crowd behaviour, for I was after all a Jewish and Communist child in Nazi Germany. Tolstoy could never have seen anything to beat the Nuremberg Rallies, and Leni Riefenstahl's spectacular choreography of the 1934 rally in her film *Triumph of the Will*. The multitude thrilled to her ecstatic and mystical production, which established Hitler as the sacred head of the nation who came near to worshipping him forever more.

In Britain new depths were reached in 1979 and after, when the impressarios who had conducted Billy Graham's revivalist meetings were brought in by Mrs Thatcher's Tory Party. When that party's conference waved Union Jacks as one, stood up as one, shouted as one 'Maggie, Maggie, Maggie', when the ecstasy spilled over to the vast television audience and I heard them sing 'Land of Hope and Glory', even as my skin began to tingle, I thought of Tolstoy.

I also thought of a man called Albert Mason. He was a Jewish doctor whom I met just before I met Bill, and like all doctors he dabbled in power of a kind. This power was not on the face of it related to politics, yet it gave me an insight into certain aspects of political power. I took a course in Medical and Dental Hypnotism and he taught it with great flair – it was certainly not his looks that attracted me to him. The course touched on mass psychology, and demonstrated how the power of suggestion from one individual to another is nothing compared to the power exerted by one individual over a crowd. When this individual, a religious or secular leader, plants an idea, it infects the crowd and spreads like a plague bacillus, only immediately. I heard *Sieg Heil* roared by a thousand voices as if they were one, I heard 'Aryan' children jeering at me and other Jewish children as they jostled us during the pogrom of 1938, I saw the sea of arms raised in a Hitler salute, the goose-stepping legs of Storm-troopers. The mob is then exactly as Cannetti described it in *Crowds and Power* (some time after Albert's course and many years after Tolstoy): a beast with a thousand legs and a thousand arms moving as one. It is the Tory party shouting 'Maggie, Maggie, Maggie', it is the phenomenon so deplored by Tolstoy and which I learnt about when I was a child.

And always in a corner of my mind was the image of me aged six, the only Jewish, foreign and Communist pupil amongst the children assembled in the playground at the end of term to sing *'Deutschland über Alles'* and shout *'Heil Hitler'*. Had my behaviour been mindless or was it prompted by a deep wish to conform?

My mother never talked about hypnotism but she did talk about demagogy, and the word is as familiar and emotive to me as 'barricades'. Demagogues were unscrupulous politicians who roused a crowd by exploiting their baser natures. Yet there was nothing that satisfied her more than when she herself roused an audience. According to her, she did it by appealing to their better natures, their reason and the fine principles of Communism. Therefore Tolstoy's criticism did not apply. And anyway, unlike the Nazi rabble-rousers, she did not rouse but 'inspire' and 'convince'. I was sensitised by Nazi ranting but also by my mother's rhetoric, and I have always winced when a crowd is enthused by a speaker, especially when I feel myself caught up in the response. This allergy is a handicap if one is married to a politician. I know full well that to be effective one must indeed inspire and rouse, and that this applies to a rally as well as a Party conference and a democratic election.

Not all my comics were political and not all my reading was enlightening. Zille, Heine and Ibsen were relieved by *Struwwelpeter* and fairy tales. They were not exactly cheerful reading but they were compelling and, though she disapproved, my mother never added them to her index of forbidden books. Perhaps she was too preoccupied to watch what I read and she may have thought the cautionary tales of *Struwwelpeter* good for me.

*Struwwelpeter* is more like a horror comic without a single happy ending: from the eponymous hero who becomes a figure of ridicule, to Kaspar the fat boy who is finished off by anorexia in five days flat, and Konrad the compulsive thumb sucker who is left with bleeding stumps and nothing to suck for comfort. But for me, Paulinchen, the little girl who played with matches, was the most tragic character and her red slippers among the smoking ashes the most haunting image. I put myself all too easily into those poignant little shoes. Though I never played with matches, I was always in fear of fire breaking out at night. I could only too well imagine the little girl's horror, her pain of burning, her panic, but above all no one coming. The warning not to play with matches was plain. But the other message – 'Parents, do not leave your children alone in the evenings' – only I noticed.

As for the tale of Nikolas, who dipped three boys deep into his enormous inkwell because they had taunted a black boy, its anti-racist message went unnoticed by all its readers. Not that *der grosse Nikolas* went so far as to proclaim that black was beautiful, only that the boy could not help being black. And as punishment he makes the villains blacker than the little Moor.

From her index of banned books, my mother exempted not only books and pictures of social and industrial violence but also the horrors of war, ancient and modern. From raw scenes of war of the twentieth and earlier centuries – disembowelling, mangled skulls, crushed faces – I grew up knowing exactly how dreadful war is even without nuclear weapons. I did not need to see films of the Vietnam war. She disapproved of Grimms' fairy tales – too fanciful and violent – but as she never banned them I lapped them up. If Bruno Bettelheim is right, then they did me a lot of good. Fairy tales reassure children. All those ambivalent feelings, all that envy and sibling rivalry, the self-doubt, the fear of abandonment (I know that one particularly well), the hate and anger towards those you should love, and do love but also hate, the ambivalences of growing up – that, says Bettelheim, is the stuff of fairy tales and only in fairy tales can these fantasies and emotions be played out and resolved. You know it will be all right in the end. They may have abandoned you, but they, or someone even better, will come to the rescue. You may go as far as shoving your bad mother into an oven, as Hansel and Gretel did with the witch, but the good mother survives and loves you still.

I am still stuck with the wicked witch part of my mother. If Bettelheim had predated Marx and Engels, Grimm's fairy tales might have qualified as Opium of the People or the Children.

My mother never told me any fairy tales but she did tell me stories about Russian peasants. The one I liked to hear over and over again is about a hungry peasant who on market day buys a loaf of bread, eats it, but is still hungry. He buys another loaf, eats that too, but is still hungry. He buys and eats a third and still he is hungry. He goes to the next shop, buys a roll, eats that up and his hunger vanishes. 'Why didn't I buy that roll in the first place?' exclaims the peasant. My mother enjoyed this joke at the expense of the poor peasant. She would never have told a similar tale about a worker. She had about as much respect for peasants as had Karl Marx.

Marxist and progressive edicts banned other things for children, not only books, though not everyone went as far as depriving their daughters of dolls. Had I been a boy, I might have been allowed to play with dolls but not with toy guns, toy tanks and lead soldiers. And any form of aggressive games like 'bang, bang, you're dead' and Cowboys and Indians would have had to be played out of sight and earshot of parents. Children of pacifist and progressive parents may have been saved from caning and slapping, but they were at the same time frustrated by the ban on war games and books. The little readers would have nightmares, get neurotic and, even worse, turn into warmongers and arms salesmen. Pacifist protection – cocooning? – on the other hand, would turn them into peaceful and well-balanced children and adults. This simplistic notion of child psychology is still with us.

# NINE

# She Was My Rosa Luxemburg

Most of the books I read were on Hitler's index and burned by Hitler's mobs. But before these vandals became the official arsonists, they had lit another fire. On 27 February 1933, five days before my fifth birthday, they fired the Reichstag, an event that has left an indelible if blurred imprint in my mind. There was near panic at home when my parents told me that during the night the Nazis had set fire to the Reichstag and were blaming the Communists. Four thousand members of the KPD were arrested that very morning, including some of my parents' friends. The KPD and its newspapers were banned. Even SPD meetings were broken up. On 3 March, my fifth birthday, Ernst Thälmann, leader of the KPD, whom my parents knew and admired, was arrested, eventually to be murdered. I doubt that my fifth birthday was celebrated.

The Reichstag fire had been dramatic enough, but it was eclipsed by the trial that followed. The cast list of this compelling theatre consisted of Nazi villains, a Dutch victim who was deranged, and a Bulgarian hero who was one of four Communists in the dock. The villains tried to pin the crime on van der Lubbe, the innocent Dutchman. The KPD, they claimed, had duped him into starting the fire. But Dimitroff, the Bulgarian, saved the day – though not the cause or the poor Dutchman. In a brilliant speech he exposed the Nazi Party as the guilty pyromaniacs. He and his three comrades were set free; only van der Lubbe was executed.

This drama was played out repeatedly at home: my mother's excited account was a *tour de force* in itself. To me and anyone else, and with promptings from my father – as if she needed them – she would give a replay of the examining and cross-examining, who said what and to whom, and especially how. That brave and fine speech by Dimitroff! A true hero! How it reverberates throughout the world! How it puts the Nazis to shame! It really did sound like a speech Spencer Tracy might make in a Hollywood courtroom to the cheering of the brave and good. Her telling of it kept all spirits up, at least while we – I and the loyal comrades – listened. My mother talked about it till the end of her life, her enthusiasm gradually becoming tinged with sadness and nostalgia. But it always cheered her up, like going to a film where against all odds the baddies get the trouncing they deserve, or like an old woman looking back to better times, which they so clearly weren't.

Sometimes she ended on a bitter note by reminding herself that the Reichstag fire had served the Nazis' purpose and been the prelude to elections which on 5 March gave Hitler not an overall majority, but the largest number of votes. My parents and their comrades always held this against the German people. Hindenburg may have helped Hitler – what did you expect of that Prussian aristocrat who always hated the Left? But it was the people, the mass of ordinary Germans, the *Proletariat*, who voted for Hitler. In 1914 they had fallen over themselves to enlist to fight their brothers. Now, nineteen years later, came the second betrayal. It helped Hitler to push Hindenburg into signing the enabling decree which gave Hitler absolute power.

Hitler's accession, though part of a period of terror and intimi-dation, is a blank in my memory, but another pyromaniac spectacle has left at least some scorch marks. Less than three months after the Reichstag conflagration, Hitler's mob illuminated another German evening and further alarmed my parents and comrades. On the night of 10 May, huge bonfires lit up the insolent faces of men in brown uniform as they fuelled the fire with books from the Nazi index. Unlike later ones, this pyre burnt not the witches (those accused of bringing evil to the German nation), but their words.

Though nearly all the books I read were turned to ashes, I continued to read my copies of them even until 1939. If during a house search these books had been discovered, if some informer had betrayed their existence on my parents' shelves, a prison sentence and probably worse would have followed. But my mother was stubborn and she loved her books. Considering the risks she took for them, it's almost as if she loved them more than her children.

Hitler organised the burning of the books as if to celebrate his victory. It was also the time his gangs had their first taste of pogroms. A full-scale pogrom was still to come but the gangs stepped up their intimidation. As Jews and as Communists, the danger for us was twofold. It's not the details I remember but the tightening of a vice.

By the time Hitler became dictator, the cells of the KPD were well underground. My mother and her comrades had to be very cautious about each one of their members. There was danger from infiltrators, but also from their own deserters who could easily turn into informers and betray their former comrades. Too many joined the Nazi bandwagon. 'From the SPD as well as the KPD,' my mother pointed out to Bill in 1979, and with wicked satisfaction. The desertion was unstoppable. Hitler had won. Everyone, the most unlikely and the most good-natured, was a potential informer. The only way to survive, to get a job, to keep a job, to keep out of prison and avoid being beaten up, was to leave the KPD and the SPD and to keep quiet. It was more sensible still to join the Nazi Party and pin a swastika on your lapel. Those who lost no time and joined in March 1933 were known as *Märzgefallene* (those who fell in March). Others remained in limbo for a while before they donned that pin and the brown uniform.

One defector from the KPD was Fritz Walter. He was not particularly close to my parents, but lived near enough to come to our flat occasionally between cell meetings. This pleasant, quite ordinary man of about thirty worked in a factory and had been a good member of the Communist Party. But even before Hitler took over, he had gone to my parents' flat and had 'talked like a different man'; the next time, he turned up in Nazi uniform. My mother and father were stunned. This man, their comrade, stood there in those brown boots, that coarse-textured, diarrhoea-coloured uniform, with the aggressive armband of the black and bent cross in its white circle on red. He stood there among our furniture, by our book shelves with the forbidden books glaring at him, in the very room that was the venue of clandestine cell meetings – and he praised Hitler. The Führer, he insisted, was good for Germany and good for the German people. My parents were disgusted and afraid.

Yet he never denounced my parents and that remains a mystery. It would have given him good marks with his new bosses. Perhaps he was afraid of betraying his own Communist past. If he was a good man at heart, what, I wonder, happened to him and his soul later on?

Fritz Walter was one of many to cross over to the Nazis, but others were less open about it and gave pretexts: we are joining the Nazis in order to spy, in order to sabotage, in order to persuade people they were in the wrong place – 'to enlighten them!' A telling word, and used by the Nazis as well. Some Communists had indeed embarked on these dangerous missions of enlightenment. But each one of them was handpicked by the Party. Some were found out and murdered by the Nazis.

My parents and their comrades were constantly on their guard against those who had gone over. I have on tape a conversation between my mother and Bill, one of many they had shortly before she died, in which she describes an incident with one such ex-comrade. She is walking along the street when this man calls after her. She does not turn round and keeps walking. He keeps calling her by name. She keeps walking. Another man stops her: 'Madame, I think he is calling you.' 'He can't be,' she says without stopping and turning round, 'that's not my name he's calling.' Bill does not grasp the point straight away and why should he? He has never lived in a police state and can't possibly grasp the logic and details of its terror. The point is that she knew the man wanted to denounce her, to point her out as a member of the KPD to an agent of the secret police – the man who stopped her. It was how Judas betrayed Jesus, and my mother had no taste for crucifixion or martyrdom other than the occasional domestic one.

Each Party member had to assume an alias for protection, which was all part of having to go underground, and nothing new to my mother with her Polish experience. She took the name Maria Bielska. With her accent, it had to be a Polish name.

Some cells had withered completely. My mother's cell – it was my father's too, but I think of it as hers – was much shrunk and had to meet in unlikely places far out of town or, if in town, in

rundown and disused sites. Sometimes they met in sheds, sometimes in cellars, sometimes in private places, occasionally in our flat
when my mother did not want to go out, especially after my
brother was born. Great secrecy and security shielded those meetings, and it took my mother back to her youth in Poland. As for
me, I was both frightened and proud. It was then that I first
experienced the thrill of political plotting with the need for secrecy
– mere discretion was inadequate.

Some evenings my parents and the comrades were so concerned
in case I overheard anything that the Danielsohns brought their
daughter Leah to keep me out of earshot. We would sit in the
kitchen and she would tell me plots of films she had seen. She was
five years older than me and was more entertained by the telling
than I was. They were mostly love stories and I got muddled,
though it took my mind off what might be going on in the next
room and any danger that lurked outside. The only story I
understood was of a man who cheated his brother in money and
love, was found out in the nick of time – I remember exactly how
he was found out – and got his just deserts.

When Leah could not come, I was put on my honour – as a
Communist of course – not to listen at the door. When the meeting
broke up, I had to reassure them that I had not heard a thing. One
evening I admitted I had heard one word, the word 'banana'. It was
ridiculous but no one laughed. I had either misheard or the word
was code or a password. They were not afraid I would inform on
them – many children did in the Third Reich, but they were all
good little Aryans – but that I might inadvertently and in front of
mischievous ears drop a tell-tale remark. I can hardly blame them,
but this exclusion made me feel diminished and superfluous.

Cells could never meet regularly, and to be one step ahead of the
authorities they had constantly to change their venue. There was
one case late in 1937 when a cell of eight men had a meeting in a
cellar. It was not in my mother's district but she knew some of the
men. It was the first meeting the eight had ever had in that place
and they felt perfectly safe. Suddenly, the Brownshirts marched
in. They took no one away. They simply locked the place up so

that the cellar could not be opened from the inside. No food, no water, no air. The eight men died within two weeks. Eight martyrs whose names are unrecorded.

The German secret police took no real interest in my parents until 1936. Then came that dreaded knock at the door – dreaded by all who have ever feared the police – and three men entered without being asked and carried out a house search. Everything was turned upside down and inside out but they found nothing. The moment the gang left, my father picked up my mother's iron, fished out their KPD membership cards from this hiding place, tore them to shreds – minute shreds – and shouted at my mother about the futile and insane risks she was taking. 'You're responsible! You'll bring death to us all!'

Membership cards stuffed into an iron are risky enough, but what about all those proscribed books? Luckily the house searchers were careless, in a great hurry, or illiterate and ignorant. They missed all those books which their fellow vandals had burnt with public celebration. Those volumes stood defiantly in their rows watching the mayhem. Only Marx's and Lenin's were poorly disguised in brown paper covers.

Being a foreign national and having a Polish passport was no protection from the secret police, and my father with his stateless papers was even more vulnerable. Not a single governmental or diplomatic soul would bother about him. This probably applied to my mother, too. It was inconceivable that the Poles with their right-wing government – the first target of my mother's political agitation – would ever have made a fuss about a Jew and a Communist. As late as 1938 Goering was invited to Warsaw and as 'our friend Goering' was treated with all the pomp and circumstance due to an honoured guest.

Had the searchers looked inside the iron, had they recognised the forbidden books, I would have come home from school, and found . . . I don't know what or who I would have found. Would they have taken away both my parents? Would they have vandalised the flat? As agitators against the Reich, as the Jewish agents of the Bolshevik state, there was no defence, certainly not the colour of a passport.

Few of the comrades escaped house searches. One afternoon my mother took me to see Marthe, a dress-maker who lived in a flat that had a living room I still hanker after: enormous and almost empty. A grand piano stood at one end and some low chairs round a smallish table at the other. There was nothing else except a beautiful oriental rug on the parquet floor and a huge mirror for Marthe's clients. Marthe was slim, pale and self-effacing, with lank and mousy hair that straggled onto her shoulders. She lived with Hugo. Hugo was tall, with the sang-froid of an Englishman. But Hugo was German and a Soviet spy. That afternoon, Marthe looked paler even than usual and her hands quivered as she smoked one cigarette after the other. A gang of secret police had burst into the flat that morning and she had stood in the kitchen and watched them search every drawer, every cupboard, every jar. 'How could they possibly have missed the note – it was right under their noses! Right there on the kitchen table!' The incriminating piece of paper would have told them that Hugo had departed in the direction of Moscow that very morning and not long before they arrived. They could easily have caught up with him. But the secret police, though eager, did not always live up to their stereotype and had lapses in competence.

What difference did these events make to me? My Marxist education certainly did not stop in 1933. Quite the contrary. Though primed in basic Marxist dogma, I was only beginning to learn to read and hadn't yet begun with Heine and Ibsen. But had it not been for 1933, I might have questioned the dogma earlier, even if not when I was six and in thrall to my mother. What is certain is that in the Nazi climate, with the KPD in opposition to a regime that was so clearly evil, and then in England during the war with Soviet Russia as an ally, my faith could only be strengthened.

But I learnt to keep quiet about my faith, and I learnt this lesson very quickly. I also learnt fear of the outside and of strangers and what may happen next, when before I had only been afraid and in awe of my parents and being left alone at night. 'Never tell anyone we are Communists, or even that we are interested in politics. Or that we are against Hitler. Don't tell anyone who our friends are.

Say you don't know anything. And don't be tricked; someone may be very nice to you but . . .' I assume they must also have warned me not to take sweets from strangers.

It was all the more shaming, therefore, that I was beguiled into revealing our secret. She was a tall, serene woman in neat dark clothes, whom my mother had engaged to take me for walks while she herself did her work for the Party. I liked this gentle woman. I wanted to give her something and I gave her this confidence which was barely mine to give. When we got home from our walk, she told my mother what I had told her. I was mortified and worried, even though she assured my mother she was sympathetic to Communism. Was she telling the truth or was she an informer? Luckily, she turned out to be what she seemed and my mother had been less worried than I. The woman was Jewish and that was some safeguard.

I had another lapse some forty-two years later. I was back in Berlin, it was 1986 and I was staying with Tim and Josiane Everard in East Berlin. Josiane had warned me that the house was thoroughly bugged and I must never refer to any German we met at a function. 'They blackball people for mixing with foreigners.' That evening we went to a party, met a woman writer who had difficulties getting published for lack of Communist fervour. At breakfast the next day, I asked Josiane, 'What was the name of the woman writer we met last night?' Josiane hesitated, and I apologised later when we were out in the open air.

Apart from learning to be careful and that paranoia was appropriate and justified – though paranoia was not a word I knew at the time – there were many moments when I was frightened: when the comrades met in our home, when Nazi uniforms milled round the streets, when *Stürmer* posters warned of the devilry of Bolshevik Jews, and when Nazi bosses blared out their message of hate over the radio and the loudspeakers all over Berlin. Or on the way home from school when Aryan children from other schools loomed near. I don't recall feeling cowed, not even during the pogrom of 1938, only upset and afraid. There were many times when I should have been frightened had I known what was going on, and after a while this condition of fear became the norm and it felt different – less acute. One cannot go round pulsating with fright all the time and I must have put a dampener on my fear. It wasn't till 1939, when we were on our way out of Berlin, that I allowed myself to acknowledge just how intense the fear and foreboding had been all those years.

The dampener did not always work, especially when we listened to Radio Moscow and my parents and their comrades huddled over the radio to catch the precious and forbidden words. The noise of the jamming was excruciating and it would have been crazy to have turned up the volume. To minimise the chance of being overheard, the radio was positioned as far from the door as possible, but not too near the window. The comrades, about half a dozen including my parents, took turns to sit by the front door in the hall and listen for footsteps on the staircase outside. It was pointless to wait for footsteps to turn into that dreaded knock at the door; by then it would have been too late. Many years of forced labour, or worse, rewarded those who listened to forbidden stations.

As not one of the comrades was keen to miss a moment of that precarious link with the promised land, it was mostly my turn to be the listening post. I was only five when I started. I sat in our hall furnished with Bauhaus-style chairs and table, and my heart thumps now as I remember the dread as I listened for footsteps and how, when I heard any, I rushed to tell the comrades. One of them was always ready to retune to an innocent station.

I don't know how many precious words made it through the din of the jamming, but each transmission from Moscow ended with 'Arbeiter aller Länder vereinigt Euch', which carried us into the happy illusion that one day the workers of the world really would unite, followed by the strains of the *Internationale* as it filtered through the jamming and waxed and waned on the short waves. That anthem gives me goosepimples to this day.

It's no wonder that from the abyss of the Nazi state my mother and comrades regarded the Soviet Union as a haven bathed in the light of freedom and equality. *Die Rote Fahne* was still being clandestinely distributed, and added to the bits of information that came over the radio. My mother always insisted that 'no one ever had any doubts about Stalin'. When Radio Moscow reported the death of a comrade, the hand of the assassin was always White Russian. But in 1936, when Stalin had all the members of the Central Committee executed, 'the thinking members' of the Party were bothered, especially by the claim that all the victims had confessed their guilt. The victims were after all heroes who had risked their lives for the Revolution. Would they have sabotaged the factories, spread lies about Stalin, cooperated with capitalist spies? 'Absurd! Only a madman could believe that,' declared my mother, who was one of the sceptics and was later punished for her doubts. Before that purge, no one had an inkling of what might be going on. On the contrary. 'It was wonderful! It was paradise!' (That tendency of hers to see things in the idiom of heaven and hell.)

What happened in 1933 affected me in the short term and the long term, but the effects on my mother were also drastic. They transformed the pattern, atmosphere and expectancy of her political work and therefore her life. She remained active in politics until 1939, but her ambitions to become a member of the Reichstag were finished. Hell had caught up with her; it was like being back in Poland, only much worse, back underground and no Orpheus was expected. Furthermore, she was no longer seventeen; she had a husband and a child, though this did not hinder her work as much as it might have done. But I would never have thought of questioning my mother's continuing work with the Party even though it put me, and later my brother, at risk. I admired her for her beliefs and courage. She was my Rosa Luxemburg.

Though I was only five when our life was so changed, and despite the risks, she and my father kept me informed and gave me the Party line on special events, national and international. I was fed these even before the age of five, but the conflagration at the Reichstag is the first of Hitler's exploits I remember. Then in 1935, when Hitler annexed the Saarland, I knew the plebiscite had been doctored. When he marched into the Rhineland in March 1936, I knew the Allies let him get away with it because they wanted Germany to grow into a military power that would crush the Soviet Union, which is also why they watched him rearm in contravention of the Treaty of Versailles. Their protests were quite insincere, my parents assured me. I knew that we could never buy white bread, imported fruit, pure butter, because all currency was spent on buying metal to manufacture weapons. It really was guns instead of butter.

I learnt about Mussolini, another Fascist, when he invaded Abyssinia in 1935. 'He is only aping the English in their colonial adventure,' my mother told me. She always said English, never British. She extolled the brave and peace-loving natives who fought on foot and with spears against Italian tanks and guns. She gave daily accounts of the to-ing and fro-ing of this unfair struggle and of Haili Selassi, that noble and brave man. She never said a word about him as emperor, an emperor by divine right and one who exploited this right without mercy. A popular song at the time had the first line '*Mit dem Roller nach Addis Ababa*' (Off to Addis Ababa on a scooter). It was a Nazi song but we all sang it. Bill sang a similar song in Liverpool.

The civil war in Spain was only a hazy background for me. I was aware that Hitler was using it as a practice war and of the anguish it caused my parents. But I knew nothing, or more likely remember nothing, of the daily details.

The next event came much closer. When I was ten, I had a bad attack of measles and the light in my bedroom was kept dimmed. My father was opening his newspaper, the *Deutsche Allgemeine*, as he walked into my room one morning. He stopped dead, exclaimed, 'I don't believe it!' and drew the curtains to let in more light. The day was 12 March 1938, the headline '*Unsere Truppen in Österreich*' (our troops in Austria) and the event the Anschluss.

By then I was old enough, if not in years, in upbringing, to understand what was going on in Germany and elsewhere politically. Apart from reinforcing my Communist identity, it affected what I thought and think of myself as a Jew. Did I know anything about being Jewish before 1933? I knew I was a Communist as well as I knew my name, my age, my gender and my address. It was my identity. But a Jew? My mother contended that in the KPD being Jewish was not really an issue, at least not until Hitler came to office. She knew Hermann Mendelsohn was a Jew and from

Poland at that, and the Danielsohns too were Jews, but otherwise, so she said, no one ever bothered about who was and wasn't Jewish. Whether some of this was due to supression, because in Marxist dogma ethnicity is of no importance, I have no idea.

My parents never denied their Jewishness, and when in 1938 the decree forbidding all Jews to attend the theatre was promulgated, neither of them ever saw another play in Berlin. My mother, as a Polish and not a German citizen, could have attended any theatre but she did the honourable thing and kept faith with her Jewish family in Poland. It was a sacrifice because she had been an avid theatregoer. When one of her comrades asked her why she had stopped going, my mother had to explain. Even as late as 1938 some of her comrades had no idea she was a Jew.

Leaving aside the overt anti-Semitism of the Brownshirts during Weimar, it was during a meeting of the cell, shortly before Hitler came to power, that my mother had her first face-to-face encounter with anti-Semitism outside Poland, and then not from a German comrade. There were perhaps a dozen people in the room when she noticed a new face, a young man's face; she was uneasy, but the organiser of the cell reassured her that he was a comrade. When they had drawn up the programme for the week, this young man stood up and with a foreign accent familiar to her said: 'I hope we have no Jews in our Party.' My mother was flabbergasted. She wiped the floor with him in such a way that even now I squirm with embarrassment, rather than with pride or fear, both of which would be more appropriate. In the circumstances, her behaviour was extraordinarily reckless.

'Where are you from?' she asked. 'Lodz.' 'And have you been in the Party long?' 'For some time.' And no, he had had no experience of Jews, he had never known any, 'but I don't trust them.' Of course, he had heard of Pelzudski but no, he didn't know this national hero's view of Jews. My mother boomed at him in triumph: 'Pelzudski said the Jews are the best fighters against Tsarism, and against capitalism!' 'Oh . . . did he?' The young man's voice had become meek and nervous. 'Have you not read his article in praise of Jewish Socialists?' 'No,' cringed the young man. She delivered her *coup de grâce*. 'Yes, and by the way, I am Jewish!' He melted away and never came again. She warned the comrades to be on their guard against him. 'If he is against Jews, he can't be a Socialist.' But what madness to have antagonised and humiliated him when he could have denounced her and the whole cell.

The wretch from Lodz was of course Polish. My mother never had any experience like this with German Communists, and in general anti-Semitism in Germany had been far weaker than in Poland. 'To tell you the truth,' she told Bill in 1979, 'I preferred the Germans to the German Jews.' She explained that Socialists were found in most sections of German society but, with a few notable exceptions, not among the Jews. German Jews looked down on the working class and on all Jews from Eastern Europe. German Jews were Germans first and foremost, whereas they saw East European Jews as Jews and *Ostjuden*, Eastern Jews, at that.

*Ostjuden* was a doubly derogatory term, and used not only by non-Jewish Germans. Germans regarded, and regard, Poles in the way that some English people have regarded the Irish: backward, slow-witted peasants. This prejudice was shared by the German Jews. I hate Irish jokes in Britain and Polish jokes in the United States, beyond all reason. They make me furious and bring me to the edge of tears.

My mother, for her part, came to look down on the German Jews because they were so *bürgerlich* (bourgeois) and, above all, such fools. Fools to think of themselves as Germans first and foremost and as Jews only by religion. They were deluding themselves simply because most of them were prosperous and admitted to the professions. Anti-Semitism was there beneath the surface all the time — since at least the Middle Ages and certainly in Luther's time. Equal rights for Jews in Germany were a late achievement: 1871 in theory and law, but much later in practice. For my Marxist mother, being Jewish was a nonsense, but not in the face of anti-Semitism.

As late as 1938 she came across a German Jew still rooted in illusions. This was just after she suffered her second attack of inflammation of the middle ear. The ear survived but she went to consult an ear specialist who was Jewish. At a time when other Jews, including German Jews, were preoccupied with the chances of leaving Germany, this one boasted that his family had been living in Germany for 800 years. 'Why don't they just persecute the East European Jews? If they would only throw out that lot, it would be all right with me.' Could this ear specialist have been deaf to her accent? In her outrage, and in the same manner and tone she used with the comrade from Lodz, she asked him: 'How many East European Jews have you met?' 'None, actually. I do have two patients, but I don't really know them.' 'Well, you have now met a third!'

When my mother took me to Poland in 1934, I saw a country that was indeed backward and a Jewish community that to me, brought up in Germany, did look bizarre, as if from a previous century or another world. This is ground for prejudice, because we are all suspicious about people different from ourselves, but it is no excuse.

# TEN

# The Best Place on Earth

In the autumn of 1990, the National Film Theatre in London screened Wajda's new film *Korszac*. It begins with a scene in an office, switches to a lakeside, and then depicts the German onslaught on Poland in September 1939. A bomb falls on a Warsaw street, and it is as realistic as any documentary. Even so, I managed to watch. But then the scene changes to the Warsaw ghetto where the shabby street, the houses and pavements looked painfully familiar. A very ordinary German soldier batters a Polish peasant woman with his rifle butt. '*Polnisches Schwein!*' he curses. She is not even a Jew.

I clambered across knees and feet, rushed out of the auditorium, along the corridor, into the Ladies and wept. Foreboding and alarm had gripped me even during the scene by the lakeside. I felt ashamed as I saw myself in the mirror – a pink-eyed coward who couldn't even watch a reconstruction on celluloid of what friends and relatives had to suffer in reality. In that small, white-tiled room, I shuddered with grief and also with confusion about the ghetto. On my one and only visit to Poland before the war, the Warsaw ghetto seemed one of the best places on earth. To me the ghetto was, is, *the* place of warmth, love, excitement and belonging. But to everyone else it is a symbol of all that was most cruel and horrific during the last war. I am reluctant to fuse the two images. I have seen many photographs of the ghetto, but there on Wajda's screen the very cobblestones of the streets pierced my gut.

It was in 1934, when I was six, that my mother took me to spend a couple of summer months in Poland. All her family was still there, apart from her brother Charles, who had run away because he did not want to be a rabbi. It was such a balmy experience to be surrounded by relatives and I revelled in it. I had never met any of them except my grandmother, who had spent some time with us in Berlin for an eye operation and whom I could not remember. Our only relative in Berlin was my father's sister Hella, and she was treated more as a servant than a relative.

My mother and I must have travelled through the Polish corridor, but I have only a vague memory of carriage windows being closed and covered and I may be making that up. Nor do I remember which of my mother's family I met first. My aunts, I suppose. Mania and Sonia probably met us at Warsaw station; Regina was already living in Paris. After sophisticated Berlin, Warsaw was an enormous shock. Men, women and children walking barefoot on the streets of the capital, which were made up of uneven cobblestones! Didn't their feet hurt? I asked my mother, but she said they were poor peasants who had come in from the country, they had no shoes, were quite used to walking in bare feet and didn't notice it. It was also the first time I saw men wearing beards, long dark gowns and caps. I did not see that sort of dress again until we came to London and visited a Lubliner friend of my father's in Whitechapel.

The ghetto was not yet famous, but for me it was remarkable and unforgettable – a favourite memory. Its architecture was mean, its pavements barely made up, the inhabitants seemed uniformly poor – much poorer than anything I had seen in Berlin – and the attire of the men was bizarre. The Nazis were to use the ghetto for documentaries; to show how backward and despicable Jews really were: true *Untermenschen*, easily cowed by superior people.

Whatever German propoganda films tried to tell us, this was not how Jews looked or what they wore in Germany. Some years ago, a BBC film about the plight of German Jews in the Thirties used shots of Jews in the streets wearing the dress of Polish Jews. I wrote to the producer to point out that the footage was misleading. He wrote back, telling me tetchily that this was footage made and used by the Germans; it was the only material available and therefore had to do. What this poor wretched producer had done was to use film that was part of Hitler's campaign to justify anti-Semitism by showing how different Jews were from the rest of the population in Germany, when in fact they were indistinguishable.

Some parts of Warsaw, the boulevards, government buildings and houses for the wealthy – in fact all the bits they rebuilt after

1945 – were lesser versions of formal Berlin. The main boulevard was the Marszalkowska and I was more taken with the rhythm of that name than with the street itself. For the most part the buildings were poor, as were the people.

I loved the ghetto because of my relatives and the way they loved me. We had most of our meals with Tante Channale and her husband Leibu, who lived in the ghetto in a narrow house on two floors. It was to this house that my mother had fled from Lublin to escape the secret police, where, had Channale not been quick to deny all knowledge of her, they would have caught her. Their rooms were so small that they seemed to have been shrunk, but they never felt mean because the people themselves were so generous and loving. Their four sons, though grown up, still lived at home. Three went to university, the fourth was a carpenter. They all played chess. The carpenter's workshop was on the ground floor of the house and open to the street when he worked. I was mesmerised whenever he picked up his plane to shave a plank of wood and the shavings curled and fell in heaps in a sequence that was beautiful, rhythmic and aromatic. The shavings, though delicate, looked impossibly large in volume. How could they all have come from that narrow strip of wood? Decades later in my studio in Chalk Farm I used a similar tool, and as the plane moved back and forth I thought of my cousin the carpenter and his brothers. The carpenter was the warmest, the most spirited and handsome, and my favourite.

Channale looked after us with the same devotion she had looked after my mother for those few days in 1922. She and Leibu couldn't spoil me enough and one way was to give me delicacies to eat. My favourite dish was Tante Channale's chicken soup followed by tinned sprats. I could not get enough of these thin fish. In Berlin I had only eaten the fatter sardine.

The chicken soup was kosher, as was all the food in the house. My relatives were practising Jews but mainstream in their Ortho-doxy and laughed at some customs they labelled superstitious. This must have been behind an incident with a female relative who came to lunch. My mother and my aunts kept telling me for days that I was not to be afraid of her, or laugh at her. Within my hearing, they discussed endlessly how I was not used to such things and might be alarmed. The object of concern was a hat called, or so it sounded to me, a *chipeck*, worn by Orthodox women. My mother, in her hostility towards religion, had inflated this modest headgear into something not only superstitious but mad and grotesque. In my own imagination it had grown into a wild concoction that would have made anything that topped a lady-in-waiting of Marie Antoinette look tame.

By the time this cousin arrived I was so worked up that as we all sat down at the long table I was convulsed with hysterical giggles, though I noticed nothing even faintly peculiar, ridiculous or alarming about this unassuming woman. The hat she wore looked like a small and old-fashioned bonnet. But I could not stop giggling and my mother told me to lie down on the sofa. As I was lying back, still shaking, this elderly woman got up from the table, leant over me, and blew and spat into my ear. My giggles stopped, I screamed, ran out of the room, and was caught by my favourite cousin the carpenter, who took me into his workroom. I stayed there until the visitor had gone. Poor woman. She was only trying to help by blowing away the evil spirits that had got inside me. Little did she know that those spirits had been introduced by my mother and her sisters.

Before we left for Poland my own head had been adorned, not with a hat but with a hairstyle suitable for little girls at that time. The top layer was kept longer than the rest of the very short hair, worn as a topknot and called a *Hahnenkamm* or coxcomb. My mother had promised I could have it cut off in Poland and she had kept her promise. On a photograph taken of my father's sister Paula, her boyfriend and me as we walk along the Marszalkowska, Paula wears a beret at a rakish angle, and my hair is quite straight and flat. I had undergone the rite of passage that made me feel more grown up but did little for my looks.

I remember an outing to an opulent house in Warsaw which was in direct contrast to the house in the ghetto. It was my aunt Sonia, the youngest of my mother's sisters, who took us there. Now, in her early seventies, Sonia is still strikingly beautiful. In 1934, she was ravishingly so. She was much the youngest and had had a different education and a less strict and orthodox upbringing. She had even gone to a school that took both Christian and Jewish girls. She had started at university and though she did not finish the course, she was proficient enough in French and other subjects to have become governess in one of the few wealthy Jewish families. We made two visits to their splendid house, which seemed to have marble walls and floors, and furniture covered in velvet. The first visit was for coffee and cakes, when the women and I sat round a damask and lace-clothed table and were served coffee in delicate china cups. I was the only child there and a tray of luscious cream cakes was offered to me first. I took the largest and richest cake. Everyone laughed and I felt awful. It is still one of the most embarrassing moments of my life.

Our next visit was brief. The house was empty, the prosperous chairs and sofas and tables were covered by white sheets and looked as lifeless as any corpse. The marble halls were cold and hollow. The family had gone on holiday.

For part of the summer, we stayed in the country near the town of Nowodwo. My mother and her sisters rented a farmhouse while the farmer, his wife and their many children moved out into the barn. This was common practice among farmers to supplement their meagre living. I can't remember whether we had one room or two, but my mother and her sisters cleaned and sprayed daily after lunch to keep down the fly population and then hung fresh fly-papers. I used to watch quite unmoved as the new flies got themselves fatally stuck and more and more of their bodies gradually filled up the yellow sticky space on either side. It is not a sight I would watch now, when even rows of whitebait under the grill evoke lines of bodies in concentration camps. The flies would have done better to keep to the lavatory which was outside in a field, quite a walk from the house and where flies and wasps buzzed round in huge swarms.

The flies were a nuisance but what really hurt and troubled me was sunburn. With the freckled and ultra-sensitive skin that comes with ginger hair, I had to be careful enough in summers in Germany. But here, where the sun was stronger and the countryside poorer in trees, shade was harder to find. I don't know how my mother could have let me get so burnt; perhaps she was too involved with her sisters. Sunning lotions were far less advanced than they are now, and my sunburn was extensive: face, back, shoulders and arms – my legs never hurt like the rest of my body – and there was at least one day when I had to stay in bed with my skin sore all over. The sheets became covered in the fine debris of tissue paper-thin flakes of my skin. Dead blisters. When I did get up and out again, I had to wear my towelling gown to cover my back and arms. I felt self-conscious walking along the fields and country roads wearing a gown in the middle of a hot day, but it was either that or staying indoors. As I got older, and this applies mainly to England, I sometimes wore long sleeves in the summer to hide the freckles on my arms. They weren't at all fashionable.

But most days in Nowodwo I wore no more than my bathing suit. A pale yellow thing of tricot or *Bleyle*, a heavy scratchy jersey consisting of trunks held up by a pair of crossed straps and worn before I minded about my bared chest. It was so hot that my mother and her sisters, with their different shapes and hair colour, used to walk round the room naked. One of my aunts wore a sanitary belt with a towel but I did not then know what that was.

One morning that summer, dressed in frock and knickers, I came across some of the farmer's boys and their friends by the pond. The sun had begun to scorch and we could not decide whether to jump into the water. None of us had swimwear – an absurd idea when I realise they were country boys in Poland in 1934 – and jumping into the water would mean taking off our clothes. I told them I didn't mind at all, but sympathised with them. It was all right for me, as a girl, but awkward and embarrassing because they, poor things, looked so funny in front. Funny in front or not, we all got into the water and had a lovely time splashing around. My mother and her sisters came along and the boys told them in Polish what I had said. Everyone laughed. I don't know how those boys and I managed that conversation by the edge of the pond; we had no common language.

The only Polish phrase familiar from home was a curse my mother often hurled out when there was some domestic mishap. It translates into 'dog's blood', sounds like 'Bee Juckreff', is spelt *Psia-krew* and is of no use whatsoever to me. My father hated it and I was warned never to say it. As it turns out, even now it is an unsuitable word for a woman to use. In the train from Berlin to Warsaw, my mother taught me to say 'I don't speak Polish' – '*Nie rozumiec po polsku* – and '*dziekuje bardzo*' – 'thank you very much'. I got to know the punchline of the Polish national anthem, '*Marsz, marsz, Dămbrowski*', but I learnt no Polish song.

Mania taught me a Yiddish ditty that mocks Chassidic Jews, played games with me and cooked delicious food. Her speciality was *piroschkies* (pastry turnovers filled with red fruit) and she would always give some to the farmer's younger children. When the smallest son, who was only two, fell off the very high hay-laden farm cart, my aunt baked some *piroschkies* especially for him. The large grin on his face was smeared with tears, dirt and the delicious purply, jammy filling of plums or cherries. I had never come across those baked goodies and I don't know if they are Jewish, Polish or both. It was that summer too, but in Warsaw, that I first came across beigels. Now my daughters, Rachel, Lucy and Juliet, buy them in Hackney and Manchester. My aunt Sonia sits in her luxurious apartment in Miami and eats them with smoked salmon and cream cheese for breakfast. I don't much like them wherever they come from.

That Polish summer was the first and only time that I dug up potatoes. Such a mundane and yet mysterious process to dig gently through the soft soil heaped into a ridge and topped with white flowering plants, and to trace the branches to find the egg shaped tubers and then to lift it all up with the fork while the soil drifts and sifts down between the prongs, leaving a cluster of new potatoes. It was the first time too that I discovered stubble and the only time I tried to walk over a stubbled field. The stubble in Poland is like the stubble in Hampshire, Berkshire or anywhere else. Then the haystacks too were universal in shape. I was photographed – and, with peculiar dress sense, I am wearing my green satin dress edged with tiny roses – in front of a Polish haystack with two other children. I have always thought them to be a couple of peasant boys, but my aunt Mania tells me they were the sons of friends of my mother. You can't always tell 'real' Poles from Jews.

To see my grandparents we took a train going east. First we stopped off at Lublin, but only for half an hour. We met a small, frail and timorous old man wearing the now familiar beard, coat and cap. This was my father's father and I was told to kiss him. We sat in the station café and he kept looking at me. But he was very ill at ease and shy, only spoke Yiddish, and communication was difficult. My mother did nothing to help. Even that half-hour was irksome to her.

We spent rather longer with my mother's parents in Lubartov. In that very poor house, poorer even than those I had seen in Warsaw, I shared a bed with my mother in a sleeping area partitioned off from the main room by a piece of material. I watched a couple of *Wanzen* climb up and down the damp wall. These harmless little bugs, plus my grandfather's red beard, his gentleness and pleasure in me, are my strongest memories. He too wore the inevitable coat and cap. I can't remember when my mother began to tell me about her father, his fecklessness, and his irritating good nature. What mattered to me that summer and ever after was the love for me that flowed from my grandfather, that his beard was the colour of my hair, and that he allowed me to pull it. I still love him.

I don't remember my grandmother at all. She was the one person in Poland I had met before when she had stayed with us in Berlin at the time of her eye operation, but I have no recollection of her whatsoever, either in Berlin or Poland. My memory is not even jogged by photographs taken in Berlin of my grandmother, my mother and me sitting on a rug on the grass. My grandmother is an imposing presence and she looks exotic: her hair is tied up in a scarf, her skirts flow and cover her legs, she is not from a western developed country. Her strong will is emphasised by the protrusion of her lower lip; a hereditary dental condition that surfaced in Juliet, our youngest daughter, but vanished with orthodontics.

My grandmother was the cleverest of three sisters. She had been taught the Talmud by her father, who did not want this knowledge to die out in the family simply because there was no male issue. For a woman to learn the Talmud is not only unusual, it contravenes the patriarchal tradition, but my great grandfather regarded his daughter Malle as having a brain to equal any man's. Paul Gradstein, the widower of my aunt Regina, likes to talk not only about what an unusual woman my mother had been, but what an unusual and remarkable woman her own mother had been. Men used to seek her out to discuss their problems and take her counsel, something which was very uncommon for a woman of that time and milieu. I wonder whether I have blocked out my grandmother because one powerful mother figure at a time is more than enough. Perhaps as I cannot block out my mother, I block out a substitute, her mother.

But in 1934, I was unaware of any such symbolic equations. The summer for me was all present and no past, and, thank God, no hint of the future. Only fields of stubble, ponds with naked boys, haystacks, burning sun, flies, potato lifting, tinned sprats and Tante Channale and four young men, her sons, marble halls with cream cakes and chairs draped in white sheeting. And in Lubartov, bugs on walls, the red beard of Menasseh, my grandfather. Being loved and being spoilt.

That is all I remember of a whole summer, except for the last day, and then only the goodbye at the station. Everyone in Warsaw came to see us off: my aunts, Tante Channale and Leibu, their four sons. Bleak sadness. I wept a little. Sonia wept too. She had such striking eyes that maybe it was more obvious in her than in the others. We were right to weep, and with hindsight we should have howled, lamented, beaten our breasts, torn our clothes, thrown ourselves to the ground. All in Lubartov, and all but two of those waving us goodbye as the train pulled out towards Berlin, came to a gruesome end, and I never saw them again. I did not think I could ever bear to go back to Poland.

Although it was my first time inside a Jewish community, I learnt little about Judaism and Jewish religion. I was as much in the dark as before. Nevertheless some traces of Jewishness grafted itself on to my Communist identity. What puzzled me was the look in the eyes of Jews, especially the Jewish women. I was not able to find words for it as a child but it was a look of resignation, of melancholy, and it may have been the look of a despised minority. I did not see it in my mother's eyes.

When my daughter Juliet was in her second year at Manchester University, she decided to go to Poland on a student exchange. I desperately wanted her not to go. 'I want to see where my roots are,' she argued. 'But there is nothing left, not even roots. They have all been pulled out, twisted, trampled on, mangled and obliterated. Nothing is left. Nothing.' I only half understand why I get so agitated about Poland. I feel more emotional, or rather a different kind of emotion, than I do towards Germany. A deep loss, an unhealed wound, a bottomless grief. I did go to Poland in 1992. I did not sob the whole time as I had feared, and the grass has certainly grown over the dreadful grounds of Birkenau, but have I achieved any healing? The ghosts of the people or the country have not been exorcised and the very idea of Poland torments me still.

When Juliet came back from Poland, she talked about the male chauvinism. But she did not tell me for several years how disappointed she had been in general. The countryside was flat, plain and ugly. The towns looked odd because much had been rebuilt in exactly the way it was before the war. But worst of all, and far worse than the chauvinism, was the anti-Semitism. 'It was everywhere and so out in the open I had no feeling that this country had anything to do with you.' My father would have agreed.

The image of what I had loved in Poland tumbled into my mind on a most unexpected occasion. In 1975, I launched a Royal Navy ship. As the wife of the then Minister of State at the Ministry of Defence, I was eligible to launch nothing less than a destroyer. I, who was brought up as a pacifist! So one Tuesday in March, as the grand lady on the launching platform, I was at the centre of much British pomp and ceremony and the fate of the destroyer depended on me. The rest of the party glittered with gold braid, titles and smart hats. The audience below the platform was more plebeian. If my ex-Communist soul was a bit uneasy, the refugee in me was relieved, though neither was uppermost in my mind – not at first, anyway.

*My mother's family in Lubartov before she left home in 1921. From left: my grandmother, my mother, Maria, Sonia, Regina, Charles, my grandfather.*

*My maternal grandmother in Lubartov.*

*Benny Biderman, my mother's first cousin, who converted her to Communism and was the love of her life.*

*Dedicated in Lublin. My mother (third from left) with her comrades in the Communist Party.*

*The anti-Semitic Polish army. My father fled to Berlin to avoid conscription, but his brother Joseph (bottom row, left) served.*

*Lublin compatriots in Berlin in 1921. Bottom right, my father. Bottom
left, Max Waldberg, who helped my mother burn her forbidden books shortly
before we left for Britain.*

*My father in Berlin in the early
1920s.*

*The comrade.*

Top left *My mother with Sister Beatrix, the nun who saved her life after I was born.* Top right *Screaming.* Above left *With my father at Erkner. Like many Berliners, we often made Sunday excursions to the Berlin lakes.* Above right *In my* Glockenkleid, *or bell-dress, which I loved but which one day, in a tantrum, I destroyed.*

„Ja, mein Kind! So ist unser ganzes Leben!"

Top left *With my teddy bear on the Lustgarten in 1930.* Top right *On the Michaelkirch Piatz, where I played daily, in 1931, with my mother and my grandmother, who was in Berlin for an eye operation.* Above *A cartoon by Heinrich Zille, whose book of cartoons was my Communist picture book before I could read. The caption reads: 'Yes, my child, that's our whole life.'*

*Adalbertstrasse, where we lived till I was three, cut in half by the Berlin Wall when I photographed it in 1987.*

*In front of the Reichstag: my mother and father on the left, with friends.*

*It is not surprising that I confused Hitler's private army of Brownshirts
(top) with uniformed Communists, the Rotfront (bottom), as they
demonstrated – and fought – on the streets of Berlin when I was a small
child.*

On the Michaelkirch Platz at the end of my first day at school with the traditional Schultüte, *filled with goodies.*

*At the Tempelhof airport with a Zeppelin.*

*A doll's pram that I remember more vividly than my tall friend Mia, to whom it belonged. My father is in the background.*

Part of my role was to pull a lever that activated a device to smash the champagne bottle against the ship as she glided into the water. 'Don't worry,' said the shipyard owner, 'it never fails.' But it did and I had to smash the bottle in the old-fashioned way, by hand. I found myself out on the ocean, balancing on the narrow prow of the harbour master's tug as it faced the bow of the destroyer, grasping the bottle of champagne in my right hand. The Admiral encouraged me – 'Go on, give her a good bash!' – and I did. With two men holding on to my legs so that the momentum would not pull me into the sea, I hit the bottle against the bow of the destroyer. But the reluctant bottle stayed whole. My heart sank. Would I end up like Mrs Eisenhower, who tried thirty-two times before the bottle broke?

And it was then and there out at sea with the fate of a Royal Navy destroyer in my hands, with those self-assured Englishmen, the Admiral and the shipyard owner, watching me, judging me and no doubt cursing me, that I invoked my own ancestors. I invoked my own poor, unbraided and untitled Jewish ancestors, who lived in that shack-like house in Lubartov. I saw the room, the bugs on the wall, the thin curtain, my grandfather's thin black coat, his red beard. I saw Tante Channale and the tins of sprats in the Warsaw ghetto. I saw her sons, their energy and then their dreadful fate. 'For their sake I am bloody well going to bash this bottle into smithereens.' I did. The Admiral hugged me and called me Silvia.

# ELEVEN

# Berlin Schools and Bible Stories

Not long before I went to Poland I started proper school. I had been at nursery school, but I was now six and the German school year used to start at Easter. Apart from the nursery school, I went to three schools in Berlin: a *Volksschule* (state primary school), a primary school attached to a synagogue, and a Jewish progressive grammar school.

In every one of these schools, and in the ones I went to later in England, I felt marginal, an outsider, whether as foreigner, Jew, or atheist. The possible exception was my nursery school. Even there I must have been potentially marginal, and unequivocally so to the adults since my mother spoke with a strong Polish or Russian accent. I myself spoke a non-accented *Hochdeutsch*, and it never occurred to me that I was in any way different from the other children. For this, credit must go to my Montessori Kindergarten that I look back on with such pleasure, though I cannot recall a single individual. Playing and learning were all mixed up and the atmosphere was warm and stimulating. We learned to plait, to lace up our shoes, tie bows and knots, and wash up. When I dry a plate now, I am back in that place – a large low-ceilinged room with sinks fitted against one wall – watching the last damp rings vanish from the surface of the plates.

My first day at the local *Volksschule* ended the way it did for every German child: my mother met me and presented me with a *Schultüte*. A *Schultüte* is a 2 ft long, usually hexagonal cone made of highly decorated cardboard and filled with goodies: sweets, fruit, pencils, rubbers, sharpeners, notebooks, tiny toys – and for some lucky girls, tiny dolls. The *Schultüte* had no religious, political or nationalistic connotations for my mother, and so in this rite of passage she allowed me to conform. She did not surprise me with any dolls but I did find some forbidden sweets at the bottom and narrowest part of the cone, and just like each of the other children

I was photographed on the Michaelkirch Platz hugging my own cornucopia and looking very pleased.

On recent travels through Germany in late summer I noticed *Schultüten* displayed in shop windows. So the custom still goes on but has moved to autumn along with the start of the school year. Because the traditional start of the school year was Easter, the *Schultüte* was called *Ostertüte* (*Oster* means Easter) in some parts of Germany. What a good thing it was not known by this name in Berlin or my parents would surely have banned it, as they banned the Christmas tree.

I was very much the odd one out in the class and the school. Less because I was the one and only Jew among Aryans – and, in 1934, it would have been the norm for them to exclude me – but because I had set myself apart. Each school day began not with an assembly as in England, but with the pupils saluting their Führer in their own classroom. It was compulsory and I was the only one who did not conform, the only one who did not stand up, who did not raise her hand, who did not shout '*Heil Hitler*'. I abstained not because I was so principled and brave but because I did not dare defy my mother's strict instructions. She reminded me, almost daily, that I was not a German citizen. I was on her Polish passport, and therefore not only morally bound (as a Communist) but legally entitled to opt out. None of the other children looked down on me or mocked me, but I wasn't much part of the class, either. Ironically, Jewish children in state schools would soon be forbidden to salute the Führer in school. It was a very effective way to brand outsiders.

We still lived in Köpenikerstrasse when I started at the *Volksschule*. I could have stayed there till September 1939 because the decrees that made life unpleasant for Jewish children in state schools applied only to those of German nationality. But towards the end of the first term, we moved to the west part of Berlin and my mother registered me at a Jewish school in the area. The headmaster of the *Volksschule* was very concerned when my mother told him I was leaving. He hoped the other children had not been taunting me; he was constantly discouraging his pupils from anti-Semitic behaviour. This must have accounted for my getting away so easily with not saying 'Heil Hitler' every morning. It was after all 1934 and Hitler had been in absolute power for over a year.

What a very brave man this headmaster was. He is one of only three individuals who come to mind when people say there were some good Germans – with the exception of my mother's comrades. The second was also a schoolteacher and lived on an island in the Baltic; the third was the caretaker of 12 Bayreutherstrasse, where we moved to next. The second and the third showed their goodness and guts within the same twelve hours in 1938.

Before I started at my next school, I had to get through the end of term ritual when the whole *Volksschule* assembled in the playground. Every right hand of this dense crowd was raised in the Hitler salute, everyone shouted 'Heil Hitler', everyone sang 'Deutschland über Alles'. I was on the edge of the crowd, but I allowed myself to be drawn in. My hand went up to the glory of Hitler, my voice sang out to the glory of Germany.

If only I had placed myself well in the middle of the crowd. For at the school gates stood my mother and her comrades and they had a perfect view of my treachery. All of them, not just my mother, laid into me with contempt. When partisans during the German occupation of their country revealed names of their comrades to the Nazi enemy, did they feel as I did then – heavy with shame and guilt? My sin was greater as no one had tortured me, but mitigated because I had betrayed not a person but an ideal; even so, that group by the gate made me feel I had betrayed not only every one of them, but every unknown comrade too. I carried that dark secret round with me until I was in my mid-forties, until one night when Bill and I were sitting up in bed reading, I told him the whole miserable story. He made no response and I saw that he had fallen asleep. But the confession has washed away my guilt.

In September 1934, I started at the Jewish school in Fasanenstrasse which was attached to one of Berlin's largest synagogues. Kaiser Wilhelm visited it in 1910. Hitler never did, though in November 1938 he sent his troop of arsonists.

The most important thing for me about that school was our form teacher. She is still one of the most important people in my life. Her married names were first Friedmann and then Petrushka, but she used her maiden name of Freundlich. A good name for her, since *freundlich* means 'friendly' and we all loved her and for us she was never anything else but Tante Freundlich. To say she was always friendly is doing her an injustice. She had great warmth but she could be serious, very cross, critical and questioning. She always looked middle-aged and I see from school photographs that this is not only the perception of a child. I saw her again after the war in 1962 when Bill and I went to Israel as guests of the government – and she still looked middle-aged.

I was sent to a Jewish school partly because of anti-Semitism but mainly because of our political allegiance. My parents deemed it safer in case I revealed our left-wing tendencies and activities. But there were dangers in a Jewish school, too. Especially in one attached to a synagogue. What was at risk was not my personal safety but the integrity of my Marxism and atheism. The constant exposure of their Communist-nurtured child to Jewish beliefs and customs, and mixing only with Jewish girls, might have converted me, I might have started to believe in God!

When I started at the school, I was much too serious and very touchy. But after a couple of terms Tante Freundlich wrote in my report that 'Silvia is no longer so hypersensitive'. I loved Tante Freundlich and realised later how significant a mother figure she was to me. When she left to emigrate to Palestine, she wrote in my autograph album that the blood of our forefathers runs deep in our veins and there was nothing anyone could do about it. I kicked against it when I read it, but it insinuated itself like a magic spell and like a magic spell I have been unable to throw it off.

I am not a Jesuit, but I know that early influences are very tenacious. Many of the Marxist ideas that I absorbed in my early years have stuck. But my mother could not keep me isolated in the Communist equivalent of a monastic enclave, not even up to the age of seven. Other influences swirled round me and penetrated the Marxist boundary: other people and other children as well as films and books. Teaching me to read opened me to the socialist ideas of Zille and Heine but also to ordinary children's books with little girls pushing dolls in prams, and mothers happily slaving away over their stoves and sinks. And my mother was right to fear the influence of school and particularly of Tante Freundlich, no matter how that impressive woman tried to reassure her. There was no deliberate effort to convert me. She was too wise for that and I never was converted to Judaism. But a slow process had begun which turned me into a Jew, and not only because Hitler classified me as such. Like my trip to Poland, my school experiences became part of my consciousness as a Jew. The process will never be completed; it is like the negative of a film left in a slow-developing solution with the prints never quite coming into focus.

What marked me out in that class and in that whole school, was not that I did not raise my hand in a daily Hitler salute – no one did – nor that my parents came from Poland – there were a few other parents who were not German-born – but that I was the one and only atheist. It marked me out but no one looked down on me for what was heresy in a school that belonged to a traditional synagogue. We were all bound together by persecution, but even so their tolerance was remarkable and any differentiation was my doing. I alone knew the truth, I was the only one in the school who was not befuddled, and I zealously tried to enlighten the others. I was a real little fundamentalist. That I was unique in my belief did not bother me or make me feel unaccepted and Tante Freundlich did not make an issue of my atheism. I was the cleverest of her pupils and a favourite. Until she left, I was blissfully happy. Tante Freundlich had given me the confidence and strength that I never had before. I was top of the class and always first with the answers. To be the cleverest, to be preferred above everyone else, was exhilarating and must be one of the greatest joys, especially for a child.

Tante Freundlich only let me down once. She was seriously provoked but it took nearly fifty years for me to recognise that. During a morning break I had had an argument with Bella Trachtenberg, a plump and pallid girl in my class. Bella was known for being 'sehr verwöhnt', very spoiled, by her mother. We used to joke about how her mother mollycoddled her. During that break Bella and I argued about God. 'Of course there is a God; I know there is!' she affirmed with some emotion, and she became very distressed when I sailed in with my 'proof' that she was wrong, foolish, and duped because 'You have never seen God, have you!' I reduced poor Bella to tears, which was not my intention. I just wanted to convince her or at least put some doubt in her mind. When we came back into class, Tante Freundlich asked her why she was weeping and Bella sobbed that 'Silvia says there is no God.' Tante Freundlich frowned, lifted her chair, banged it down on the floor and said: 'Silvia thinks she knows better than the rest of us.' She looked angry and no one moved or spoke. Her disapproval felt like a denial of me. It hurt for many years. The contention that the majority knows best has never worked for me, but that she was sorely tried I do understand. It is only lately that I have understood how arrogant and dogmatic I can be when I think I am right.

Bella caught pneumonia. Everyone blamed her mother. Bella had gone to a party for which her mother had wrapped her into too many layers of wool and so she caught cold on her way home. Daily bulletins charted her progress until that morning when Tante Freundlich told the class, 'Bella died last night.' We were shocked and sat in silence. Only I wept, though I tried not to. I felt alarmed and guilty. Could I have hurt her all that much, and where was she now? In Heaven?

An episode with another girl underlined my marginality in the class. This time there were no arguments, no tears, but an invitation to tea. Hannelore Klein was a fair-haired, cheeky and popular girl who invited me to her home one Saturday afternoon in winter. I went there by bus, and my mother impressed on me to give my return fare to Mr Klein for safe keeping. When I got to the Kleins' flat, the family was sitting in semi-darkness without any electric light. I asked Hannelore's father to look after my money but he hesitated. Before it got completely dark, he explained that it was still sabbath and they could not switch on the light, or take money. But he did take my coins and put them on a shelf, without any reproach showing on his kind face. He knew I was an atheist and was probably sorry for me. I felt I had strayed into a strange culture and the Kleins' good grace and manners only emphasised this. But I also felt uneasy because I knew that in some ways I was part of this culture. I had never experienced this ambivalence so acutely as in the Kleins' twilit sitting room. The family emigrated to Holland, the parents died in a concentration camp, but Hannelore survived. When I look at our class photograph now, I think that by dying in her bed Bella Trachtenberg may have had a lucky escape.

My episode with Bella did not stop me from holding forth on religion and related topics. To mention Jesus, for example, was taboo. But I, in my arrogant wisdom, informed my schoolmates that Jesus Christ had existed, not as God or God's son, but as a man and a good man at that. I bet I added that he was the first Communist. As for that sacred book, the Old Testament, I may have been a dogmatic atheist but I drank in its stories as avidly as anyone. To assuage the Marxist in me, I applied freethinking rationalism – provided by my mother – whenever I had to. This doubting and cynical Thomas must have been very irritating to everyone else and made absolutely sure of my place on the margins.

Tante Freundlich embellished some of the stories and brought the characters in the Old Testament to life. Every day we would draw pictures of at least one biblical event. But it was Joseph above all who inspired me to produce whole portfolios of his life and times: his coat, his brothers getting rid of him and those fat and thin cows and fat and thin ears of corn when he interpreted Pharaoh's dreams. When I look back, he may have had special appeal to me because he was such a successful outsider. We also recorded the bad times suffered by his descendants as they became a despised minority, with drawings of the Jews building the pyramids – little figures whipped by the overseers and bent down with the burden of huge stones. I could not have had a better example of the exploitation of the wretched of the earth. 'That's how cathedrals were built – by slave labour!' my mother pointed out.

We drew the saviour of the damned: Moses in the basket, Moses being rescued by Pharaoh's daughter, Moses hearing God's voice from the Burning Bush with the eternal flame that never consumes. Our drawings of the seven plagues were very explicit. We felt little compassion for the Egyptian population, until all the first-born were slain and until the waters of the Red Sea closed over the Egyptian soldiers. But our images depicting the scenes of the Jews dancing round the golden calf, with Moses throwing the tablets at them, were as unrestrained and wild as our subjects.

The atheist in me could accept dreams so long as they were dreams and not visions. But the true child that was hiding somewhere within me enjoyed not only the dreams, but the visions, the miracles and all the other surreal images. My mother, however, always alert to the dangers of my being drawn into the beliefs of my peers, did her best to put me back on the proper rational Marxist path with a down-to-earth explanation for each picture I brought home. If the ten plagues really happened like that, one after the other, that was conicidental but not miraculous. Each of the phenomena – from plague to frogs – was endemic in that part of the world. If the Red Sea really parted, its waters were pulled back by the magnetism of natural forces. If Moses heard a voice in the bush, he was imagining it or not telling the truth. As for going up to the mountain to draw up the Ten Commandments – how very sensible of him. He needed peace, quiet and solitude while he was drawing up the laws and scratching them onto the stones.

But it was Elijah's proof that Jehovah was the one and only true God that demanded all my mother's interpretive skills. Elijah's bet with the prophets of Baal over whose god would first send down fire to consume the offering of the bull, theirs or his – that was a matter of science, insisted my mother. Whereas the superstitious prophets had chanted and danced round the severed head all day and night, tearing their beards, slashing themselves in their frenzy, Elijah prayed to the Lord God of Israel, but also showed off by soaking the offering with water before calling down the fire. 'It wasn't water he poured on; it was petrol!' she revealed triumphantly. As usual, I passed on the revelation to my classmates. I have forgotten what the source of the spark was meant to have been – something like an ancient match hidden in the folds of Elijah's gown?

The story of Esther had no need of rational interference from my mother. It had no miracles and visions, but the modest Jewish girl finding favour with the king was very romantic and we all loved it. We never noticed that the royal marriage was a mixed one or that the virtues recommended in a wife were mildness, beauty and patience, and that Esther was the opposite of the wicked Delilah, who trapped Samson, another hero of our drawings.

When we came to the end of the Book of Kings, Tante Freundlich asked us what we thought of the Old Testament heroes. We told her that we had kept thinking, 'At last, here is one who is wholly good', but we kept on being disappointed and David was the last straw. He had been 'good' almost to the end, but then he too lapsed when he became enamoured of Bathsheba. For her, Uriah lost his life and David his reputation.

How can any one of us have grown into a feminist on such a diet? But this query is hindsight and except perhaps for my mother no one was concerned with feminism after 1933. There were other more urgent problems and few of us grew up to put anti-feminist lessons to the test. The lesson Tante Freundlich intended to teach us with her question was that leaders are human; that they are neither gods nor godlike and should not be put on a pedestal. I have now seen enough leaders at close range to know she was right.

A story I carry with me was of the mother who defied a dictator and sacrificed her sons. It was the woman who refused to recant her faith as demanded by the ruler at Antioch. Rather than bow down before this king, she watched one son after the other being slain as she refused to bow down. I can't make out what I felt about her then – admiration, horror? I doubt that sitting in that schoolroom in the Fasanenstrasse, I made the link to my mother and her principles and dangerous activities, and how they might conflict with her role as mother.

The best of our drawings were put up on the walls of our classroom, and most of them were mine. I was good at art, but hopeless at needlework. Simple embroidery was not too bad, but my sewing was abysmal and so was my knitting. I never managed to knit the *Topflappen* everyone else took home to their mother. But then my mother would hardly have been bowled over by a pot-holder. She did not care that I got a 6 (the bottom grade) for needlework. Quite the contrary. It suited her feminism, as well as her view of my father's work, and proved how her upbringing of me withstood the bourgeois surroundings at school. As for me, being unable to knit was of no importance. My drawings on the wall – that was something to be proud of, rather than a knitted pot-holder. I was a feminist among girls who had never heard of such an idea.

Tante Freundlich linked the various Judaic festivals to the Bible stories. These occasions were familiar to everyone but me and I only ever picked up a few details. I learnt the symbols of the Passover but to my regret I never participated in a *ceder*. This ceremonial feast is performed entirely in the home and no one would have dreamt of inviting such a militant non-believer – not that my mother would have allowed me to accept.

Tante Freundlich also taught us Hebrew. The school's Board of Governors demanded Ancient Hebrew but Tante Freundlich argued that her pupils might come to find Modern Hebrew more useful. In the end, not one of us needed it. Of the class of twenty-five girls, two of us moved to England, one went to the United States and one went to Holland and survived the war. As far as I know, there are no other survivors.

What were my relations with the other girls? I went to all their birthday parties, though all I remember of them was that I wore my best dress, white knee socks or stockings, and maybe even black patent leather shoes – all very bourgeois. But as far as being invited to tea, that only happened once, with Hannelore Klein. Parents may have seen me, the atheist, as a bad influence, or looked down on me as a Polish Jew. On the other hand, I don't have a single memory of not being accepted. I am not even sure that I was aware that in general Poles were looked down on. Only my own Polish mother would mock the shambles in my own room, with the joke that Germans use to ridicule Poles: when Poles tidy up, they put the butter next to the comb.

In Berlin, being a Polish Jew was never a source of misery for me. I did not even know the derisive term *Ostjude*. It was not until I had lived in England for some decades that I experienced the superiority that German Jews think they have over Polish Jews. To be fair, it is only those who feel socially inferior to me, who keep reminding me of the term *Ostjude* and rubbing in the old jokes about butter and combs. It irritates but doesn't bother me, partly because in England the tables of national hierarchies are turned. It is better to be a Pole than a German.

Tante Freundlich never referred to politics, national or international. But one day she asked us to sit in silence for one minute. King George V of England had died in the night and 'he was a good friend of the Jews'. She must have meant the Balfour Declaration drawn up during his reign. In 1937, Tante Freundlich left for Palestine. We all wept. I was devastated. Her replacement, Fräulein Grüneberg, was her complete antithesis. I resented her deeply, I hated her, and she couldn't stand me either. In my unhappiness and distress I developed a habit which I have never quite lost: I started to twiddle with my hair. It drove Fräulein Grüneberg mad. Poor woman, she had to cope with a class of girls who resented her, the most implacable of whom sat in the front interminably twiddling her hair. She banished me to the back of the class and made me wear a hairnet. The halo of being teacher's pet decorated the head of a new girl whom no one liked and whom Fräulein Grüneberg pronounced the cleverest. Everyone else — children, parents — condemned her as *altklug* or precocious. It really was impossible to follow in Tante Freundlich's footsteps. Furthermore, outside the classroom the atmosphere of persecution had worsened, which only heightened our anxiety and resentment. We needed Tante Freundlich more than ever.

On our way home from school, and we never walked anywhere alone any more, we used to stop at a little grocer's to buy ten Pfennigs worth of sauerkraut wrapped in greaseproof paper. Occasionally when we came out of the shop, some boys of our age would start to jeer and jostle us till we dropped the marinated cabbage. It wasn't too awful as muggings go, but it was disturbing because it was not regarded as naughty or delinquent, but correct. It was gradually becoming more and more unwise to walk home from school without an adult, though even that was poor protection. If we weren't jostled or hit with stones, we would be jeered at: '*Jude raus, Jude verekke*' or '*Schmutzige Juden Kinder, blöde Juden Kinder*' (Jews out, Jews perish; dirty Jew children, stupid Jew children).

The synagogue and school were a ten-minute walk from home

and every day we passed the showrooms of Mercedes Benz at the corner of Fasanenstrasse and the Kurfürstendamm. Some of the pupils had managed to get some Mercedes Benz badges from the salesmen – they hadn't realised the girls were Jewish – and wore them on their lapels. I recognised a similar logo years later and have never been able to take the CND badge seriously for that reason – certainly not as a symbol of peace. To me that logo signifies Hitler in his favourite car. He stands up, his hand is raised with the elbow bent, as the Mercedes carries him slowly along the Unter Den Linden or in triumph along the main street of the capital of a vanquished country. If I ever had the money, a Mercedes is not what I would buy. For years I felt this about all German cars. Now I happily drive a Volkswagen. I never saw a Volkswagen in Berlin, though its name was famous. The notion of that car was a symbol of propaganda and of Hitler deceiving his own people. The deception of the German people – *das Deutsche Volk* – of that time does not bother me one bit.

Of course, my boycott is irrational. Some of my best appliances – like some of my best friends – are German. In a way each one is an alibi for my tolerance. Apart from my car, I have a Rowenta iron, a Bosch fridge-freezer and an AEG oven. But I shall never buy anything from Krupps, the firm that waxed fat on slave labour. Were any of my family among them? Shouldn't the firm have been disbanded, shouldn't the shares have been given to survivors? They now trade as Krups; they may have lost a 'p', but not their guilt.

Back in the 1950s I would not have dreamt of buying anything German. Just before we were married, Bill and I went on a Fabian trip to Yugoslavia and our plane had to land at Stuttgart. Sitting in the plane was bad enough, but we had to get out and I hated it when my feet touched German soil. The tarmac burnt right through my shoes.

At Easter 1938, when I was ten, I transferred to a grammar school. The Holdheim Schule at 66 Nürnbergerstrasse took boys and girls, was associated with the Reform Community but not attached to a synagogue. I don't think we learnt Hebrew and I can't remember any Old Testament lessons either, though they must have been on the timetable and the school closed for Jewish holy days. I was once more the only atheist and the only pupil who never went to synagogue, but it was less of an issue. And if there was hardly another girl or boy whose parents were not born in Germany, again no one looked down on me and I never heard the derogatory word *Ostjude*. At the same time, and without any dimming of my Marxist fervour, I grew more aware of being Jewish as the persecution grew more and more vicious. Studienrat Ofner, our headmaster, warned the school: 'Never walk home by yourself and if any one shouts insults at you, don't react, don't answer, just walk on home.' He repeated this most gravely in late October, the day after a German diplomat had been shot by a seventeen-year-old Jewish boy in Paris. Within a few days this act triggered off the *Kristallnacht*, and Studienrat Ofner, with thousands of other German Jews, was led into Sachsenhausen concentration camp.

At the same time, *Der Stürmer*, Julius Streicher's anti-Semitic paper, was becoming more and more virulent. One side of the Wittenberg Platz was occupied by rows of glass cases of blown-up pages of this most horrific of all tabloids. Too many people stopped to snigger at the exaggerated stereotypes of Jewish faces: huge and deformed noses, swarthy stubbled skin and the evil leers of Jewish men killing gentile male babies, raping gentile women, conning gentile men, betraying the Fatherland, and conspiring to rule the world together with the Bolsheviks. The pages were covered with every fantasy of horror that inhabited the minds of the authors. Witchcraft fantasies of the Middle Ages are children's stories compared with what was displayed for the German people to absorb on their daily shopping trips.

Despite the frightening atmosphere out in the streets and the wretchedness brought into our homes – jobs lost, financial ruin, desperate applications for visas – we were happy while at school. I certainly was, even if no one took the place of Tante Freundlich. The syllabus was ambitious and the competition exciting; I had far more competition than at Fasanenstrasse, especially from the boys. The arts were a joy, too. We discovered watercolours and saw our first Shakespeare play when the Sixth Form performed *A Midsummer Night's Dream* in German. No other performance has ever lived up to this one, especially the scene with the crack in the wall. The actors who peeped through it had great style.

And we began to learn English. We had the choice of French or English but most of us chose English for the simple reason that our parents had hopes of emigrating and there were more English-speaking than French-speaking countries. By now anti-Semitism had reached such a pitch that everyone was desperate to leave and to go anywhere no matter what the language – English, French, Spanish, Chinese. Our grammar book was called *Current English*. It had an orange cover and I remember the feeling it gave me, but not what I learnt from it. Apart from rudiments from this orange book, we learnt a crazy song that told us it was a long way to Tipperary but not what or who or where was Tipperary, or the 'Lucifer' or the 'fag'. Nursery rhymes were bizarre fantasies where a cow jumps over the moon while other domestic animals and things from the kitchen got up to all sorts of tricks, and where an oversized egglike creature tumbles off the wall as all the king's soldiers march by. We were fascinated by those absurd images. Only King Cole was boring.

I discovered that I excelled at sports. Not gymnastics and not the kind of team games I later played in England, but running and long jump. We practised in the playground and at weekends on the playing fields outside Berlin that belonged to Maccabi, the Jewish sports organisation, and were soon to be claimed by the true Germans. I was small but could jump further and run faster than anyone else of my age. A certificate declares me first in the *Sportskampfe* on sports day for my age group but I was frustrated that I was not first overall.

In our class of just over twenty there were seven girls. We met in different homes each Tuesday and called our group *Das Kränzchen*, a circle of little women who meet over coffee for a *Kaffeeklatsch* (to gossip and talk about home and children). Daisy Meyer was my best friend. Daisy was a smart and enviable name. It was English and everything English was smart. Like pictures of the Houses of Parliament, slow-marching guardsmen in bearskins, and gentlemen in knickerbockers playing golf. Daisy's father was in the rag trade but not a tailor like mine. Herr Meyer was a wealthy merchant who dealt in cloth and owned a comfortable house in Grunewald, the smartest district of Berlin. His family was German, not Polish, and his name was not encumbered by that alien 'sz', like ours. This tall man had fought in the Great War, and regarded himself as Prussian. His German was faultless, unlike that of my parents with their heavy East European accent, which I may not have noticed, though I am quite sure they did.

Frau Meyer was well-groomed, had a sophisticated manner and a dry humour. But she could be offputting and never more so than later in England when I was already grown up and she told me that whenever I had visited them in the Heerstrasse, I had always worn everything inside out – jumpers, blouses, dresses. She laughed at the memory but I was embarrassed and annoyed. No doubt she meant no harm, but I felt she was not only laughing at me and my mother, but mocking my Polishness.

For all their Prussian demeanour, the Meyers were practising Jews and, though liberal, celebrated the sabbath every Friday evening, began the Passover with a *ceder*, and went to synagogue on Yom Kippur and Rosh Hashanah. My father used to accuse me of liking Daisy for all the wrong reasons: for her family having more money and living in a large house in the best area and with living-in servants. The Meyers' house on the Heerstrasse stood in its own large gardens where roses grew, Daisy's room was decked out with pink furnishings embellished with frills, ribbon and lace, and her dolls sat on shelves, on chairs, and on her bed. I loved every bit of this thoroughly bourgeois household which contravened all my parents stood for. Staying there was a treat for me and a threat for them which I did not understand at the time. But they should have realised that my Marxism was not up for sale.

Daisy and I were complete opposites but it had little to do with any German/Polish or religious/atheist dichotomy. I had short ginger hair, freckles and a flair for sport, Daisy had brown corkscrew curls, pretty clothes, a baby voice, and an awkward gait. She always behaved well and never complained. I became a tomboy – a little feminist wanting to be a boy? – and Daisy, the good girl, admired me for this delinquency. But what endeared her to me was her good-naturedness. She was still like that when she died in her forties. She had also kept her baby voice and her slightly hysterical schoolgirl giggle. Though she died so young, she was one of the few of our class who lived beyond childhood and had children of her own. She left Berlin very early in 1939, but a few weeks before she left she nearly died of diphtheria. Our class received daily bulletins but the crisis passed and, unlike Bella Trachtenberg, she survived.

I sometimes spent the night in Daisy's frilly room in the Grunewald and we talked till dawn. But what did we talk about? She was perplexed by my heathenism, that I never went to synagogue and knew so little of Jewish customs, but we never discussed that. Nor did we discuss the opium of the people, Marx, Lenin or Rosa Luxemburg. We talked about the things that girls of ten do talk about: what had happened at school, how cheeky I had been, what we thought about the other girls, which boys we fancied, and sex.

One of the girls had revealed that the boy's thingy goes into the girl's whatever it was, and that if grown-up women did not do this often they went crazy. That was why when Fräulein Warschauer, our form teacher, took a few days off, our *Kränzchen* knew that she had gone to a place where they cater for that need. We had reversed the traditional pattern and dreamt up a male brothel for the use of women. Such an institution occurs in Kästner's *Fabian*, but all we had read was his *Emil und die Detektiven*.

All too soon – after the *Kristallnacht* in November 1938 – the main topic of conversation changed to who had been taken away and who had come back from the concentration camp and in what state, and who was leaving the country and what was their destination.

# TWELVE

# Hélène and André

Two children who affected me for ever came into my life when I was eight – Hélène and André. Hélène was my cousin, André is my brother. Hélène was the only child of my aunt Regina and my uncle Paul and she and her mother came from Paris to stay with us for part of the summer of 1936. Hélène was four and still wore her hair in a topknot. I was twice her age, we had no common language, but we got on like sisters, only better. She picked up German very quickly, though the only French I learnt were a few songs. Someone told me that the way to pronounce French words was always to omit the last letter. This has caused me no end of confusion ever since. Considering the lasting impact this encounter has had on me – a day does not go by when Hélène is not somewhere in my mind – I have extraordinarily little recollection of what she and I did together. We went together to the shop that sold sauerkraut by the Pfennig from deep barrels. We ate ice-cream in pretty shell-shaped wafers, and from ordinary wafers, licking the ice and watching the gap between the two halves close up and each trying to be the last to finish. We bought similar pairs of sandals – hers were white, mine were beige, and very smart in either shade. Hélène and her mother taught me 'Frère Jacques' and 'Au Clair de la lune'. I don't know which German songs she learnt and what on earth could she have thought of them later when she was ten. I do know we were inseparable and that I loved her.

This apparently irritated my mother, who kept trying to turn me against her. She would tell me, for example, that Hélène had upset something but had tried to pin the blame on me. My feelings for Hélène were not affected in the slightest, but it may well have been the beginning of my doubts over my mother and foreshadowed future mischief: her tendency to come between me and my friends, as well as me and other relatives.

Hélène and her mother stayed till the end of the summer. For all those weeks I had a sibling, a person all to myself, someone I could play with, someone who wanted my company more than anyone else's, someone to be with when the adults were preoccupied, and who was not drawing Marxist conclusions all the time. To judge from the photograph of her and me on Wittenberg Platz, there must have been an element of mothering in it. I look like the protective big sister; she looks very fetching and cuddly. I had been asking my mother for some time why I couldn't have a sister or brother, and Hélène fulfilled that need. Perhaps she was in part a replacement for the doll I never had.

The day they left to go back to Paris still distresses me. Hélène and her mother stand in the living room, then they are in the hall. They are dressed to go away, they are surrounded by suitcases. The flat has been emptied of all their belongings. I start to sob, to scream, 'Don't go, don't take her away. I shall never see you again.' I throw myself at her, she is torn away. I throw myself to the floor. The front door is open and I crawl forwards and by the front door I bang my head against the ground as they walk down the stairs. I howl. I know that I shall never, ever see her again. I lie weeping, sobbing on the floor. Someone hauls me back into the flat. The flat is as it was before they came, but such a void.

I never did see her again and my premonition has haunted me all my life. Six summers later, on 16 July 1942, she and her parents were rounded up by the occupying Germans in a special drive to clear Paris, and indeed most of France, of all Jews. Her father was taken directly to Auschwitz. Hélène, with her mother, spent her tenth birthday in a camp at Pithiviers, not far from Paris. Then her mother, with every other mother – even mothers of babies were torn from their children – was taken to Auschwitz. On 16 September 1942, Hélène and two cousins of a similar age were herded into a Nazi train full of children and sent to Auschwitz, not to be reunited with their parents but to be thrown into the gas ovens on arrival.

The Lubartov survivors in Paris have published a book, a record of those who did not come back. It is written in Yiddish and contains a photograph of the three little cousins and a letter one of them had written and all had signed. They threw it out of the window of that train and miraculously it found its destination –

more miraculous than any missive in a ship's bottle coming in to port. To say the letter reached its destination is only partly accurate because one of the people to whom it was addressed was Hélène's mother, my aunt Regina, who was already in Auschwitz. But it did reach some members of the family in Paris.

My uncle Charles had fled into Vichy France when the Germans marched into Paris and was living in Perpignan on the farm belonging to his wife's brothers. Late that summer, via the underground network, he got a message to tell him that his sister and her husband had been taken to Auschwitz, but that Hélène was still in Pithiviers. He rushed back to save Hélène, to try to smuggle her out – to buy her out, perhaps? They showed him the letter the children had thrown from the train; it was found in two pieces and pasted together: *'Nous nous dire je ons surmiedz {?} rejoindre mama tout vas bien arriverons ce soir espère trouver maman Courage! nous nous reverrons bientot. Ric, Thérèse, Hélène.'* He loved her so and he was too late. They say he was out of his mind when he returned to Perpignan.

Charles was then married to Germaine. Germaine was pretty, Catholic and French and, according to my mother, reluctant to become pregnant as she feared she would lose her figure and therefore Charles. That dilemma may well have been resolved had it not been replaced by another. When Charles came back having failed to save Hélène, he was not only out of his mind, he became temporarily impotent. Germaine then took a lover, he caught her – and that was that as far as he was concerned. My mother always told me a completely different tale of why their marriage had broken down: Germaine could not stand being married to a Jew in the circumstances of Vichy France and so she left him; she was a silly woman anyway who only cared about her figure. I wouldn't be surprised if my mother had exaggerated this tale of vanity, or even made it all up. It is far more likely that Charles left a wife who would not bear him children. I am sure my mother resented and was jealous of any consort of Charles'.

While she was always ready with tales of Charles and Germaine and Charles and other women, my mother never told me what had happened to Hélène. I knew nothing about the letter or the train.

'Hélène has disappeared and we don't know what has happened to her' was all my mother ever reported after the war. Missing presumed killed must be one of the cruellest and most futile of phrases. Hope is engendered and imagination stimulated, and all in vain. How can one come to terms with the death that is left vague, how can mourning be completed? For years after the war, I fantasised about finding her. There were stories of Jewish children, or perhaps they were non-Jewish children of Slav nations, who had been taken by the Nazis to be given to childless Aryan mothers. I felt sure that my beautiful and clever Hélène must have been singled out and saved like this.

I discovered the awful truth by chance. In the 1950s I went to see some friends of friends of my mother and aunts who were on a visit to London. They talked about Hélène and her mother and the circumstances of their deaths as if I knew all about it. I refused to believe their story. So they fetched the Lubartov book they had brought with them to give to their London relatives. I saw the chapter devoted to Hélène and her mother, their photographs, and above all that letter, and I collapsed into despair, grief, horror, I felt betrayed, of no account. Why had it been kept from me? Who did my mother think she was? God? Was sainthood no longer enough? I did not want to upset you, she said, with that familiar expression of hers: indifference, irritation at being questioned, discomfort at being found out, and pretence of innocence and caring.

Even then, the truth was adjusted and I was told that Hélène and other children had been burnt in a forest in the French countryside. I suppose they meant Pithiviers. I could not read Yiddish and so they got away with it. But I can read some French and I discovered the facts a few years ago when I read the booklet Paul Gradstein wrote and published privately about what happened to him, Regina and Hélène. The truth is that Hélène and her cousins were tossed into the ovens at Auschwitz/Birkenau the moment their cattle train got there. It was seven weeks after her tenth birthday.

Back in 1935, in Bayreutherstrasse 12, after my aunt and Hélène had left, after I had quietened down and was no longer weeping out loud, only inside, and feeling flat, my parents told me they were going to have a baby. They had not intended to tell me just yet, but I was so upset about Hélène's departure and they wanted to cheer me up. I felt no pleasure, no emotion other than vague surprise which turned into outrage. How could they even begin to think that anything could heal my despair and misery, and that an unknown, unborn baby could compensate for my lovely Hélène!

I don't remember my mother's pregnancy, only the day my brother was born. Our circumstances had changed considerably since the day I was born in the Jewish Hospital in the *Rote Wedding*. My little brother started life in a nursing home – a Jewish one, of course, given the political climate. He was born in the afternoon, and in the evening, on our way to the nursing home, my father took me to dinner in a Hungarian restaurant to eat a delicious goulash. At the nursing home my mother lay in a small cosy room and bewailed, not the baby's hair which was suitably dark without a hint of red, but the baby's length. 'Only 51 cm!' she cried. 'He'll never grow tall!' She was sure he would end up smaller even than my father, who was 5ft 6. My brother is now over 6ft.

In a traditionally Jewish community, as in many others, a daughter is not as valued as a son. This could have lingered on in the unconscious of my progressive and feminist mother; in any case, she came to dote on André. He may of course have been a more lovable child, or perhaps it had to do as much with her psychological make-up and the Oedipus complex. I now believe more in Freud than in Marx.

They had André circumcised. Not, they hastened to tell everyone, for religious reasons but for hygienic ones, and it was true that no rabbi was anywhere near the scene when my baby brother lost a snip of tissue and some drops of blood. They called him André after a French Communist and martyr. I never found out which one and I did not care for the name. Ideologically sound it may have been, but I would have liked my sibling to have a more ordinary name.

My mother was by then a statuesque shape and breast-fed the new baby with fervour. She liked me to watch but I was not keen to be an observer of their close relationship. I was also less than keen on my own contribution to the baby's nourishment: I had to carry shopping nets full of empties to the *Konsum*, the local co-operative store, and hump back full bottles of *Malzbier*. This dark and rich Guinness-like beer was reputed to increase the volume and richness of a mother's milk. The nets got heavier and heavier as I trudged back and forth. I was the family drudge. The Hella substitute. When they took the new baby out in the pram, my parents, with a great show, encouraged me to push the pram. I was expected to feel proud, grown up and grateful but I would have been happier pushing a dustcart.

I sound a hard-to-please child. But mine were the common problems of the first-born, only aggravated. My position had always seemed precarious; I had never been the centre of my parents' universe. That place was held by the Party. But as I looked at my mother feeding her son, I saw that he was the apple of her eye: why had it never been me? To make matters worse, as well as the fact that I was no longer the only child and was being pushed further to the periphery, the birth of my brother signalled the abrupt end of childhood itself, not necessarily a concomitant of becoming a sibling.

Daily trundling to the *Konsum* for nourishing malt beer was only a minor part of my new adult role. To emphasise the end of childhood, my parents took away my teddy bear. My one and only cuddly toy, my only doll surrogate, my brown teddy bear, was given to my baby brother. They kept reminding me that I was too grown-up to need it, that I was no longer a baby. As if I needed reminding. I can't in fact remember the moment my teddy bear was taken from me, only my mother's subsequent justifications. I have suppressed the pain, but it is not too deeply hidden for those who live with me to notice some of the effects. Our daughters were in their early teens and younger when they began to tease me about the huge number of cuddly animals I continued to give them. How right they were. It was ridiculous: each had at least twenty or thirty soft toys and dolls. They were a source of pleasure but also a cradle for moths.

If I can't remember exactly how it felt to have a teddy bear taken from me, I know exactly how I felt when my parents left me in charge of my tiny baby brother, a few weeks old at most, while they went to the cinema for the evening. They were amazed at my request for a baby-sitter. I was no longer alone, I had a companion, I was now the big sister. But to be a big sister as well as a Communist was just too much, and I sat in that flat and screamed and screamed. No one came, just as Hella had not come in Adalbertstrasse. Those flats in Bayreutherstrasse were custom-built for people to mind their own business, to maintain a bourgeois front, to enable them to turn a deaf ear, though also good for cell meetings and listening to Radio Moscow. It was only to an American or British bomb that this solid block succumbed in 1945.

But on that evening in 1937 I was in terror of the indifferent walls, the loneliness, and my utter helplessness. The baby lying there fast asleep throughout my ear-splitting screams seemed an object of nuisance and terror, rather than another human being. I yelled and yelled. My throat ached but I yelled until they came. They, who with a couple of Party friends had gone to the local cinema to see *Sous les toits de Paris*, were livid with me and scathing.

That is all I remember of my brother in Berlin. Was the amnesia due to losing my place as the only child, coupled with the loss of Hélène? Because what made the advent of a baby brother even more difficult was that my parents kept offering him to me as a substitute for Hélène.

André was my first and only sibling and an unbeatable rival, but even he did not come before Party. The Party mattered more than either of us. André's birth, like my own eight years previously, did not stop my mother from her political activities. He was only a few weeks old when a couple of comrades turned up and asked her to resume her work for the Party. My father was dead set against it. Less committed to the cause in the first place, his main concern was that she was putting all our lives at risk.

My mother too hesitated. She told them she had two young children and one of them was a baby. If something happened to her, and it might, what would happen to the children? Furthermore, she had no time, what with the children and the domestic responsibilities. They offered to provide her with a daily help. Fräulein Pelz was older than my mother, wore her hair in a splendid bun, looked respectable and bourgeois. I don't know where she came from and who paid her, but she must have been safe. A household like ours couldn't risk anyone who was not. My mother continued her underground work – same friends, same cell meetings, same secrecy. If I was not at school on wash day, Fräulein Pelz took me with her to the *Hängeboden*, a huge area formed by the attics of one whole block running into each other. All the washing was done there: the scrubbing, the rinsing, the wringing out and the hanging up. I watched Fräulein Pelz and helped her, and sang the song of the *'Lustige Waschfrauen'* or merry washerwomen. That vast Valhalla of attics had such strange magic for me that I thought I might have dreamt it. But when I went back to Berlin in 1966, the Aschersons showed me their *Hängeboden*. I had not dreamt it.

Later, in London while I was attending a rather poor state school, André was sent first to a prep school and then to Godolphin and Latymer. He qualified as a doctor, emigrated to South Africa, and was glad when Margaret Thatcher replaced Ted Heath. 'Ted Heath is not right-wing enough,' he told me. He remained the apple of our mother's eye.

# THIRTEEN

# King for a Day

André's birth and the subsequent weeks were not the happiest time, but in the following summer I had ten days that almost made up for the weeks of misery. These were ten days that my father and I spent in the Sächsische Schweiz (the mountainous region near the border with Czechoslovakia) all on our own. My mother and my baby brother stayed behind in Berlin. I have no idea who got in the supplies of malt beer; maybe they requisitioned Hella.

On the way, my father and I stopped at Dresden, less to see the old town than to walk round an architectural exhibition of real houses, all of them modern. My favourite was a Danish house — simple, elegant, and with large and long windows that went right down to the polished wooden floors. I did not see windows like that again until I went to England. We came out of the house into a storm of hailstones as large as sugar Easter eggs. It is a strange memory to have of Dresden, now famous for being destroyed by missiles as hot as the hail was cold.

From Dresden, my father and I headed for Schmelka near to where the Elbe flows across the border from Czechoslovakia. We got off the train at Bad Schandau, crossed to the east bank of the Elbe and walked all the way to Schmelka, in soft and steady rain. My father and I were the only people on that path, and walking in warm gentle rain has been an almost sensual pleasure ever since. It rained quite a bit that week with typical mountain rain that is not heavy but persistent. Even so there was enough sunshine to bathe in the river, play with my new, huge beach ball and start swimming lessons in the Elbe. A kindly middle-aged instructor with a moustache tied me to a harness and from the jetty advised and encouraged me as I struggled in the water. When my father and I turned up on the third day, a notice had been pinned up telling us that '*Juden sind hier nicht erwünscht*'. The same message had made me leave my sausages and potato salad in the KaDeWe. Six lessons had been paid for, but we turned back. The instructor had to draw his own conclusions. Maybe he already had. I did not learn to swim until the summer of 1939 in the Prince of Wales baths in North London.

We were still free to walk and that area was superb for walking. We walked up and down mountain slopes, through forests of beeches, and past outcrops of rocks of all sizes. Some rocks that looked across the Elbe were known by names corresponding to their anthropomorphic shapes. From one particular mountain top we would look yearningly over into Czechoslovakia. Unlike other visitors to the area, we could not cross the border. My father, with his stateless papers, needed a special visa.

Favourite outings were to two rock caves called the *Schneiderloch* and the *Pfarrerloch*, because one had hidden a tailor and the other a priest from persecution. I remember one in particular but not for its political mythology. We had gone there with a guided tour and one woman who was excessively plump got stuck as she tried to climb up into the narrow refuge. The guide joked and laughed while, like a midwife, he eased her out, slowly and painfully. After that little scene, the guide waited outside to collect his tips. Two trees stood there, intertwined but of different species. The guide quipped 'Rassenschande', all too common a Nazi joke about the disgrace of racial pollution. Everyone laughed as they fished out their tips. My father hesitated before taking out his wallet, but the guide walked up to him and prompted him.

When it rained we ate our picnic lunches of cold meats, rye bread and lots of tomatoes topped with raw chopped onion, in a *Laube* (a cross between a garden shed and conservatory). An even greater treat was to have lunch or dinner in the local hotel that overlooked the Elbe. My father could not get enough of their veal escalopes. To me they tasted like fish rather than meat but for my father they were perfect, with not a hint of pork. He was relaxed about everything: a man who at home in Berlin had the tendencies of a paranoid tyrant was now a gentle and understanding father. We shared a room and I woke up one night to find I had wet my bed. At home he would have flown into a rage. Here, he was sympathetic and helpful even though I was sitting in quite a puddle.

We were not the only Jews holidaying in Schmelka, and sometimes we went on outings together with a Jewish couple who had a son a little older than I. My father started to tease me about him and made me feel very self-conscious and shy. It got so bad that I could not even look at the boy. His face was rather ugly and bony but it had nothing to do with that. I was just becoming sexually aware. His parents did not escape the Holocaust but the son did. They had put him on a Kindertransport to England. After the *Kristallnacht* in November 1938, trains carrying children of all ages, but without their parents, left Germany for England. My father located the boy some years later. He was then an undergraduate at Cambridge and visited us in London, but only once. My father kept making inept jocular references to his parents and we never saw him again.

The holiday with my father was a particularly joyous episode for me. No one else mattered. I had his whole attention, and apart from our being banned from swimming lessons, no politics interfered. But all holidays, with or without parents, were happy interludes from life at home. Bourgeois pleasures were allowed, my parents had time to spend, and politics were irrelevant. Like the shooting season, politics did not start again till the autumn. Memories of the earliest holidays are hazy but in photographs of these sojourns in German seaside resorts I look like any other little girl. On the sands of Ahrendsee I hug a huge beach-ball animal and on the promenade I look stylish and boyish wearing a towelling gown and holding a kaleidoscope upside down, trying to work out where the jewelled lit-up bits are hidden.

The first seaside holiday I remember clearly was spent in Zopot, the year after my unforgettable summer in Poland. Zopot was then part of East Prussia, hemmed in by but not part of Poland, and so my father could come too. Most of our days were spent on the beach where the three of us had built a wall of sand to surround our *Strandkorb*, a beach basket-cum-chair large enough to shelter three people. That summer, we were still three. On sunny days we would lunch within the *Strandkorb* but evening meals were mostly eaten in restaurants. My favourite was the Mirabelle, which sounded like the name of my favourite aunt, and served cauliflower sautéed in brown butter.

Two highlights of the Zopot municipality were a fireworks display, which frightened me, and a carnival of flowers that provided the one and only political lesson of the holiday. A dozen or so black, elegant and smug limousines drove at funereal pace along the promenade. Each was decked out in elaborate floral arrangements but my mother warned me that the beauty of the display was irrelevant; to win one had to be in with the judges and that depended on one's social position. She was proved right when the dullest and stiffest display, made up solely of maroon gladioli, won first prize.

My mother took me on a brief trip to Danzig to see the sights but also to meet my aunt Paula, whom my mother despised as superficial and vain. Unfortunately, when we met her, she seemed to prove it. Her feet were tortured by new shoes. My mother pointedly asked poor Paula what size shoe she took, and when Paula went red it was obvious that the silly woman had brought shoes a size too small. To wear shoes that were too small, had high heels, open toes and slingbacks – that was a sure give-away of an unliberated and bourgeois woman. Not acceptable to my mother, and therefore not to me. But our main purpose in going to Danzig was to see the old town with its houses so narrow that they seemed to be drawing in their breath. It was my first time as a tourist and my shoes were all too sensible.

Our next summer holiday was in Denmark on the island of Fanø, and the only one the three of us ever took abroad. I was still the only child, the hotel was the best we ever stayed in, and I shared a room with my parents. There were no politics, no unpleasant scenes, but many intriguing first encounters: Englishmen and amber and lobsters and ballroom dancing. It was the most bourgeois of our holidays and I enjoyed every bit of it.

The hotel was owned by a tall man who had all the withdrawn charm of Englishmen I met years later. Each morning before breakfast as the tide went out, he would walk along the beach searching for amber. He had a fine collection and in the end we too had filled a box the size of a half-camembert box with amber pieces. I am still enthralled by that semi-precious stone whose process of formation took millions of years, and was due to earth movements, oceanic upheavals, climatic changes and the extinction of huge forests. Adult words but they reflect the ideas that excited me then and were first stimulated by museum visits and books on fossils given to me by my parents' comrades and friends, the Danielsohns. Evolution is important to Marxists.

The owner of the hotel had one of those rare amber coffins containing an insectiform Snow White whose prince had never turned up: an insect caught by a drop of sap from a tree and through time transformed from an object of distaste into a jewel. My own favourite pieces of amber were deep-red chunks that look like large drops of clotted blood. We had one or two among the yellow and brownish pieces in our box of uncut amber. The box survived our exodus to London but was then stolen by the miserable removal men who moved us from Chalk Farm to Ealing. The loss lingers and I still hope it brought them bad luck.

Quite apart from the amber, the beach was full of more commonplace interests: bathing machines, donkey rides, and marvellous sand for building castles. My parents, my mother in particular, got carried away with this silicone architecture, and feverishly indulged in ever more extravagant engineering and artistic feats. I thought of them years later when I climbed through the crazy complex of the Gaudi Cathedral in Barcelona. I also had two playmates of my own age: a blonde girl who was not Jewish and a plump dark-haired girl who was the daughter or niece of the Kempinskis of the Berlin hotel and there with her nanny.

The meals in our hotel seemed like banquets. Cold buffet lunches spread out over mile-long white linen-clothed tables were splendid but outclassed by dramatic displays of lobsters on Saturday evenings. Waiters carried dishes of whole lobsters round all the tables to be admired. Ohs and ahs came even from our table but I was appalled by those angry red armour-plated bodies with limbs of machine tools and cranes. What had these things to do with food and how could my parents feast on these monstrosities and with such relish?

I had no idea then that Orthodox Jews avoid shell fish as well as pork. I must have been in my late twenties when I first learnt of these prohibitions, and by then I liked lobster. Later still, at a dinner party of Woodrow Wyatt's, I sat next to Harold Lever, who when the first course was served asked me to 'be a darling and pick out the shellfish for me'. His eyesight was bad, he said. I suspected he was being ostentatious in his religious observance, but I now think he was reinforcing a bond. Wasn't he really saying, 'You and I belong to the same tribe or group. We two are Jews unlike the others supping here'? Actually there were two others, but Nigel and Vanessa Lawson – who looked like a beautiful Egyptian woman from those ancient wall paintings displayed in the British Museum – did not seem to want to be conspicuous by giving up their delicious prawns, any more than I did.

Back in Fanø, when I was seven and when these creatures far larger than the prawns served up at that smart London dinner were carried round the dining tables, they were simply an abomination to me. I didn't know that this is exactly the word in the edict in Leviticus: as shellfish are neither fish nor flesh and do not fit into any categroy determined by God, they are abominations. It is not hygiene that is the reason for the prohibition of either pork or shellfish.

Of course, my child's mind never gave a thought to the classifications in Deuteronomy or the abominations in Leviticus. In any case, unlike other Jewish children I knew little of biblical laws. Nor was I a mermaid sitting on the ocean floor where I might have admired the lobster for their beauty. As a Berlin child in a bourgeois restaurant, it was perfectly obvious to me that lobsters were an abomination – even all dressed up and lounging on silver trays. It had nothing to do with the rules of God, in whom as a devout Marxist I did not believe in anyway.

Like the slave who is king of Babylon for a day, I played the little bourgeois to the full for a month. The high point was the weekly Children's Ball on a Tuesday at the Kursaal, or was it Monday at the largest hotel? Chandeliers sparkled, adults and children dressed up. I wore a simple but decidedly bourgeois white muslin dress with smocking, albeit not done by hand but factory machine. I danced in a perfectly bourgeois way with a partner, a boy of similar height. We did not talk and I don't know what nationality he was. We were self-conscious and had to concentrate on dancing, but we managed. The evening always ended with a game of musical chairs and me coming second. The winner stood on the last remaining chair, was applauded and given a box of chocolates. There was no glory or prize for coming second. I played this game during a Labour Party event up in Stockton-on-Tees. I ended up not with a prize – not done for the Member of Parliament's wife to win – but with a neat hole burnt into my black crushed velvet skirt. One of the men whose lap I had landed on had not put out his cigarette. I wore that skirt for many more years, always over a black petticoat, and always thought of Fanø and my white muslin frock.

It was on those Mondays or Tuesdays in Denmark that I realised how much I loved to dance and how good I was. Back in Berlin I dared to ask my mother if I could take ballet lessons, but she squashed my bouregois ambition with contempt. What was all right for the Bolshoi later was not all right for a Berlin Communist then.

Each year on a special night in July, they burnt a witch on Fanø. It was similar to the burning of the guy on Guy Fawkes night, but the witch was a woman and more in keeping with medieval persecutions. A female effigy of straw, wood and cloth was thrown onto a fire which lit up the dark beach. I kept my distance, although I had no premonition of the scapegoating and witch-hunts that would include the burning of my little cousin. Witch-craft accusations and hunts had by then been going on in Germany for two years but I did not make the link.

Among the many firsts for me that summer was my first meeting with an Englishman. To say Englishman is to anticipate the adult-hood of some boys I met on a stroll along a beautifully kept stretch of golf course. The ground was luscious and springy and made up of different kinds of grasses and herbs smelling like nothing I had ever smelt before. We had no common language and they were less forthcoming than the boys I had met by the pond in Poland. More polite and in keeping with their Englishness, I now realise. But we did establish where we all came from and what languages we spoke.

I had two very enjoyable holidays without either of my parents. For part of the summer of 1935, my mother arranged for me to go to a holiday camp for children in the country round Berlin. Everything was friendly and jolly. The younger helpers entertained us to a show in which a very tall young man dressed up as a woman and shrieked in a falsetto voice. I have a photograph of the actors surrounded by us children. Our hair is garlanded with elaborate daisy chains and we look so typically German of that period. How well I fit in! Other photographs remind me of the sylvan setting with meals eaten in the open air and the large, rotund matrons wearing white uniforms and caps. There is one photograph I treasure because of its political absurdity: I'm not on the edge but right in the middle of a group of five children; we are perched on a fence and one boy holds a full-size swastika flag. Far from looking askance, I smile contentedly.

Suddenly, unannounced and well before the camp was due to close, my mother arrived and took me home. I have no idea what excuse she gave to those in charge but in the train she told me she had heard the camp was run by Nazis. She shuddered to think of me in their midst. She did not think they would hurt me, but it was ideologically and morally wrong for me to be there. And there was always the danger of my being indiscreet, followed by the inevitable denunciation. I did not tell her I had liked the camp and wished she had not come.

In the early summer of 1938 my mother sent me to another camp, but this one was run by Jews, for Jews, with not a swastika in sight. Anyway, by now the mistake she made in 1935 would not have been possible. I felt I really belonged in the camp, and my time there gave me respite not only from the parental regime but from the tensions of a Berlin growing more and more onimous and anti-Semitic. When I look back on this idyll, this interval of relief from fear and persecution, I see sunlight and pleasure: the easy atmosphere, the other children, the staff, the grounds of meadows and trees and bushes, the sky uninterrupted by cloud but patterned by branches and leaves of tall trees. Iridescence. Here we, the children of Jews, had fun and looked forward to the next day and the next.

I learnt to play table tennis and it is here that my ESP got to work again. Though never recognised, it had been active once before with my premonition about Hélène. Here it helped me to locate nothing more than a missing table tennis ball. Everyone had been searching for this small, brittle object for hours. I closed my eyes and saw the large area planted with bushes of red and white *Johannisbeeren*. I walked over to one particular redcurrant bush and picked up the ball. It was that simple. I was uneasy about my ability and didn't discuss it either at the camp or later at home. Extra-sensory perception did not go too well with my mother's super-rational atheism.

I also kept quiet about two rather shameful episodes. Both bothered me and one I was really ashamed of because it revealed the Gestapo within me. There had been a rash of petty thefts and I knew — again through intuition rather than evidence — that the thief was one of the girls who shared my small dormitory. I collared her one afternoon in the dormitory, and told her that I knew she was the culprit: 'But if you own up to me now, I promise I will not tell anyone.' She wept, she said yes, she had stolen the things. I went immediately and told one of the staff.

The other episode shows me up as nothing worse than a silly goose. I had taken a fancy to one of the boys, and he to me. We never spoke, we just gazed at each other from a distance, but we had a go-between, his friend, who evolved a plan for the two of us actually to meet when we got back to Berlin. This was the last thing I wanted. I insisted it was impossible to meet without my parents knowing, but the boys persisted. I felt trapped and the boy I had fancied now repelled me. The only solution was to leave the camp.

I told the director of the summer school I wanted to go home. He was perplexed. He knew I was very happy at the camp yet I kept saying I wanted to go home, and behaved like a two-year-old. He telephoned my parents and my mother came to take me home. I had expelled myself from paradise. I never had a chance to re-enter.

# FOURTEEN

# Martyrs Should be Childless

1938 was hardly the year for holidays. It was the year Hitler walked into Austria, Czechoslovakia was betrayed by Britain and France, and Hitler knew he was free to burn synagogues, smash windows and Jews. For me personally, it was a devastating year. Any good moments were smothered by illness, a dreadful pogrom, my father's departure from Berlin, and then my mother's expulsion from Germany.

Anti-Semitism was fulminating by now and our social life was much restricted. There were no more visits to theatres and cinemas, and we stopped going to cafés and restaurants, an integral part of a Berliner's life. On occasions my parents had taken me with them when they met their friends for dinner on the Kurfürstendamm, usually at the Café Wien. It was a wonderful treat to sit there in the crowded and animated atmosphere and watch people at the other tables, and to eat *Rostbraten*, beef roasted with that special German flavour. It is the café atmosphere I still hanker after, as well as the cacophony of bustle and lights on the Kurfürstendamm that had still not recovered its full glamour and vibrancy by 1991.

The early part of the year was not too bad. I liked my new school, I made lots of friends and I had enjoyed my short stay at the summer camp. Then in September the Munich crisis over-shadowed everything. I associate it with an evening in our flat. It is twilight and my parents and a few of the *Genossen* are sitting round our table by the window that overlooks Bayreutherstrasse. The atmosphere is tense and solemn. I ask what the matter is: 'We are waiting for the news,' they tell me. Chamberlain (I knew who he was) has come to Berchtesgaden to talk to Hitler. Hitler wants the Sudetenland (I knew that, too). The world is waiting to see if England (it is never Great Britain and the British, but England and the English) will stand firm and, if Hitler does march into Czechoslovakia, declare war on Germany. 'That's what we're hoping for; it must happen. Anything else will be a disaster.' I am alarmed. 'Won't that be the end of us?' Oh, yes, everyone round the table agrees. But, they assure me, a war now might be the end of us but would save millions of others. Hitler is rearming at breakneck speed, Germany gets stronger by the week, better to start the war right now. It is inevitable anyway.

The logic of their case, their altruism, the readiness for self-sacrifice — even a child of ten could understand that and admire it, though most children of ten are only required to admire heroes in story-books. But this child of ten was also terrified. I was in no way ready to sacrifice myself but I couldn't show my cowardice. Not in front of these heroic grown-ups who faced their demise — the consequence of a war declared then and there — so coolly. I often think myself back into the ten-year-old girl that I was, to the admiration I still have for those grown-ups, and to the fear I had to keep hidden. When twelve days later, on 28 September, the communiqué of the sell-out to Hitler had been broadcast, I walked with foreboding, relief and guilt along the streets of Berlin. Down Bayreutherstrasse, across Tauntzienstrasse, along Nürnbergerstrasse, and further — and I looked with amazement at upturned tree trunks. Clumps of soil were trapped by the roots and clung to the underbelly of the trunk. Broken branches were strewn over pavements. There had been a fearful hurricane during the night. Or have I imagined all this? I have never dared to check the weather reports. Was the hurricane a fact or a symbol of the turmoil of that month and made manifest only in my mind and memory? Unlike that other brazen concrete symbol of dread, the Berlin Wall, there for anyone to see, the storm is an inextricable part of my purely personal memory of the Munich disaster. When there is talk of Munich, I see the storm, when I am in the middle of a storm, I think of Munich.

Not till the hurricane that hit southern England in October 1987 did I see trees so injured. Bill and I happened to be in Hyde Park the day after the storm and because of the extent of the damage and the danger the park was shut except to guests at a private view at the Serpentine Gallery. The show was disappointingly tame, but the scene outside with broken and fatally wounded trees provided acutely dramatic images. It was sad and spectacular to see those giants lying on their sides, their roots which had been hidden for decades and centuries now exposed and useless. In the West End of Berlin in 1938 there were far fewer trees, but they were all damaged – whether in reality or only in the turbulence of my soul.

This turbulence was due mainly to fear but also to my parents' indifference to my feelings and fortunes. Where were those parental instincts? How did they square them with the risks they took? I know the answers and the logic, but ... My parents were not the first or the last to put the greater good before that of their own children; to reason that without a moral society children do not prosper. The anti-apartheid activities of Ruth Slovo, the South African Communist, led first to prison and then assassination, leaving her children abandoned. The mother in the Book of the Maccabees, rather than bow to the idol and the tyrant, watches her seven sons being put to death. And there was William Tell. What did his son really feel about his father's brave exhibition? Who was the greater hero? Perhaps martyrs should be childless.

I am confused. There is no doubt that when in 1990 the Communist librarian in East Berlin introduced me as the daughter of members of the *Widerstand*, or Resistance, I was so thrilled that I shivered. He had made my day and I was proud. But back in 1938 in March, notions of pride were not uppermost in my mind. My feelings were quite out of tune with my parents' ideas. It was certainly unthinkable for me to express relief that I wasn't going to die just then or be torn from my parents, to those selfless people sitting round the table.

It is barely acceptable for me here and now to admit how relieved I felt when Chamberlain did not declare war for the sake of 'Peace in our Time' or peace in my time. I have never admitted it, and I affect to despise those in Britain who were relieved. But how can I blame ordinary British people who were glad to have peace rather than war and could not foresee that they would be at war anyway, even worse for the delay. I do have a deep contempt for Chamberlain who went crawling to Herr Hitler, and for those who supported him, including those who wrote leaders in *The Times*. They knew the facts and should have known better.

Chamberlain apart, the man who epitomises Munich for me is Lord Halifax. He was so typically English in appearance: his height, his leanness, his hat, the way he wore his clothes, so elegant, casual, such disdain for everyone and everything around. Is it odd that I make him sound attractive? Not really. Any small refugee child is bound to be just as impressed as repelled by such a figure. However, if I hear any reference to him now I shudder because of his stance over Munich.

With the carte blanche marked 'Munich' that Hitler received from Britain and France, anti-Semitism became more rampant still, and the hunt for visas to emigrate even more frantic. During the post-Munich summer several more decrees marked out the Jews from the rest. As this was still before the war, it could only apply to those of German nationality or stateless people like my father. As well as being banned from attending the theatre, every German Jewish man had to add Israel to his other forenames, every German Jewish woman had to add Sarah. My school report from the Holdheim Schule is signed by Curt Israel Ofner and Ernst Israel Breisacher.

Another decree that summer ordered all Jewish owners of shops, firms, businesses and cafés to paint their name in white regulation lettering across their windows, shopfronts, and nameplates. We lived on the first floor of Bayreutherstrasse 12 and my father's plate – black letters on brass – was mounted by the front entrance. He should have painted those white letters across it, but suspecting something malevolent in the intent of the order, something rather more than simply showing Aryans which shops to avoid, he took a considerable risk and ignored the edict. In Germany the name Schulmann (for business purposes he did not use the correct spelling, Szulman) is not particularly Jewish and he escaped official attention. Had he heeded the order, our home, every bit of it, would some months later have been smashed to smithereens.

In the meantime, my recurrent tonsillitis turned out to be tuberculosis. The bacilli were proliferating in the lymph glands along the right side of my neck; and in my mind the spread of this disease is linked to racist edicts, racist attacks, hunts for visas, people packing up and saying goodbye and families being separated. The first treatment that was tried was to expose me to ultra-violet and so I spent the summer not by the seaside or the Elbe, but on a table under a sun lamp. I turned up two or three times a week to lie first on my back and then on my front. The cubicle was dark apart from the treatment lamp and filled with that unearthly aroma of ultra-violet. I imagined and still imagine it will be the smell one smells the moment before death.

However, the bacilli ignored the treatment and one gland got larger and larger till I had a lump on the side of my neck that looked like a marble covered by skin. I had a consistently high temperature, though I was unaware of this until my mother appeared with her thermometer. This went on throughout the summer and into the beginning of term when my mother made an appointment with a surgeon. But when we arrived at his consulting rooms, no one took the slightest notice of us. The place was in chaos. Everyone was feverishly pushing every item in sight into packing cases. The surgeon, a Jew, had that very morning and at long last received his visa from the United States and was getting out as fast as he could. In any case, facilities for a Jewish surgeon to operate were by then nil, and an Aryan surgeon could not and would not operate on a Jewish child. My mother and I left the building feeling very low. We did not talk much on the way home.

The episode underlined our circumstances. The lucky surgeon had a precious visa to the land of milk and honey and the free, and we were left among the hopeless and helpless. It must have been hard for my mother, and I marvel that more mothers do not go out of their minds when faced with the merciless reality that there is no help for their child. In my case, it was my father who was more obviously upset by the state of my neck, and it was my mother who mocked him for being too sentimental. I felt warmed by my father's concern but suppressed whatever I felt about my mother's detached and sensible attitude. To be fair, it was she who again was left to cope – with that and everything else.

In mid-October, my gland was close to bursting. As surgical

help was now out of the question, my parents sent me to a nursing home for Jewish children on the North Sea, in the vain hope that the sea air would blow away the tubercular bacilli. The home itself had a resident doctor who happened to be in Berlin that October. My mother took me to the Lehrter Bahnhof to put me in the care of this cold and unlovely woman whose lower jaw stuck out and whose eyebrows bushed over small, dark, suspicious eyes. The two of us set out and I was glad I had a book to read. We stayed the night in Hamburg and shared a room. I was fascinated when this stranger undressed, albeit with her back to me. Her bottom was the largest I had ever seen and as ugly as her face. The next morning we took the ferry to the island of Föhr. The skies were grey and the sea thick and yellow. A woman was sick over the side before the boat had even sailed, but the waves were not really threatening and I felt fine. I had always felt queasy on swings and on Berlin buses, but sea sickness never plagued me till we crossed the Channel in March 1939.

The children's nursing home, which was in Wyk-auf-Föhr, had been reduced to an annexe after the main building was burnt out. It had a staff of two plus the doctor, and only five children, four girls and a boy, who shared the dormitory. I don't know how long I stayed in that place – it could only have been a matter or two or three weeks – but I was miserable the whole time. Two of the staff were domineering and the third was good at being their servant. None of them really liked children, though they blatantly favoured the boy, who knew how to ingratiate himself.

The tyranny of that Jewish sanatorium in Wyk-auf-Föhr, like the Jewish boarding school in Sussex less than a year later, is caught perfectly in an episode of John Le Carré's television film *A Perfect Spy* when he describes his own childhood in his uncle's repressive household. How much boarding schools have in common with concentration camps is powerfully shown in another film, Lindsay Anderson's *If . . .* For a Jewish home off the coast of Nazi Germany to be such a totalitarian regime is of course ironic.

A strict rule in the Wyk-auf-Föhr sanatorium was that every morsel of food, however unappetising, had to be eaten. One particularly nauseating soup stuck in my mouth as it has stuck in my memory: a dull beige sludge with all its taste derived from a surfeit of salt. The last mouthful of this gruel was beyond me, too disgusting to keep in my mouth and too disgusting to swallow. I was the only child left sitting at the table with the malevolent doctor keeping guard over me till I had cleared my plate. My taste buds and muscles rebelled and, mumbling that I had to go to the lavatory, I ran out and spat the soup into the bowl. The doctor ran after me and shouted, 'You are not to pull the chain! Do you hear?' She looked down at the bowl, grew red with anger at the floating gruel, and let everyone know of my misdeed.

Another daily routine I disliked – it made me feel helpless, and the lack of privacy and the erotic undertones embarrassed me – was the taking of temperatures. This was done not under the arm, as is usual in German homes and doctors' surgeries, but with the thermometer shoved into the rectum, with no privacy whatsoever and to each child in turn, the boy included.

My gland was not cowed by the doctor's presence, or by the North Sea air – quite the reverse – and a few days after I got there it ruptured and poured out its pus. A good metaphor for my feeling towards that wretched place. The fund of pus was inexhaustible. The dressing was changed daily but never in time to prevent the sticky discharge from showing through.

We were the only Jews on the island and did not meet any of the inhabitants. All five children were ailing anyway, and in the late autumn chill by the North Sea would not have moved far from the annexe. Sometimes, and on my own, I walked in the grounds. Mists like chiffon scarves hung round, veiling the ruins of the burnt-out main building. It was a setting from a Hans Christian Andersen fairy tale. I don't remember mists in Berlin, and just as storms evoke Munich, any fog or mist always evokes that island, that institution and the event that followed.

One evening when everyone had gone to bed, we were woken by a loud and persistent knocking at the door. We heard the door being opened, loud peremptory male voices, the door banging shut, silence, and then sounds of consternation. The staff came into the dormitory, told us to pack all our belongings and then go back to bed. The SA had ordered us to leave the island early in the morning.

I can't remember if the staff explained what was happening. There had been enough persecution around us for the last year to make us jumpy and afraid without any further explanations. I dimly remember them telling us that similar things were happening to Jews all over Germany. Did our parents know we were coming? Were they all right? If things were happening all over the country . . .? The staff were up all night, and none of us children could sleep because we kept on having to pee. We were reassured that it often happens when one is nervous.

I cannot now remember how we made our way to the quay but we each carried our own baggage. Only the boy got some help from the overladen staff. When we arrived at the quay, we children were astonished to find the whole quayside humming with children who should have been at school. Because of our seclusion, we had no idea there were so many people on the island. The whole of the local school, hundreds of pupils and some teachers, had assembled to bid us farewell. Their farewell was to boo and jeer and laugh: *'Judenkind das, und Judenschwein dies.'* One of their teachers, a man and one of my 'good' Germans, rushed in vain from one jeering group to the next trying to prevent some of the worst jostling and jeers. But it was in vain and the ugly noise filled the air while we embarked.

But there was no sign of the steamer that had ferried me across a couple of weeks ago, with cabins and all the usual facilities. Down there in the water rocked a small rowing boat with only a pair of oars and just large enough to take the eight of us. We clambered in and the oarsmen cast off as the mocking reached a crescendo. Our teachers gave us strict instructions: 'Keep your eyes down, and your heads! You are not to look at them!' But that was exactly what I had to do. I was not going to turn away. I was not going to bow down to them or in front of them. I looked squarely into the rows of sneering faces and thought, 'I am going to remember these faces as long as I live.' These thoughts are as clear to me now as they were then. I concentrated on the face of one of the children, a blond boy whose large angular features and jeering grin are fixed for ever into my memory. If a child of ten can have contempt, then at that moment when our little boat cast off I added contempt to my dislike of the staff. It must have been the force of my contempt and anger that kept me from being seasick because the sea was very choppy and the boat very tiny. I can rarely muster such mind over matter now.

We did not stay in Hamburg but took the next train to Berlin, all of us fitting into one compartment as we had crammed into the boat. I fell half-asleep but overheard the staff talking about what they thought and feared had been happening throughout Germany. They also made some not very complimentary remarks about my mother: she had kept phoning them; she was a nuisance, she was foreign. Our parents met us at the station in Berlin, and my mother took me home in a taxi. I usually relished a taxi ride but this one was horrendous. The streets between the station and the Westend where we lived were littered with the broken glass of shop windows, the contents spilt out and trampled on all over the pavements. My mother said it was the same all over the city. As the taxi drove into Bayreutherstrasse, my mother pointed to the food trodden into the pavement in front of the ruins of the Café Adler, where earlier that day even the dogs had been prevented from licking the *Judenkuchen* (Jew cake).

This was 10 November 1938, the day after the *Kristallnacht*, the pogrom so named because of the sight and sound of so much shattered glass. I sat in the taxi and what reverberated through my ten-year-old atheist mind was: 'This is what Hell is like, this must be Hell.' Throughout Germany homes had been demolished down to the last tea cup; pianos tossed out of the window; doctors' medical instruments and tailors' sewing machines tossed over balconies, men rounded up in the squares, stripped and forced to lick each other's bottoms; young men fettered in cattle chains and beaten by women and children; synagogues not only burnt but their sacred objects desecrated; a *sofar* (the sacred horn) blown by boys in the street outside; prayer shawls used to wipe the pavements, or taken home by the women to be used as dishcloths; men taken to concentration camps; people beaten up, and a woman murdered by children. The catalogue of humiliation and terror is long and would be longer still if everything had been recorded.

An elderly Jewish picture framer and his wife worked and lived opposite our house. His neat shop looked as if a band of frenzied hoodlums had gone berserk with pickaxes and stamped the contents into the pavement – exactly what had happened. The inside and outside were a mess and there was no window or door to separate them. The framer himself had disappeared. On the door of Bayreutherstrasse 12, the rampaging Brownshirts had seen our SCHULMAN nameplate. But the porter of the house had been a member of the SPD and hated the regime, and so when they knocked at his door he shook his head and insisted that we were not Jews. He showed them a nameplate three doors away belonging, as it happened, to a von Schulman. A *von* is unlikely to be a Jew and so we were spared. The porter was the third 'good German' I knew as a child.

If my father had not disobeyed the decree to paint his name in white letters across the nameplate, the Brownshirts would not have needed to consult the porter before ransacking our flat and destroying it – before tossing the sewing machines out over the balcony, before crushing the lamps and bookcases, before mutilating the books, before terrifying and ill-treating my mother and my little brother. There is no telling what these state-licensed vandals might not have done. What they could not have done is drag away my father. He was no longer there.

My mother was first alerted to what was going on when she heard the breaking of glass and shouting in the street. From the window, she watched the mob of SA and ordinary un-uniformed Germans including children, mainly boys, breaking the windows of the frame-maker's shop opposite, splintering everything with their axes and terrorising the elderly and frail couple. My mother was alone with my brother. My father had taken a train to England that very evening. She resented this, even though it was extremely lucky for all of us that he got away when he did. If he had not, he might never have got out at all and then neither would we.

My father had a far worse time that night than my mother, and the narrowest of escapes. This is what he told us when we saw him five months later in London. When the train reached the Dutch frontier, the German SS herded all Jews off the train and put them singly into various rooms in the station building. A group of young SS men ordered my father to strip naked, and began to taunt him. He pretended not to be frightened and talked to them as he would to equals and reasonable human beings. He told them how the Germans had not always treated the Jews so, and cited details such as when Ludendoriff, dropping leaflets over Poland during the last war, addressed them as '*Zu meinen lieben Juden*' (to my dear Jews). He must have put some doubt into the minds of these men in their uniforms of terror; he may have found a group less than completely brainwashed. After a few hours they told him to get dressed, and he was put on the next train to Holland with his papers and luggage. I am not sure if they gave him back his watch. It sounds an extraordinary tale, but he did get through, he did arrive in London, and the Dutch at the border were amazed to find him on the train – he was the only Jew who had made it.

A week after the *Kristallnacht*, there was a ring on our doorbell. The kind of ring my parents and their comrades had always dreaded. My mother opened the door but the uniformed men had not come for her; they knew nothing of her political activities, and as for transporting Polish Jews over the border into Poland, they had finished with that. But they had been collecting Jew after Jew – men who were German or stateless – for days, since 9 November, and now it was my father's turn. My mother told them he had gone to England. Of course, they did not believe her but luckily she could show them a postcard from London that had come that very morning. It was from my father. letting her know he had arrived. The men left to collect other Jews for Sachsenhausen, the concentration camp near Berlin.

My old school and the synagogue in Fasanenstrasse had been vandalised and then set on fire during the pogrom. The mob that attacked it – the standard mob of SA men and civilians – beat up the nightwatchman and threw him into the sidecar of a police motorcycle. They beat up a passer-by who had dared to express his indignation. Then they tossed the organ over the balcony, tore the Torah into pieces – some of the brown-shirted vandals actually put bits into their pockets for good luck! – ripped the rabbinical prayer shawls into shreds, ripped and defaced the prayer books and then, to round it off, the arsonists of the Third Reich poured petrol over the benches. Police had diverted traffic from the area and a fire engine was standing by. When the reader of the synagogue ran into the burning building to drag out sacred and precious items, and cried to the chief of the fire brigade to turn on the hoses, he was told, 'I am only here to stop the fire spreading into neighbouring buildings.'

The synagogue was to smoulder for days, and a similar fate was suffered by all the synagogues of Berlin and the rest of the country. I did not go to look at the synagogues and my old school in ruins and smoking. I did not go there again until 1966, when it was heartbreakingly unrecognisable. But by then I was unrecognisable too. I tried to tell the man selling memorabilia from a stall just inside the new building that I had been a pupil at the school. I wanted to tell someone. 'Yes, yes,' he mumbled tetchily, 'there was a school here,' and tried to sell me postcards posted from Auschwitz during the war, as if I were an American tourist.

The excuse for the pogrom had been the assassination of a German diplomat in Paris by a young Polish Jew called Grynspan. Goebbels' propaganda line was that the German people, fed up to the teeth with the evil deeds of the Jews in their midst, had reacted spontaneously to the murder of a German by a Jew and were determined to avenge his death all over the country, in every street, in every village. Christabel von Bielenberg describes the pogrom ambiguously as 'Hitler's interpretation of the spontaneous reaction of the German people'. But there is enough evidence that this pogrom had been in preparation for months, that Grynspan's deed could not have come at a better time for Hitler, though to say it was God-sent would be blasphemy. The night of 9 November, fifteen years earlier, was when Hitler's Munich putsch had failed, and he probably chose this date deliberately and in advance. Or was he aiming for 11 November, the anniversary of Germany's defeat in 1918?

An additional piece of evidence for the meticulous planning of the pogrom is usually overlooked, though it is so obvious. This was the edict issued in the summer of 1938 – and ignored by my father – that made all Jewish premises so conspicuous to passers-by. Those white letters painted on every Jewish window and nameplate made a pogrom easy to carry out. As easy as when the blood of the lamb was smeared across the lintel of each Jewish home in Egypt to help the angel of the Lord smite the first-born of Egyptian homes only. The mark of blood had warned: 'Keep out, Pass over.' The mark of white paint now said: 'Smash your way in.' How wise of my father to have recognised it for what it was.

Rabbi Hugo Gryn, who had been a child in Auschwitz, drew my attention to a sinister thread running through the episodes: the involvement and corruption of children. The Nazis had made sure that children took an active part in the pogroms. They were certainly the worst offenders on Wyk-auf-Föhr; and my mother described how schoolboys joined in the ill-treatment of the picture framer in Bayreutherstrasse. I have seen photographs of the *Kristall-nacht* where schoolchildren are jeering in the front row; not just a few individuals but several classes. In archives there are many instances of children aiding the SS, and sometimes taking an initiative which makes their participation in Wyk-auf-Föhr look angelic. In several places they did their best to desecrate and destroy the synagogue and its sacred regalia. In one place, they murdered a Jewish woman.

When my mother talked about the *Kristallnacht*, it was 'the pogrom in the street where we lived'. Her tone was casual and I dare say if one is a Jew brought up in Russian Poland a pogrom is nothing out of the ordinary. I myself did not think of the *Kristallnacht* as a pogrom. A pogrom is something that happened in little places in Poland, in a backward country, in another age. I do not know if the superior German Jews ever recognised the *Kristallnacht* for what it was. Could they, and can they, face the fact that they had come so low as to experience the same humiliations as the despised *Ostjuden*? In my school in the Nürnbergerstrasse no one referred to it as a pogrom. *Kristallnacht* is a musical-sounding euphemism. *Kristall* has nothing to do with the sound of breaking glass, or glass splinters. *Kristall* is the word for crystal, and the sounds of crystal are harmonious and imply gracious living. If you want to emphasise the sight and sound of the broken windows of the pogrom, call it *Splitternacht* or *Scherbennacht* (night of splinters or broken pieces). *Kristallnacht*, or 'The night of the crystal', sounds more like a tale of mystery by Wilkie Collins.

I still carry round with me a symbol of what happened that night. It is a very personal symbol: it is the scar on my neck. The suppurating wound from Wyk-auf-Föhr, became integrated into the general picture of destruction and chaos. When the pus exhausted itself, the scar formed into something puckered up like a poor piece of sewing. Little blackheads appeared in the folds and it was unsightly, though it bothered my father more than me. When I was twenty, he paid for Sir Archibald MacIndoe, the pioneer of plastic surgery for Battle of Britain airmen, to tidy up the scar. Sir Archibald took out most of the lymph glands on that side – they had all been infected – and cleaned up the scar itself as far as possible. Like the event for which it is a metaphor, it has resisted complete removal – tubercular tissue often forms a keloid or thickened scar – and it is still visible, especially when I am tired, not well or under stress. I have never tried to hide it with cosmetics. It is not that bad and is now merging nicely with my wrinkles. How lucky I am to have escaped with only this and not a tattoo on my wrist.

# FIFTEEN

# Broken Families and Burnt Books

The first days back at school after the pogrom were very subdued.
The building of the Holdheim Schule was intact. It was not part of
a synagogue and there was nothing obvious on the building to
show its religious and racial denomination, or perhaps the vandals
in their frenzy simply missed it. Its front entrance did not open out
into the street and any regulation white lettering would have been
in a passage hidden from passers-by. But nearly all the male
teachers were missing, including Studienrat Ofner. The remaining
teachers gave us yet more strict instructions on how to behave on
the way to and from school: 'Be as invisible as you can.' This
invisibility was now as advisable for me who had never had German
nationality as it was for the most Prussian of us, including Daisy
and her parents. We could no longer kid ourselves that we belonged
to this country we were born in. We weren't even on the margins
now but well beyond. Our only hope of escaping persecution was
to keep out of sight. It was being virtually out of sight that had
saved the school.

There were no more school sports for us out on the Maccabi
fields where little boys and girls in brown were now running or
marching and singing to the glory of Fatherland and Führer. There
were a few new pupils from schools that had been destroyed and a
few new teachers who had not been taken to Sachsenhausen. The
new music teacher played the 'Turkish March' with great brio but
had a tough time keeping order. I was one of the worst offenders
and not allowed to forget it. Even years later, when were both
adults and living in England, Daisy used to remind me how I had
thrown an apple core at him and said 'Catch!' A misdeed she still
thought hilarious.

After some weeks Studienrat Ofner returned with his head
completely shaven. He introduced a new teacher, Herr Breisacher,
whom he had met in Sachsenhausen. Herr Breisacher had not only

a shaven head but a freshly withered right arm – 'Due to frostbite in the camp,' he told us. Those shaven heads were a great shock and the sight of that arm certainly affected us, but I am not at all sure how. There must have been some pity and sympathy. But we mainly felt discomfort and even resentment. Did we resent Herr Breisacher because he was the substitute for a popular teacher, because he was tetchy and too strict, or was it because we saw in his presence and his withered arm the awful reality of our own and our parents' circumstances and things to come?

Before I left the school in March 1939 to go to England, I passed round my autograph album as was the custom. Herr Breisacher wrote that if one has to choose between two alternative courses, the right one is never the easier, but the more difficult. It is one of two entries I remember; the other is Tante Freundlich's reminder of the blood of my ancestors in my veins.

Herr Breisacher and his family did not survive. They could not find a government anywhere to grant them asylum. Fräulein Warschauer, who had been succeeded by the tetchy Herr Breisacher, had managed to get a visa to London, but she returned just before war was declared. Her old mother either could not or would not join her in London, and she chose to stay with her. Nothing more was heard of either. Studienrat Ofner, a widower, came to England and stayed. He got a job teaching maths in a small boarding school and married the matron. Frau Meyer, Daisy's mother and his cousin, was very snooty about that. The matron was the wrong religion, and definitely the wrong class.

Apart from Daisy, I have never come across anyone else from Holdheim Schule. When I was about eighteen, I thought I recognised a young man serving in a bookshop but I was too timorous to go up to him and ask: 'Do you come from Berlin and did you go to Holdheim Schule?' I was reluctant to make a mistake and look foolish; but what really kept me back was a reluctance to make this contact at all. I felt a vague fear that he had come here on his own on a *Kindertransport*, which I did not want to confront, and a vague disappointment that a clever boy had ended up not writing books, but selling them.

Just after the New Year, and nine months before the war, Daisy

Meyer left Berlin and travelled to England with her older brother. Her parents followed a couple of months later. My father had had some success, too. A Jewish firm he had been working for in Berlin was well established in London, and sent him an affidavit. On the strength of this the British consulate gave him a temporary visa to go to London, though it did not give him a work permit and until he got this permit he was not allowed to send for us. My mother used to read out bits in his letters that described how the loneliness and anxiety of his waiting was made more miserable by the English winter and the English heating system. 'I am sitting with my right side on the equator, and my left side in the North Pole.' I found out later exactly what he meant. He had been sitting in front of a gas fire in a room that was otherwise unheated and where the doors and windows did not fit their frames, and draughts had free rein. My mother also read out how he was grieving that my gland had burst and was still suppurating. 'I wept,' he wrote. With her distaste for any show of emotion my mother scorned his *'sentimentaler Quatsch'*.

But she must have been desperately anxious when week after week my father sat in front of his gas fire waiting for the British government to grant him that permit. Without it we were stuck. But the British officials were in no hurry. After all, we – all four of us – might become a burden on the British taxpayer, and British taxpayers, with their latent or active anti-Semitism and their xenophobia exacerbated by unemployment, were hardly likely to rush the Home Office into issuing permits to refugees. But neither British xenophobia, the anti-Semitism of the Cabinet and the Foreign Office or the inertia of the Home Office were in my mind then. I was just apprehensive about losing my father and being left behind. It was only in 1993 that I learnt the extent of the actions taken by the British government and the Foreign Office to hinder Jewish immigration.

Through my nearest and dearest friend Barbara Sands I had met the historian Martin Gilbert. We were all having dinner when this topic came up; I don't know how because it was a jolly occasion. Martin Gilbert recounted how Malcolm MacDonald, son of Ramsay, and Dominion and Colonial Secretary at the time, had refused to save some thousands of Polish Jewish children. On 18 September 1939, Chaim Weizmann asked MacDonald to allow 20,000 Jewish children from Poland into Palestine. MacDonald refused because the chief concern was to win the war, and: 'However brutal it might sound, to remove 20,000 children from Poland at this moment would *pro tanto* simplify the German economic problem.'

Martin Gilbert sent me his article on 'British Policy Towards Refugees', which included the details of this episode. The material is mainly drawn from Cabinet, Foreign Office and Colonial Office papers and demolishes the complacent myth that Britain has always welcomed refugees. It also makes nonsense of the excuse that no one really knew what was happening, and refutes the accusation that the Jews could have got out had they wanted to. The British government and the Foreign Office knew only too well of the atrocities committed during the *Kristallnacht*. Consuls in various towns had sent reports of the vandalism, sadism, arrests, murders and suicides. As early as 1934, the British Consul General in Munich and Dresden had sent shocking reports of conditions at Dachau and Buchenwald concentration camps to Lord Halifax. But however dreadful the accounts, none evoked compassion or a rush to help. Quite the reverse. A few days after the *Kristallnacht*, Roger Makins, who after the war became British Ambassador in Moscow, wrote: 'The pitiful conditions to which German Jews will be reduced will not make them desirable immigrants.' Immigration was indeed curtailed: to Britain, the Empire, and Palestine. In the House of Commons some MPs insisted that though 65,000 Jews had reached this country, many more should be allowed in. The Home Secretary, Sir Samuel Hoare, explained that he would not allow 'alien immigration on a big scale' because it could lead to 'a definite anti-Jewish movement'. He would 'keep a check upon individual cases of immigrants'.

The curtailment, and in July 1939 the suspension, of immigration to Palestine had nothing to do with anti-Semitism among the British people. As Malcolm MacDonald told the Cabinet, it was 'out of the question' to 'antagonise the Muslims within the Empire or the Arab kingdoms of the Near East'. Throughout 1939 and even into the war, the British government put strong pressure on other governments and shipping agencies not to allow Jewish refugees to board ships bound for Palestine. Ships that did arrive were turned back. Immigrants who had landed in Palestine were hounded out. All these actions were applauded by the King, son of George V whose death we had mourned in our Jewish school in Berlin. In February 1939, George VI conveyed to Lord Halifax how glad he was 'that steps were being taken to prevent these people from leaving their country of origin'. These people were 'Jewish refugees . . . surreptitiously getting into Palestine'.

In March 1939, Lord Halifax went so far as to instruct Sir Neville Henderson to ask the German authorities to prevent Jews without visas from boarding German ships. 'They attempt to land in any territory that seems to present the slightest possibility of receiving them. This was a cause of great embarrassment to His Majesty's Government and . . . The American Government.' On 1 September, even as the Germans were bombing Warsaw, a British ship fired on the *Tiger Hill*, a ship carrying immigrants, killing two.

Throughout the first winter of the war, the British government pursued its campaign to prevent Jews from reaching safety with ever more zeal. Royal Navy ships intercepted immigrant boats, and the British government persuaded Greece and Romania to outlaw this traffic. Other countries promised to do the same. And as for entry into Britain itself, all visas granted to German Jews were rescinded when the war started.

Having learnt of MacDonald's refusal to save 20,000 Polish children, I was not surprised that he was one of the chief instigators of the drive to keep persecuted Jews out of Palestine. The Palestine White Paper of April 1939, which severely limited Jewish immigration for years to come, was mostly his work but he felt safe to admit to the Cabinet that there were aspects of the policy that met 'Arab pressure' rather than 'strict merit'. It was after all a cabinet headed by a Prime Minister who in a letter to one of his sisters in July 1939 wrote: 'No doubt Jews aren't a lovable people; I don't care about them myself: but that is not sufficient to explain the Pogrom.'

While they were closing the doors to Palestine, MacDonald and

Halifax blamed the victim. The Jews, they claimed, had always refused to co-operate with the Arabs; therefore, if Arabs were hostile to further Jewish immigration, it was the Jews' own fault. But there were some voices that spoke out against the pitiless immigration policy. One of them was Josiah Wedgwood, who during a debate in May in the House of Commons scorned the fervour with which the White Paper was being applied as 'conduct worthy of Hitler'. He warned Malcolm MacDonald that if he succeeded in stopping this immigration, 'the report of it will stink in the nostrils of posterity.' This was before MacDonald refused to save 20,000 Jewish children. Malcolm MacDonald flourished, and after the war the Labour Government sent him to Southeast Asia as Commissioner General.

I never met any of the political or diplomatic actors in this drama, except for Patrick Reilly, a diplomat very much on the side of MacDonald in his drive to keep Jews out of Palestine. When Bill was a junior Minister in 1964 and we stayed in Paris in the splendid residence of the British Ambassador, the Reillys were the newly arrived incumbents. Lady Reilly was thoroughly unpleasant. I thought it was only because she resented any Labour politician but now I wonder if there was not something else she could not abide because she would have known of my origins. Her husband showed no hostility, but to judge from some of his minutes written in 1938 and 1939 his wife's demeanour may have displayed not only her prejudice, but his also. He was much too professional to show it. I can't decide whether it wasn't a good thing I didn't know then about his part in preventing Jews from escaping Nazi prosecution.

In April 1939, Patrick Reilly minuted that the Jews who were trying to emigrate from Czechoslovakia to Palestine had no reason to leave and that some were 'definitely criminals or spies'. On 7 May, he indignantly rejected a suggestion to land refugees from a ship bound for Palestine on Cyprus: 'Why should the British Empire take these refugees? We have nothing to show that they are in any way suitable settlers.' On 9 June, he was incensed by 'the Romanian Govt's complete failure to stop the scandalous traffic of illegal immigrants into Palestine.' On 24 July, he assessed Jewish refugees from Czechoslovakia as having 'panicked unnecessarily . . . many of them quite unsuitable as emigrants and would be a very difficult problem if brought here'. But this is nothing compared to his reaction on 18 August to accounts of horrendous persecution of Jews in Slovakia. His worry was that Jews were fleeing and that some had reached Palestine, and he advised using governments funds 'to get the Slovaks to reduce pressure on Jews to leave'. To be fair, most of his colleagues shared his attitude – it was in perfect harmony with Foreign Office policy. I have singled him out only because I have met him.

Nowadays we only remember how Bevin callously turned away boats of Jewish refugees trying to reach Palestine after the war, and most of us deceive ourselves that before the war Britain had received Jewish refugees with open arms. But given the reality of British policy in 1938, 1939 and 1940, it is not surprising that not one of Tante Freundlich's pupils joined her in Palestine and that only two of us reached England.

While back in 1939 in Berlin we were waiting to hear the good news from my father, my mother went to the Polish consulate to renew her passport and have André's name added. She needed it for immigration purposes anyway, but she thought the three of us might have to go to Poland. Earlier that year Poland had decided to refuse passports to anyone who had not lived in Poland for five years, but the consulate in Berlin was more humane and made out a new passport straightaway. One of the Secretaries called her in to his office to hand it to her in person and to warn her in Polish: 'Mrs Szulman, I strongly advise you not to go to Poland.' Of course, he knew why she might want to go, but he urged her against it: 'Go wherever you like, but don't go to Poland. War will soon break out and you will have the Nazis in Poland.'

One morning the post brought not the longed for news from London, but an expulsion order from the Third Reich. My mother had to leave the country, in one month or three, I can't remember. And still there was no visa, still my father waited in his Maida Vale bedsitter for the work permit from the Home Office. Despair and hopelessness were unnatural in my mother, but I did detect some panic. Even now I get wild with anger when people in Britain wonder why the Jews had not made the effort to get out of Germany. Jewish families were getting desperate to emigrate. They had tried just about every consulate but the acceptance rate was minute. Britain was not the only country whose doors were closing. Some people had their visas revoked if any disability was discovered. Luckily the British authorities never found out that Daisy's brother was mentally handicapped. A German family with two children whom my parents knew slightly had applied early on to emigrate to the United States. They couldn't believe their luck when in 1938 they received a visa. But the consulate discovered that their four-year-old son had Down's Syndrome and was therefore deemed unfit to be admitted into the US. They offered the parents the option: 'You may enter the United States with your daughter so long as you leave your son behind.' It was a choice of one certain death against four almost certain deaths. They chose to stay.

My parents, too, had tried to get into the United States but they did not stand a chance. That land of the free was no more willing to take ordinary Jewish refugees than Britain or indeed other countries. It was no secret that to get into the US one had to be an Einstein, a Thomas Mann (a distinguished political refugee and not a Jew), a film star, or to have started applying many years ago, or to have impressive affidavits from well-off relatives. And it was better to be German than Polish-born. Since 1917 the United States had had an immigration quota that favoured 'old' immigrants or Protestants from northern and western Europe, at the expense of the 'new immigrants', the Catholics and Jews from eastern and southern Europe. No matter what was happening in Germany, this quota remained rigid. They changed it in 1965.

Our friend Max Waldberg from Lublin got a visa to Argentina and early in 1939 my mother and I went along to see him off. The platform was packed with men, women and children and humming with the sound of sobbing. The sobbing grew wilder as the men pulled themselves away and got into the train. Then, sad-faced, they leant out of the windows. To mop up tears and to wave, they took out large white handkerchiefs, one of the last items ever to be washed at home. All the men were Jews, each one was on his way to South America, on his own. The condition of their visa had been to leave everyone behind, and left behind they were, on the station platform. Britain had been ready to take only children; Argentina, only men. No one knew if they would ever see again their husband, father, son, daughter, wife, girlfriend or boyfriend. Most of them never did. And as the train began to move, and heads and white handkerchiefs got tinier and tinier, the pain was intolerable, like the moment when the coffin is lowered into the earth. I too wept, and I weep now. Add that to the farewell on Warsaw station in 1934, to say nothing of Hélène's last journey, and it is small wonder I have problems with seeing my daughters off at stations.

Of my mother's comrades, the only Jews left were Jaques Mendelsohn and the Danielsohns. The Danielsohns were marked out not only as Jews but as Communists and with a political prison record. The chance of any country giving them refuge was nil, nor could they buy their way out as a few very wealthy Jews had managed. The Danielsohns were quite poor but gave my parents a few items of modest value: a gold ring, two fountain pens, a watch. They had sent their daughter Leah to Palestine and they wanted these things to go to her. My parents pledged that if they succeeded in getting out of Germany they would see that these things reached Leah. But they never managed to trace her; I only wish I could be sure their search had been exhaustive. Her parents had since vanished – a euphemism for a terrible fate – and it might have been too painful for my parents to meet Leah again.

Hermann Mendelsohn, whom I never knew, had died before 1933. But his younger brother Jaques, who had followed him into the Communist Party, did manage to escape in 1938 and later became a British Member of Parliament. My mother had only met him twice in Berlin, once when he was a schoolboy and she visited Hermann as he lay dying in his mother's flat, and the second time in 1938 at a cell meeting. Everyone used an alias but she broke the rule and asked: 'Isn't your name Mendelsohn?' He looked exactly like Hermann.

I do not know if this encounter was before or after November 1938. I know that in the perilous period after the *Kristallnacht* while she waited for the postman to bring the good news that the Home Office had issued my father's permit, my mother continued with her clandestine activities. Quite as likely as the postman's knock at the door was a more ominous one preceded by the thumping of jackboots. But that did not deter my mother. She went on typing Party material at home until she had to start packing, and she went to cell meetings till she left to catch the train to London. The cells were sadly depleted. 'We realised there was not much point any more and war would come soon anyway.'

By now, some non-Jewish comrades had disappeared or gone to the USSR, such as Hugo the Soviet spy, and Ernst Neumann, whom my mother did not know well but admired, and whom the Russians later shot as a German spy. Helga – she who had got me into such trouble over the stains on her friend's dress – lost her father. Sometime in 1938 he was taken to hospital after a thorough beating up by official thugs in brown or black uniforms. His wife came to see my mother and sobbed: the doctors were experimenting on him and he was dying. It seemed that the hospital authorities had been told he was a Communist and they could do what they liked with him. His death was that of an experimental animal. *Die Grosse Käte*, who with her baking had made my birthdays such joy, lost her daughter. Like Helga's mother, she came to see my mother and wept. *Die kleine Käte* was lost to the Nazis and had gone off on one of those Hitler Youth weekends whose function was to increase the German Aryan race.

My mother, too, lost something precious. The loss was not of a person but deeply painful and never made good. It was the loss of her books, all that proscribed literature still braving it out on her shelves. It was too risky to keep them, too risky to pass them on to friends, and far too risky to take them out of the country – should we ever get that far. But how do you destroy hundreds of banned books? Do you burn them as did the Nazi vandals in 1933? Even though they scorned the books and you love them? In any case, all we had were *Kachelofen*, tiled ovens that are decorative, efficient for heating the flat, good for softening apples, but useless for anything on a grand heroic scale. So my mother went to see my father's *Landsmann*, Max Waldberg, shortly before he left for South America. She knew no one else who had a suitable fireplace and whom the Nazis did not suspect of subversion. When she asked him if he would let her burn her books in his fireplace, Waldberg, who was apolitical but had moral courage said: 'How can I deny you the only chance you have to save yourselves?'

On the tape recorded shortly before she died, my mother tells of the deed in a quiet, sad voice. 'Oh, my books, all the books I had, all the books I valued, all the books I loved, I took them all one day in a car to Waldberg's. And I burnt them over two days. One half one day, one half the other day. In two open fireplaces. Ah, it hurt me so much.' A pause, and her voice is quieter still and her accent stronger: 'It was Lenin, it was Trotsky, it was a *Kapital* of Karl Marx in German, and Engels and biographies of all these people. And works of the Russians you call the Decembrists.' Another pause: 'Oh, yes, it was tragic. I cried over each book.' I can hear the sobs now.

She told this story to Bill a few weeks before she died. She does not often move me to tears of sympathy and sadness for her. But in the telling of this, there is no defiance, no resentment, only a deep sorrow.

The air of apprehension and insecurity was everywhere. At school a few gaps appeared, left by the few fortunate teachers and children who had managed to leave for a variety of destinations. My mother had been expelled but still she had nowhere to go, and still the Home Office in London was dragging its feet. It looked as if we were going to be stuck. But finally the Home Office issued the permit and, as it turned out, with a good six months to spare before Chamberlain finally declared war. On 23 February 1939, my father got the precious document that saved our lives. I had not thought of it like this before – 'the document that saved our lives'. I must be mellowing. Usually when I think of or look at this bit of paper, browned rather than yellowed, with torn edges, the splitting centre crease held together with dark brown sticky paper, I feel anger, sadness and bitterness and think: it took them long enough, those indifferent, unhurried, spoilt British, so relaxed while we despaired in a Berlin which was getting more frightening by the hour. I see their patronising and callous words which tell my father to be out of the country by 28 February the following year, adding graciously that 'the Secretary of State does not desire to raise objection to Mr Szulman's employment' up to that time.

It was lucky for us that the war began before that last day in February. They – the Secretary of State's minions – would have shipped us back to Germany, probably on my birthday. Of course, we had to be grateful. That permit to work for a year and five days was not to be had just for the asking, or for pleading persecution where we came from. But I feel bitter rather than grateful. I look at a school photograph and all twenty-five of us were ten years old in 1938. Only four of us were seventeen in 1945.

# SIXTEEN

# Goodbye to Berlin

The precious permit that allowed us to become refugees is dated 23 February but the officials at the Home Office were in no great rush to post it. My father said he received it on 3 March, my birthday, and that my birthday has always been a lucky date for him – a loving thing to say. My mother got the news in the first week of March after my eleventh birthday, one that was not celebrated. We were both standing in the hall by the front door when she opened the envelope. At first we could not believe it and then our relief was transformed into frenzy. The books had already been burnt, but everything else had to be sorted out. For a few days we lived in utter chaos, but when we had packed everything up the flat was bleak. For the few days before we left we lived on bare boards with a few bits of furniture, some borrowed, some we were leaving behind. We had rudimentary curtains, a couple of mattresses, some boxes and a chair, a small rickety table, plates and knives and forks. The lack of soft furnishings gave the flat a hollow sound and that suspension in a vacuum, that betwixt and between feeling, was overwhelming. But we survived on prayers – if atheists can lay claim to prayer – like: 'Let there be no last-minute hitches. Let there be no sinister knocks at the door.'

We were not the only lucky Jews getting out and for all of us the usual decisions about what to take and what to throw out were complicated by decrees. These stipulated what Jews leaving the country could take out. There were financial restrictions, as well as those controlling the quantity and the age of objects. All over Berlin, trees outside houses and a few hastily erected wooden posts began to sprout pieces of paper with handwritten lists of things for sale. On one tree, for example, you would find a pale blue piece of notepaper with neat handwriting offering to sell: one Rosenthal dinner set, eight dining chairs, one set of brocade curtains, four damask tablecloths, two table lamps, one kitchen table, and a set of four saucepans. Everything was dirt cheap and it gave the Aryan

Germans a dignified opportunity to loot from Jews. But Jews bought too. It was a kind of exchange. You sold what you could not take out, or what would not be practical to take wherever you were going – you would not want a mink in Kenya, or a chandelier anywhere – and you bought what you might need and were allowed to take out. My mother bought a baroque coffee set decorated with blue-grey roses. I can't think why. It was ugly and she didn't need it, but she clearly liked it. Most of it is now broken but I still think of the remnants as the cups and saucers that grew on trees.

A man in Nazi uniform sat in our flat for two whole days while under his scrutiny my mother packed things into huge boxes to go into a still larger container called a *lift*. After all, we might have stuffed a treasure of the German nation into our nightshirts, or a bar of gold bullion – let alone a volume of Heine. Then another uniformed functionary came to do random tests. They missed the Heine and the Zille. Maybe my mother stuffed them among her sanitary towels – an old trick.

While we were packing, Helga and her mother came to say goodbye. Her mother looked very down. She had lost her husband, now she was losing her close friend and comrade; but as if that wasn't enough, there was still another reason for her wretchedness. Helga looked far from unhappy, only very detached and superior. When I said something to her about her mother, that ten-year-old girl drew herself up and declared icily: 'My mother? That's not my mother! Just look at the colour of her hair. My real mother was blonde like me; she was a true Aryan!' This true Aryan mother had died when Helga was born and her father and the woman who came to live with him and look after Helga had never married. Helga was now going to live with her dead mother's parents, who had been threatening to denounce the woman who had been a mother to her as a Jew and a Communist. I didn't know she was a Jew – perhaps she wasn't.

The awful fact was that *Die Grosse Käte* was not the only one of our *Genossen* to lose her daughter to the Nazis. My mother's friend, who had brought Helga up from birth, had lost her and was never going to see her again. The grandparents had barred her. They were strong Nazis and Helga too was a Nazi now. I sat among my

clothes and felt miserable and something else that I could not
understand.

On 19 March, we sat on boxes and steadied our plates on a
wobbly table someone had lent us. Our big table had by now
arrived in London, that same round table at which the comrades
had glumly waited for news of Munich. Our last *Silvester* or New
Year's Eve dinner in Berlin had been celebrated at that table,
though celebrated is hardly the word. Like the Munich seance it
had been a sombre occasion, only even more dispirited. Those
effervescent *Silvesters* now seemed so unreal. My father, instead of
sweeping me off in a waltz, was warming his feet in front of a gas
fire in a lonely bedsitter in Maida Vale. It was and seemed a
thousand miles away. And those of us left in Berlin – where would
we be next year? *Silvester* had become a victim of persecution,
emigration, separated families and despair. As for saying goodbye
to school, my memory is a blank. Had such farewells become
commonplace, or were they too fraught with anxiety both for those
leaving and those staying? I only remember the day we left when
four or five of my mother's comrades, the remnant of the old cell,
called for us in the morning and took us to the station. It was
dangerous for members of a cell to be seen together, but the only
precaution taken was for the Danielsohns not to turn up. For Max
Danielsohn, the former political prisoner, to be seen in their
company would immediately identify non-Jews as Communists.

I cannot remember how we got to the Anhalter Bahnhof. What
preoccupied me and astonished me, even at the time, is that I felt
not one grain of regret at leaving. I did not wish to stay, to cling
to the place where I was born, the places I knew, the people I
knew, our flat, the parks I played in, the Wittenberg Platz, the
school I went to. I could not get out of Berlin fast enough and I
was amazed. I was leaving my home town, my school, my friends,
so why was I not sad? Why did I not cry? I knew I was going to
see my father again, but that was not what preoccupied me. I was
not expecting much from England. It was not my promised land,
it was not waiting to overwhelm me with milk and honey. It had
fought the Soviet Union, oppressed indigenous peoples all over the
world, and was full of stately monuments and snooty men like Lord

Halifax and others who wore knickerbockers and played golf. And it had taken its time before grudgingly granting us a visa. But on the way to the station, on the platform, and above all, as the train pulled out, and even as we waved to the comrades whom we would probably never see again, I felt enormous relief. We were going to escape! We really were going to escape! Not since the *Kristallnacht* had I admitted to myself quite how terrified I had been. My deep relief was indeed a measure of that terror. I wish I knew what my mother felt, but she never told me and I never asked her. My brother was only two.

Before the train left, the comrades – *Die grosse Käte*, Helga's mother and Fritz, a tall fair-haired young man who was a special favourite of my mother's – gave me a *Bonbonniere*, a large, glamorous box of chocolates, the kind only grown-ups got. Compared to my mother's first flight from oppression, when she travelled in secret and so lightly in her red dress, this second flight was downright ostentatious and extravagant, but it was without hope and full of bitterness.

My relief at escape was interrupted twice. First, at the German side of the border where a churlish official came into our compartment and brusquely told my mother to take her children and her luggage and 'Get off the train. Quick.' He bustled us into a large, bleak but brightly lit room in the station building. No other passengers had been hauled off the train, and we were the only ones in that room. Officials of the German Reich went through what little luggage we had, and asked questions. My mother kept saying we would miss the train, but they said, 'Never mind your train.' One tall man in a dark civilian suit took my box of chocolates, tore off the satin ribbon, opened it, swept aside the pretty pieces each in its own pleated paper cup, and asked me: 'And where does your mother keep the money?' 'What money?' is what I think I said, but it may have been 'We haven't any money' or 'I don't know'. I hid my outrage at the violence he did to my chocolates but I hope I did not say 'thank you' as he gave me back the box. He had left it in a dreadful mess and the lid barely fitted. No time to put that right: the whistle had sounded, the train was about to go.

My mother, André and I, our bags half-closed, scrambled for the train which had already begun to move. No one helped us but we got on. It was unthinkable to have missed it. Better to have lost a bag, all the chocolates, sprained an ankle, broken an arm, than to have stayed in that nightmare.

We collapsed into an empty compartment. My mother tidied the bags and I tried to put my chocolates back into their original pattern. Their disarray was so symbolic of other Nazi acts. I was still unnerved and still tidying my *Bonbonniere* when the next official came into the compartment, the Dutch border official. He turned the stiff pages of my mother's Polish passport and sighed. 'I am very sorry, Madam. But you cannot cross Holland. You have a Polish passport, and you need a Dutch transit visa.' We would have to get out, return to Berlin, get the visa, and only then could we travel through Holland. Snakes and Ladders of a horrendous sort, all the way back to hell, and I burst into tears. My little brother copied me and started to howl. The Dutchman, may he have gone to heaven, softened and made an exception. Of course, he was aware of the circumstances but then officials aren't often, if ever, swayed by circumstances. We stayed on the train and did not get out until we reached the Hook of Holland. I wanted God or the equivalent to bless and look after all Dutchmen. But God proved to be indifferent once the war began.

My always efficient and highly organised mother was exasperated with her failure to get a Dutch transit visa. She remembered that my father needed one, but with his bundle of stateless papers he had all sorts of different requirements. Given the burdens she had to bear and deal with and all by herself, one lapse is not too surprising. She lived through the *Kristallnacht*, then she had to burn her books, pack up our home, cope with Nazi officials, look after her children, and all the time she was wondering if we would make it. On top of all that, she had to bid farewell to her comrades and she knew that the farewell was for ever.

# SEVENTEEN

# Opium

Had the crossing to England been calm and fair, I might have seen it as a good omen for starting anew. But the night of 21 March was very rough and to me the crossing was a symbol of the fear and violence we were leaving behind. I have never been back to the Hook of Holland or Harwich, and I shall never again make that particular crossing. But my rejection of this stretch of geography has nothing to do with being sick. And how sick I was! Sicker than either my mother or my little brother. The worst thing was being sick without having anything left to vomit. The taste of nothing is very bitter.

My father met us at Harwich, and wore his familiar dark blue homburg and big overcoat. André looked bewildered and called him 'Onkel'. I felt shy. On the train journey from Harwich to Liverpool Street, I was intrigued by my father and mesmerised by the landscape. The flatness, the tongues of water infiltrating that flat land, the thin fog merging the land with the skyline – all was in shades of grey that went on for miles and miles. The bleakness of the land crept into me. I had met flatness before, in Poland, in Germany and in Denmark, but it had been enlivened by summer fields of corn, of stubble, corn flowers and poppies and marguerites, hedges, sometimes trees, sometimes cattle, a pair of sheep. Here the grey had washed out everything green.

After that cheerless terrain came the dilapidated streets near Liverpool Street Station, and some more dejected streets as our black, square and high-roofed London taxi took us towards NW3. Nothing could depress a visitor to this country more than coming in on a dull day in March via Harwich and Liverpool Street.

My father had rented a flat in Chalk Farm and the taxi stopped at the first of the three blocks of flats, Eton Place, Eton Hall and Eton Rise, that creep up Haverstock Hill. My father looked apprehensive as he took us up in the lift to the third floor of Eton Place, along the narrow corridor with the rows of identical featureless doors into the minute flat. Our heavy Berlin furniture was crammed into the rooms and the hall. It was impossible to close a single door except to the bathroom. The bookcase touched the ceiling so that nothing could be put on top of it, the sides of the carpets crept up the walls, the dining table could never be extended by its leaf and the chairs round it could not be pulled out properly. If we wanted to sit down, we had to squeeze ourselves into and onto a chair. I do not know how my parents' bed fitted into the tiny 'master' bedroom. It was many years before I saw Magritte's picture of a huge cupboard in a tiny room.

The sash windows of that doll's flat, with the sixteen or twenty-four separate panes, were very pretty but they let through the most awful draught. We had been used to double windows, common-place in Berlin. In London, until fairly recently, the only proper double windows were those of the Royal Veterinary College in Royal College Street. I have always imagined it was less a barrier to the weather getting in than to the sounds of distressed animals getting out.

The only animals at 91 Eton Place were first a mouse and then a cat. I had never seen a mouse until we came to live in London and that awful day when my father and I tried to catch one in the kitchen. We shut the door, I was armed with a broom, my father with something that must have had an edge – was it a kitchen knife like that of the farmer's wife in the new song I had learnt? – and we chased the little mouse back and forth, from one end of the table to the other. My father managed to cut off half its tail, but that was all. I don't know how I could have been so callous. Did I want to embarrass my mother, who cowered in the living room and who was scared of nothing else but mice? But I was overjoyed when we got a cat to deal with the mice, and it was mine. Whenever my little brother was around, the animal bolted because André would pick it up and swing it back and forth by its tail. My mother called the jet black cat 'Nigger'. Now my mother was the least racist person I know and practised what she preached. When she lived in West Hampstead in the Sixties, she let rooms only to blacks to redress the prejudices all around her. When in 1939 she called our cat 'Nigger', the word for her had no racist connotations at all.

When we still lived in Berlin, the thought of a pet would never have occurred to me – not with my mother's attitude to animals. It wasn't an issue anyway: I was busy, had lots of friends at school and I felt at home. But once we were in Eton Place, all that changed. It was some weeks before I went to the school across the road, and even then the contact with the other girls was interesting but hardly satisfying. The children who lived in the same block but did not go to that school used to make fun of me for my foreignness and my sex. The girls giggled while the boys shouted 'hairy bottom'. I barely understood but I knew it was meant to taunt and degrade. I had been taunted in Berlin, but the racial taunts of German children had felt more alarming than humiliating and were hurled at me as a member of a group. Here I only had a pet for comfort. It stood in for a doll and a teddy bear and sustained me in my isolation and bewilderment. But she was not enough and I looked for something else. When I found it, I had to hide it from my parents because it was Religion.

I knew from my mother that there was no God. I knew Christ was just a man, a good man but nevertheless only a man. I knew that the only things that existed are those I could see. I knew religion to be the opium of the people, who will be rewarded by eternal bliss 'while the rich who on earth grind the faces of the poor will squirm in Hieronymus Bosch-like torment for ever'. (Bosch is my addition.) My parents mocked those who based their lives on what they labelled superstition. Their own lives were based on Marxist fundamentalism. Marxism explained the world to them, provided their *raison d'être*, the basis of their morality, their social life and for my mother, her work – like any sacred religion.

It was a tragedy, no less, that when she arrived in London, my mother applied to join the branch of the KPD in Britain and they told her, 'You have been expelled.' Someone in Berlin had overheard her criticising the purges in 1938, and she had been excommunicated from the Party without her knowledge. There was no point in applying to the Communist Party of Great Britain, not because she had little respect for them – so feeble compared with what she had known in Poland and Germany – but because they too would have refused her membership. They would have been informed of her expulsion and in any case had a strict policy of only accepting British citizens. Anyone else was considered to be too vulnerable. The expulsion was a stunning blow to her. There was no appeal and she never discussed it.

The expulsion deprived her of contacts in Britain who would have made so much difference to her, and also to us children. I ended up in the wrong school, she was cut off from the natural continuity of her political activities, the essence of her life, and at the same time, excluded from something that might have integrated her into some of the social and intellectual life of this new society. Her political allegiance had worked so well for her when she left Poland and came to Germany. It is true that in Germany the Party had a crucial and central role, whereas in Britain the Communist Party, as well as any of its foreign branches, was marginal and barely taken seriously. Nevertheless, it was still part of the culture and for my parents there was no alternative. Quite unthinkable to have joined the Labour Party, the nearest thing to the SPD. It was equally unthinkable to join a synagogue, whether Orthodox, Reform or Liberal, and so that focus of social life and integration that meant so much to other refugees was closed to us.

As for my finding religion in 1939, I have no idea which factor – spiritual, social or psychological – was strongest in triggering off my need, but I was ready for a powerful dose of the opiate. I was too young to be bothered about the afterlife, but my 'here and now' had collapsed. Relief from fear was insufficient substitute for the purpose and joy in life and the feeling of belonging I had left behind in Berlin. Finding comfort in religion is common in cases of bereavement, and though I had lost a culture and not a person, medical anthropologists have recognised that the symptoms and needs of cultural bereavement simulate those of personal bereavement.

I used to think that my own secret religion was a kind of madness, at best a craziness. But, thinking it over, wasn't it nothing more than just a trifle eccentric? I was a child catapulted into a foreign country, my English was limited to 'Hey diddle diddle, the cat and the fiddle', and I was barred from the main religions. For me to slink off to church or synagogue was out of the question.

The religion I discovered was immune to maternal edicts and gave me people who could not be detected and whom I could understand. It was as rational as it was irrational and a balm to the loneliness and uncertainty in my new life. I found it in two books written in German but which I had not read in Berlin. They were volumes two and three of the Greek legends – the first volume was missing. A pity, as it would have told me the story of Oedipus. But the other volumes were rich and potent enough. I started to read them as pure fiction, but they became my holy books and I a polytheist with Pallas Athena as my supreme deity. Zeus was unsatisfactory, capricious, and not all that powerful. Athena was not frivolous like her philandering father. Her interventions were purposeful and effective and her warnings and threats taken very seriously. She was a powerful protector if she was on your side; deadly dangerous if she was not. She was quite possibly a replacement for my mother – a Greek goddess rather than a saint?

I called frequently on Athena, but my room was also crowded with other figures and episodes, though it is difficult to remember what I learnt later and what obsessed me then. But Cassandra stems from Haverstock Hill, as does Helen. Poor Cassandra. There have been moments in my life behind the glass walls of politics when I have thought of Cassandra with empathy. Awful to see something long before anyone else does – like the character of David Owen – and I sometimes wonder if they will find me dead in my bathroom. Helen had little personality but she was the namesake of my cousin, and the scapegoat for the Trojan wars. My room was the background for those battles: all that back and forth just like the First World War but without the muddy, stinking trenches my mother had always described to me. Details of limbs severed, throats cut, blood spurting out all over the place were clinical rather than brutal, and clean. Even the corpse of Hector as it was dragged through the dust by Achilles' chariot gathered no grime. And the soul of each slain man neatly left the body and went either to Hades or to live with the gods. It was clean but noisy and tumultuous. Horses groaned as they fell, soldiers moaned as they were wounded and died, shouted as they fought, wept and wailed as their friends died. Weapons clashed, breasts were beaten, winds howled, flames flared

— all in marvellous contrast to the vacant corridors of Eton Place that were more silent than a mausoleum. The sagas gripped me like the best soap operas. There were rivalries and treacheries, friendships and marriage ties. And I met Achilles and Patroclus, whose names I had first encountered in Heine's irreverent poem about Krapülinski and Washlapski.

What captivated me most was Odysseus' voyage home while Penelope spun and her suitors feasted at her palaces at a never-ending dinner party. Even so, I did not forget my Marxism. Whenever Odysseus and his crew got into difficulties, it was the men who were sacrificed, never the master. Odysseus escaped the Scylla's tentacles, but his men were changed into pigs by Circe. Here I had the proof of Marx's thesis that wars are started by the rulers for the rulers, and that only the damned of the earth suffer. It fitted the whole saga from beginning to end. Marx had infiltrated even my secret and sacred religion.

This lack of compassion for *Proletarier* and the underdog was the only disappointment in my new religion. Otherwise it fulfilled all its roles. It brought me lots of company — noisy and lively if not alive — all of whom I hid from my parents. It gave me images of what I might find after death. My mother was certain there was absolutely nothing. I, for a brief time, knew better. The Jewish and the Christian afterlife had always been too vague, unreal, either horrific or very dull. But the scenes of the Greek afterlife were as vivid as any film at the Odeon in Camden Town, and far from dull.

I did not pray to Athena as the intercessor with Zeus, the way that Catholics pray to the Virgin Mary to intervene with God. For me, Pallas Athena was a power in her own right. My preference for a female deity did not strike me as remarkable at the time. But to attribute power to Athena rather than to Zeus, who was *Herr des Hauses* of the classical pantheon, was my first independent feminist act.

One reason for my ready conversion to this Greek polytheism was that all the characters, their society and their values were more comprehensible to me than the society I had landed in in March 1939. The characters spoke neither Greek nor English, but German.

In addition, neither mortals nor immortals were at all reserved like the stereotypical British, but spilled out their feelings constantly and without apology. They quarrelled like my parents, and their family feuds and conflicts outdid my own. Friends and families torn apart by war were horribly familiar, and any reunion was a happy ending and welcome escapism. And my religion allowed me to be in control and to redress the helplessness I experienced in my new environment. It was tailor-made for my circumstances. I have not the slightest recollection when it faded – which it had to do, unless I was going to be locked up. But I emerged as matter-of-fact and intolerant an atheist as before.

I don't like to dwell on the decade or so following the spring of 1939. Berlin had been my home full of my streets, my parks, my language, my friends. I was cut off from it for ever and had landed on a strange planet, rich with pastures for its aboriginals but for me alarming and unsettling. I began to shut myself down. It took me years to realise quite how half-awake and numb I was in that transitional period. I think myself into that ten-year-old who stood on the Wittenberg Platz and for whom nothing seemed insurmountable and daunting, and I then think myself into the eleven-year-old in London NW3. What a contrast. I had become like an insect which, sensing danger, folds inwards and feigns death. I dared not relax, I dared not be spontaneous, and my very body became rigid in order to protect myself. But I also saw myself as a two-way mirror because, although alarmed and withdrawn, I was also excited by the newness all around me and hungry to observe and learn. More than anything else, it was the deliverance from terror that obscured the anguish of being torn from my homeland, the panic of being dumb in a new environment. No more huddling over the wireless to listen to forbidden radio stations, no more dreading the sound of jackboots, neighbours, erstwhile comrades, or jeering 'Aryan' boys on the way home from school.

My religion helped to cushion some of the loneliness – not a term I knew then, only a feeling I recognise now, and remember. I had been lonely in the playground among the children who gave the Nazi salute. But it had been brief and nothing compared with my utter loneliness in a class of fifty English girls.

Unlike the assembly in the playground at the end of term, there now seemed no end in sight. Nor was there the comfort of a ghetto, a community, a synagogue or even, as it turned out, the Communist Party. The despair of my parents must have filtered through, though they never discussed it with me; which can only mean that they never comforted me. The word 'alien' is linked to the German word *elend* or wretched. This wretchedness or cultural bereavement suffered by loss of the familiar and ejection into the new is partly due to culture shock.

Culture shock has little to do with culture spelt with a capital 'C' or 'K' and featured in the review pages of the quality papers, but embraces everything from religion and language to tram cars, to the way you hold your knife and fork and whether you chew gum or betel nut, wear a suit or a penis sheath. The new verbal language was of course the main reason for our culture shock, but minutiae were also disconcerting, if interesting: the size of our flat, its draughty doors and windows, its light switches that you did not turn but flicked up and down, the light bulbs that did not screw in but clicked in, the traffic that drove on the 'wrong' side of the road and included hybrids of bus and tram called trolley buses. Even the trams were not like the squat cars that trundled in twos or threes across Berlin, but top-heavy double-deckers that wobbled alarmingly.

A delicious part of the shock was gorging myself on juicy Jaffas from the corner shop – when had I last eaten an orange? – and the whiteness of the bread and the butter. As white as the butter I had seen in Berlin in the kitchen of Jewish friends when they opened their food parcels from Holland. Less delicious were the sausages that tasted of pepper and straw.

I was delighted by cardboard notices in shop windows bearing the letters 'CP'. Wasn't England a wonderful country where one could tell everyone where the cells of the Communist Party met! I didn't realise until years later that 'CP' stood for the removal firm of Carter Paterson.

What worried me were pubs because of all those children hanging around outside, and letter boxes because my mother warned me that they were as likely to harbour bombs as letters, put there by Irish fighters against English oppression. What really depressed me were the dead Sundays. Trolley buses slumbered in Camden Town, shops were closed, and so were restaurants, theatres and cinemas. Streets were deserted. No sport was played. Everyone was meant to go to church and read the bible. This deadness chilled me even into my later, happy years – until British Sundays came to life thanks to the influx of yet more foreigners.

But it wasn't all gloom. What cheered me up no end before and after a gloomy Sunday were trips to the numerous cinemas. I had started to go to films long before I understood enough English to make head or tail of what was happening on the screen, but the whole experience was exotic and pleasurable. Every cinema showed not one but two films per programme, the programmes were continuous and one could walk in at any time. If I missed the beginning of one film, I stayed in my seat till it started all over again. If the film was graded unsuitable for children, I soon learnt how easy it was to attach myself to an adult. In the Gaumont in Camden Town, an elaborate contraption called a cinema organ rose out of the floor between films, and in the semi-darkness a man in black tie, with his back to the audience, played popular tunes whose texts unrolled on the screen. The whole audience sang while I munched milk chocolate biscuits. I had bought them from the nearby Woolworths, where sloping counters were stacked with more varieties of chocolate biscuits than I knew existed.

Round the corner from the cinema was, and still is, the fruit and vegetable market. But buying there was not easy. The first time my mother bought a pound of fruit from a barrow, we were puzzled when the man kept asking for 'tuppence hipenny'. It took us ages to grasp that 'tuppence hipenny' meant two and a half pennies.

We were also puzzled by ungainly tricycles that carried a box over their front wheel, with the words 'Stop me and buy one!' painted on the side. What could it mean? We watched other people stop him and we too bought one of those orangy things on sticks meant to be ices. It was hard, and the only taste was a disagreeable after-taste. I never bought another, but in a tiny shop on the bridge of Chalk Farm station I discovered bars of chocolate frothed up into bubbles, and I used to gobble up these bars of Aero at a penny a

time. They were even more irresistible than Woolworth's chocolate biscuits. My mother did not know I was indulging in
forbidden fruit.

English people bought real fruit but mainly to keep in bowls as
part of the furniture, like a still life. We never understood how, in
spite of all those biscuits and chocolate they consumed, English
people were noticeably thinner, if taller and more elegant, than
Germans. No doubt they all ate very little at main meals because
to us the food served in restaurants seemed like starvation rations.
At our first meal out, we waited in vain for more to be served. In
Berlin no one would have dared serve up such tiny portions or such
tasteless dishes where pepper was the substitute for flavour.

My parents and I indulged in the abundance of fresh foods,
especially oranges and bananas, the spoils of Empire, but were
amazed not only by the chocolate and sweet culture, but by the tin
culture we were in. In Berlin, no one with any self-respect would
prepare meals out of tins. Here even the shelves of smart shops
were filled with tins of all sorts of things, from baked beans – new
to me – to luxury fruit and fish. They even tinned round-the-year
vegetables like carrots, but we never ate those until forced to do so
by wartime shortages.

We also discovered that hands were hardly ever shaken – even
now there is confusion about this custom – and when someone
sneezed it was best ignored – a sneeze was almost as embarrassing
as a fart. We learned less tangible differences, like saying 'I don't
think so' when you mean 'No'. Like saying 'presently' when you
mean 'wait'. Like that very unpleasant English habit of putting one
in one's place by ignoring what one has said, which is far more
crushing than any caustic comment. Like being more withdrawn; I
am still conscious of being louder, of talking with my hands, of
asking questions English people never ask, and referring to things
English people ignore. Friendly people call it being spirited. Others
call it showing off, and not knowing how to behave.

One of these 'others' accused me of this, twenty-seven years later
when I was on the fringes of the English Establishment. A Foreign
Office wife used an anonymous phone call to tell me, 'You are not
like us and you don't know how to behave.' She said she had met

me at various Foreign Office functions, but what exactly had upset her was not clear. However, she ended by telling me that I was 'too cosmopolitan'. At the time, 'cosmopolitan' was well known as the Soviet euphemism for a Jew.

Although I had never been 'like us', no one had ever told me so explicitly. Not even when I was eleven and when the differences between my family and the English were most acute. In Berlin, I was barely aware of any cultural differences between my parents and others. German was my mother tongue even if it was not my mother's mother tongue, and I was brought up in the culture of the land even though I was taught to resist its religion and politics. I felt at home despite my marginality. Yes, I was a marginal, but never so acutely and in such discomfort as when I came to England. In Berlin I had almost gloried in being an outsider, except when it involved persecution and that was ameliorated by being part of a group. Then I came to London and I became the petunia in the onion bed and cried inwardly for many years.

My feelings of alienation were exacerbated by changes to the spelling and pronunciation of my name. For eleven years I had been Silvia Schulman; now I was Sylvia Szulman, which involved different sounds. The German 's' is pronounced 'z', so instead of Zilvia, my name suddenly started with the hiss of the harder 's' as well as being transformed to Sylvia with a 'y' because that is how the name is spelled in England, in spite of Shakespeare. I have constantly resisted that spelling; I do so dislike that 'y'. It changes the whole feel and image of the name; it conjures up a small-time model with mousy blonde hair and little character. And my surname! Schulman in Germany had never presented any problems, but Szulman in England! What kind of a name was that? It was impossible to spell, impossible to pronounce. But it was wise to stick to this original spelling just as it was wise, and of course correct, to be Polish rather than German. Once the war began, to be German was to be an enemy alien, to be Polish was not only to be a friendly alien, but a brave exile and a dashing freedom fighter.

This romantic idea of Poland originates in the 1830 revolution, but flourished beyond reason once the Second World War began. Poles were seen to be desperate for freedom above all else, when in fact until now they have fought for freedom to be oppressed by their own nationals. The British also endow Poland with a glamour which, as a backward country, it does not have. To them it was perfectly captured in the film where Cornel Wilde plays Chopin and Merle Oberon is George Sand. They imagine Poles to have grand manners and grand pianos and to be suffering the tragic fate of their country. Poland has indeed suffered by being torn into pieces by Russia, Germany and Austria. A few Poles do have grand manners, and grand pianos, and speak French. My mother used to mock the army officers for being interested only in the whiteness of their gloves. And then there is the Polish Pope, still in all his finery and glory. But in my prejudice I see most of the population as illiterate, growing beet, eating swedes, drinking and brawling, and all of them – rich or poor – hating Jews. I had to jettison part of my prejudice on a recent visit to Poland when I heard that the Communist regime had taught the population to read and write. However, I also think of Poles as vivacious and charming and wish they were not so rabidly anti-Semitic.

As for the glamour and heroism, during the war we welcomed this reputation and were glad enough of the status of friendly aliens. To be an alien was bad enough; no point in being an enemy alien. It was better to capitalise on how much the liveliness of Poles, their impulsiveness and recklessness, captivated the inhibited English. Characteristics which in everyone else they frown on as loud and unseemly, in Poles they find irresistible. I came to exploit this, together with the impulsive and hot-tempered associations of my red hair, but I did not resort to it until I was in my third school in England.

# EIGHTEEN

# The Deep End

A couple of weeks after we arrived in Eton Place, I was thrown into the deep end and I didn't know how to swim. I landed in a school where no one spoke anything but English, and then of a kind not usually taught to foreigners. Nursery rhymes and songs about Tipperary were of no help whatsoever. It amuses me to boast that I was once a pupil at what became Haverstock Hill Comprehensive and not the goal of most middle-class parents. Now it is mixed but not mixed as in working-class and middle-class, but in boys and girls and white and black. It is almost wholly working-class. In 1939, the all-girl white working-class school was unleavened by blacks or browns, and I was the one and only immigrant or refugee, and the only non-Christian.

Our flat in Eton Place was right opposite the school. From the window I had watched the girls arrive in navy school uniforms with smart hats, and white ankle socks no matter what the weather, and the spring of 1939 was wet and chilly. In Berlin we would have been wearing stockings.

These girls in their hats and white socks went to the superior part of the school, the grammar school part. But I understood no English, I had not taken the Eleven Plus, and so, a couple of weeks into the spring term, I was sent to the non-grammar section, the secondary school, in the adjacent building. I was staggered by the size of the class – fifty girls, more than double the number I had been used to. The teacher introduced me and told them they were to mind how they spoke as 'Silvia' (Silvia, not Zilvia) 'is here to learn English. You must all set an example.' She kept repeating this throughout the term and every time she picked someone up on what must have been broad cockney. No glottal stops and no cockney vowels were allowed to pass. Every time anyone said 'bu'er' instead of 'butter', 'lite' instead of 'late', 'ain't it' instead of 'isn't it', she was told to think of Silvia. It is a wonder the girls did not come to hate me. If they did, they didn't show it.

I did not understand the nuances and significances of different English accents. They all sounded equally strange to me and I was convinced that no matter what language the others spoke and understood, they surely thought in German. Even as I listened to girls converse in English, and to the teacher teach in English, I just knew their thoughts were in German – it was not possible to think in any other language! A supreme case of ethnocentricity.

The class had an elocution lesson once a week and the set text was *Alice in Wonderland*. I had never heard of it, I had no idea what the story was and I certainly did not learn it then and there. The language was well beyond me but the illustrations were unforgettable: the White Rabbit taking out his watch, Alice drinking the shrinking medicine, and the Mad Hatter's tea party. (Years later, the colour supplement of the *Sunday Times* had the same tea party on its cover with Bill as the Mad Hatter). The teacher was in the habit of picking out one word and asking each pupil in turn to pronounce it. For the word 'recognise' she judged my pronunciation to be the best, not that I had the faintest idea what it meant. I was elated. I hid my deep pleasure at this faint echo of coming top in class in the years when I knew the language and when I could participate in everything. 'Recognise' still has a delightful ring to it.

At my first morning in assembly, the school sang 'All things bright and beautiful'; on the second morning, they sang 'Jerusalem'. I was amazed. No one gave any sign of being in the least interested in either Palestine or the Jews. I was unable to ask any questions at this stage but, had I not been so handicapped, I am sure I would have found that none of them even knew where or what Jerusalem was.

Nowadays the song moves me to tears. I think of the scene in the film *The Loneliness of the Long Distance Runner* where the hymn resounds in the runner's ears and, though he is winning, he slows down and stops running for the glory of his borstal school. The pleasant land through which he runs is not for him. His surroundings are still the dark satanic mills. In my obstinately political mind I see working-class estates neglected by Labour Councils and I weep that the Labour Party has so failed the deprived. Though I suspect that, above all, I weep for every disappointment in my own life and for that bemused refugee child that I was. But the hymn also amuses and vexes me: I smile at the sexual symbolism, and am exasperated by the cheek of Blake's millenarian ambition of transferring the Holy City to England.

In 1939 I knew nothing of sexual symbolism, William Blake or Labour Councils, and daily assembly itself was a new experience. I tried to sing some of the hymns, or at least hum the tunes. Unlike singing to the glory of the Führer in the *Volksschule* in Berlin, there was no harm in singing to a God who did not exist and to all things bright and beautiful. What bewildered me was not the religion, only the foreignness of it all. It was strange and exotic – it was English. It was certainly not like that assembly of the *Volksschule*, and at the Jewish schools we had no such get togethers except for sports days. Our communal bonds were reinforced mainly by persecution from the outside.

As well as daily assembly, the school on Haverstock Hill – in common with most English schools – had a system that fostered the communal spirit by dividing itself into 'Houses'. Here each House was symbolised by a colour and each pupil wore a coloured button to show which House she belonged to. The Houses were named after the points on the compass. Red may have corresponded to South, blue to North and so on. I wore a green button. By the time I had been to other schools and read schoolgirl stories, this kind of social organisation had become familiar, but it seemed extraordinary at first. One would expect to find it, as well as the school uniforms, in Germany rather than in England. And as for prefects – but that particular hierarchy did not impinge on me until later.

The uniform in this part of the school, where the children were poor and not on a grant, was minimal: poorly pleated navy gymslips, white blouses, webbing belts, and all available at Woolworth's. At Woolworth's I also bought tennis balls and a skipping rope and learnt new games. I became proficient at bouncing tennis balls against the wall games and I skipped to: –

> My mother said
> I never should

play with the gipsies
in the wood. –

'Gypsies' touched no sensitive chord in me; it merely fitted in with some of the shcoolgirl stories I came to read, where the baddies were either Mediterranean foreigners or gypsies. I became infected with the prejudice. I did not know then that the Germans were treating gypsies in the same way as they were treating Jews.

Each afternoon was given over entirely to sport: five whole afternoons every week! One tiny girl, slightly pigeon-toed and with very dark colouring, was a natural at all sports. So outstanding was she that arrangements were made for her to have tennis lessons outside school. The school bought her a panama hat to wear when she went for lessons and tournaments. She came from a poor family and lived off the Prince of Wales Road in a tiny terraced house. The lavatory was outside and there was no bathroom. I used to have romantic images of her mother pouring water over her father in a zinc bath as in the miner's home described by Emile Zola. I never met her parents, I was never invited inside the house – or inside any of the other girls' houses. I used to hover on the doorstep and from there, the house seemed dark, dank and minute, the kind of house I got to know in Stockton-on-Tees in the Sixties but which has now been pulled down or, in London, mostly gentrified. In 1939 the Prince of Wales Road area was pure Coronation Street without a hint of modernisation.

Most of the evening meals for my athletic friend and her family came from the local fish and chip shop and did not always include fish. It was my first encounter with families whose mothers often did not cook meals but offered a standard ready-cooked meal which their children had to go and fetch. Sometimes I went with my friends to fetch the family supper. The smell was awful and the shop stifling, but I tried to ignore it as I watched how the chippie or his wife took a huge long-handled sieve and lifted out the noisily sizzling chips, and how they deftly folded the chips and the disguised fish into a sheet of newspaper, and how my friends, before they left the shop, unwrapped the newspapers and drenched their meal with salt and vinegar. It was all so peculiar: fish and chips cooked in deep, dark cauldrons, the chips cut into long sticks instead of flat circles, the fish wrapped in a thick batter that could easily be peeled off and eaten separately, vinegar that was sharp and dark brown and sprinkled over hot food that was wrapped in newspaper. It was this – cooked, hot food wrapped in newspaper – that was the most astonishing of all. I came across more strange food in the cookery classes in school: rock cakes and suet puddings that lived up to their names, and salads laid out in intricate baroque symmetry but creations without a soul as there was never a drop of dressing.

One of the girls in my class lived in a run-down flat in a crumbling house in a crumbling road, St George's Terrace off Primrose Hill – those very houses that by 1962 had become too expensive for Bill and me to buy. My friend who lived there in 1939, wore shoes that were coming to pieces. I gave her some I had just grown out of, a pretty navy-blue pair and the last shoes I ever bought in Berlin. She was happy, and so was her mother. I would have forgotten this act of charity were it not for the fury it provoked at home. I might have expected my parents to praise me for being a good little Communist, but instead they were beside themselves with anger. My father shouted at me and said that I should have given them to my aunt Hella. (She had by then joined us in London but lived in a small room nearby.) My mother, whose dislike of Hella was one of the most consistent things about her, sided with my father. I told them how the soles of my friend's old shoes were flapping away from the uppers and were riddled with holes, that her parents were poor and could never buy new clothes for any of the children, that they lived in a dilapidated house with cracked window panes, without heating, without a bath, and sharing an outside lavatory with four other families. In short I described a family whose circumstances were straight out of the pages of Zille. But they did not forgive me. I was upset and bewildered but assume their reaction must have been due to their recent and uncertain refugee status. The obsession to keep things in the family by giving the shoes to Hella could not have been prompted by anything else. At the time I saw only that they were denying all they stood for and all they had taught me.

They may not all have walked to school in torn shoes, but all the girls at Haverstock Hill lived in those tiny run-down terraced cottages or in part of a larger, equally run-down house. All the dwellings lacked basic facilities, and none had an indoor lavatory. There were exceptions in the block of flats on the Prince of Wales Road, my first encounter with council flats. I was astonished that they were even smaller than our flat. Each one had its own bathroom and lavatory and my mother told me that when flats like these were being built, British reactionaries and capitalists had objected that 'The workers won't know what to do with the baths, they'll only keep coal in them.' I agreed with her; it was indeed an outrageous thing to say, but I wondered to myself where they did keep their coal. I was no more welcome in the flats than in the houses and never had the chance to look into their bathrooms.

This lack of welcome may not have had anything to do with my foreignness or class, but was just one more cultural difference. In Berlin, it would have been out of the question not to ask whoever called, be it postman, milkman or neighbour, to come in and at least stand in the hall with the front door shut. English people can leave someone standing on the doorstep, shut the door, and no one feels embarrassed.

Some of the blocks of flats on the Prince of Wales Road are still standing, but the one I used to play in was bombed to smithereens one night during the Blitz. Were my playmates, girls and their brothers – I had a crush on one of them – killed? Evacuated? Saved by an air-raid shelter? I lost touch the moment I went to my next school. In this case Marx was right and class was a stronger barrier than nationality, or ethnicity, which was not a word I knew in 1939. But my next school proved that his views were fallible.

Before I went to my next school, I was made miserable by an experience that happened because I was an outsider not familiar with the language and the mores of English schools. The form teacher had allotted me to one particular girl in our class to be my 'minder'. She was a pretty girl, with a squarish jaw, a long bob of light brown hair, thick long eyelashes and pale grey irises outlined by a fine dark line. She had a German father and so the idea of someone speaking a language other than English was not strange to her, though she herself did not speak German. Of all the girls in my class, hers were the only parents I ever met and the only home I ever set foot in at that time. One games afternoon I had forgotten to bring my plimsoles and my friend showed me a pair in the classroom cupboard. She persuaded me that it was perfectly in order for me to borrow them. She was very insistent and watched me put them on. When the form teacher arrived she was outraged and affronted because I was wearing her shoes; she would not accept that I had not realised this. She believed my half-German friend, who swore that she had warned me not to take them. I was punished, but I am not sure how – sent home instead of playing games, I think. I felt wretched and betrayed. I walked the few steps home across Haverstock Hill, and comforted myself with the thought that at least I could tell my mother. How bleak it would have felt had I been one of those children who had come to this strange country without their parents.

I shall never know if the trick played on me was the result of anti-Semitism that my friend had absorbed from her father. It was a hurtful episode, but the worst aspect of my term at this school was that although the girls, with that one exception, were friendly, I had not one intimate friend, and I had no influence. If I had any value, it was that of a freak. At my next school I did not even have that.

It took fifty-one years for me to be fully confronted by the poignancy and pain of being the one and only child in a school from a strange country and without the language. It happened unexpectedly when Geoffrey and Pat Tordoff invited us to dinner in the House of Lords. I was fond of our hosts and I enjoyed the evening except for one awkward moment. We were discussing integration and whether children of immigrants should be taught in their own language or in English. Pat Tordoff assured us that children learn a language amazingly quickly. She recalled how at her school in 1939 a Jewish refugee boy from Vienna appeared suddenly. 'He spoke not a word of English but within three months – do you know he had caught up!' To my dismay, I felt my eyes filling with tears. It was as if one of the girls in my class on

Haverstock Hill had told of the day fifty-one years ago when a Jewish girl from Germany appeared in their class, could not understand a word but pronounced 'recognise' better than anyone else. The full extent of my isolation and singularity stared me in the face over the soggy trifle in the guests' dining room in the House of Lords. But I couldn't possibly cry in front of people I hardly knew, and especially in this place for British aristocrats who are so imbued with anti-Semitism. For all I knew, Lord Halifax had entertained his guests in this very room.

Then Pat Tordoff, a sensitive woman who had inadvertently dropped me into this dilemma, inadvertently saved me. She kept stressing that this boy, like other children, had not come over until 1939 because 'they hoped it would all pass over'. I stopped feeling sorry for myself and became angry. I told the dinner party that it was not a matter of any illusions either parents or children might have held, but that no country was prepared to take them in. I wanted to tell them about the desperate parents who had put their children on the *Kindertransport*, but I did not trust myself to remain cool. Our hosts and their friends, being truly British, did not ask me when I had come to Britain, or how.

My one term at Haverstock Hill school seems much longer now. It was an early stage of my initiation into a new culture, I had learnt so much and I am happy to talk and write about my time there. But I prefer not even to think about my next school. It brings back too much resentment and might-have-been. The cause of this misery pushed itself into my mind one winter Sunday a few years ago. Bill and I had gone to lunch with his old friend Shirley Williams at Furneux Pelham in Hertfordshire. One of the other guests was the writer Frederic Raphael. It wasn't so much that he boasted of being a tax exile, nor that he dropped the names of obscure philosophers rather than ideas into the conversation, but that he reminded me of the girls at Henrietta Barnett School.

Current news that Sunday at Furneux Pelham included the possibility of further immigration from the new Commonwealth. An editorial in one of the Sunday papers discussed whether this would be good or bad – good or bad for those already here, that is.

Frederic Raphael's views, his tone, his demeanour took me right back to that school in Hampstead Garden Suburb. He pronounced that we should be careful about letting in more immigrants; those already here did not want them, it was bound to make things awkward for them. I was enraged. Here was this intelligent, educated and privileged Jew expressing exactly what had made my life so miserable. His was the same attitude as that of the British-born Jewish girls in Henrietta Barnett. I was the immigrant they and their parents could have done without. There was no other reason for the miserable stand-offishness of the daughters. The school had been recommended to my parents as likely to welcome refugees because Jewish girls formed a large minority. I was put together with them during morning assembly and instead of singing songs about Jesus and Jerusalem, I sat in a room with a group of girls who totally ignored me. Hardly one of them ever spoke to me or was in any way curious about me. Not one of them ever invited me for a walk, a game, a party, an orange squash – anything.

I realise now that some of the Jewish community in Golders Green feared that their tenuous acceptance by Britain was endangered by other Jews coming in: by Jews who spoke broken English, or none at all, whose financial position was in most cases dire, who were of a different culture but could claim and did claim affinity with the British Jewish community and were certainly identified with it. The British Jews feared that by association they would become too conspicuous and once again attract anti-Semitism.

For who knew how long they had lived in their semis on Hendon Way or their palaces on Bishops Avenue? Or when they had moved from their wretched dwellings in Whitechapel, or which generation had come from even more wretchedness in Poland and Russia? I wish they had risen above their immediate fears. I am surprised how angry it still makes me. To be fair, the leaders of the Jewish community and most of their members did as much as they could for the refugees. But I had stumbled across this group in Golders Green and its environs who feared for their recently won security. If I shrink from Golders Green now (the school is in Hampstead Garden Suburb but Golders Green is a metaphor, not just a place), if I mock it for its taste, its style, its habits, it must stem from that period. This must also be partly to blame for the ferocity of my reaction to Frederic Raphael. He had a point, but as a victim of that point I was enraged. In any case, it was a mean point.

Yet why should the pupils of Henrietta Barnett have accepted me? I was a refugee, a Jewish one at that, but my Jewishness must have seemed very odd. My family were not members of any synagogue, I knew no prayers, I was unaware of the Jewish holidays, traditions and customs, and I may even have turned up at school on the Day of Atonement. I had ceased trying to convert anyone to my ideology, and I wonder now if I showed my disdain at their religious goings on. Indifference would have been quite enough to put them off.

If the Jewish girls upset me by not wanting my company, at least we were aware of one another. But the non-Jewish girls might have been in a different form; they didn't mix with us at all. The exclusiveness may have been mutual. I recently met an old girl of the school, two years younger than I, who agreed that the school had always been popular with the Jewish community but that quite a lot of the staff had been anti-Semitic. On every Jewish holiday, for example, her teacher used to greet the class in the morning with: 'Isn't it going to be lovely today without the others?'

Thoroughly foreign as I was, my appearance was misleading. Anyone seeing me on my way to and from school would not have noticed anything different about me. I had begun to push my true self further and further out of sight. I did so want to be like the English. They were in charge and therefore superior, enviable and to be emulated. I wanted to be accepted just like them. I was pleased that superficially at least I could pass for one of the girls in the schoolgirl stories I borrowed from the public library – not a foreign but an English girl. I did not have long curly black hair, olive skin, dark flashing eyes that played false, or lips that were too red and too full – all features that, according to those stories, revealed foreignness and with it danger and inferiority. My hair was straight, short and gingery, my eyes gingery-brown, my skin pale and freckled and my lips anything but voluptuous. But for me the best part of my disguise was that I was decked out in a complete school uniform.

This uniform, my pride and joy, was not to be bought in any old shop, and certainly not at Woolworths, but was stocked by respectable and middle-class John Barnes in Finchley Road. The basic shade was a light navy, decorated by the school colours: orange-red, green and yellow. The gymslip was well-shaped – none of those pleats that bulged in the wrong places and gave the girls at Haverstock Hill such a peculiar shape below the waist. This elegant tunic was worn with a white blouse of unique cut and a tie. The green games skirt had matching knickers, was brief and very stylish. And those gorgeous hats! A navy felt of sensuous bloom for winter, and then for spring I had that coveted Panama hat.

I learnt to play netball, hockey and tennis. I also learnt to cook English winter puddings, though to say 'learn' is to exaggerate. The lessons evaporated as quickly as the steam of the steamed puddings: spotted dick, roly-poly. I have never since cooked a pudding, or baked a cake. Unsatisfactory cookery lessons alternated with sewing lessons. They began well. I was after all a tailor's daughter and enjoyed buying the checked cotton material, making up the pattern, laying it on the material and cutting it out. It was then that my trouble started, since sewing proved no easier and no more fun than knitting and, though I finished the dress, it took me four hours to do the modest hem. Was that my mother at work inside me again and triumphing over my father?

The only remarkable, the only bizarre lessons at this very traditional school were the French ones taught by what looked like a stereotypical spinster of the time: plain, thin, flat-chested, small spectacles, grey hair pulled into a meagre bun. But the methods she used to get our pronunciations right belied her appearance. They were theatrical and imaginative, and in that conventional school quite outlandish. Each girl brought a small mirror to school and then the whole class had to practice correct pronunciation, with each of us looking into our mirror as the French vowels distorted our lips, cheeks and chin. In unison, we pursed our lips, we wrinkled them, we opened them wide, we stretched them into long slits, we pouted. Our teacher contorted her face first and then we copied. The whole performance must have looked hilarious, but we all sat there with solemn expressions. No one giggled.

My paintings and drawings were not memorable. Art classes were often based on poems we were reading in English literature and I was especially intrigued by 'The Lady of Shallot' – the metre, the rhythm, and the mystery. But the mystery was compounded and confused by my inadequate grasp of English. Not only the poet's works but the teacher's explanations were beyond me. For years I wondered: 'Why did that mirror break and why was she so upset by it?' Some of the girls did tender paintings of the lady floating down the river, with trailing hair and trailing willow branches, but my pictures were stilted and prosaic and I was vexed by my failure.

A poem of a different style was 'How Horatio kept the Bridge', which the whole school was to perform at the end of term concert. The class divided into groups, each group learning different verses. We had an audition to pick one girl to recite each verse or set of verses, and everyone judged my rendition of 'Oh Tiber, father Tiber, to whom the Romans pray' to be the best. But then they ruled it out because of my foreign accent. I haven't forgiven them yet.

In our first physics lesson I did not fare too well either but that was entirely due to my own inadequacy. The teacher put potassium permanganate crystals into a beaker of water, lit the bunsen burner below the centre of the beaker, and the purple colour rose in a central streak in the water. At the top, it curved over to flow down the edges. She placed two burners under the beaker, one on each side, and a double purple pattern played within the water. It had a beautiful symmetry, but what was going on? I could not grasp a single one of her sentences and panicked. Yet one more thing I could not understand! It was decided I should 'be excused' any science lessons until I knew more English. This was well-meant but it increased my isolation and added a grain of despair. I wish someone had taken a little trouble to explain the magic of the purple streams in the beaker, though I now wonder if my underlying problem was psychological rather than verbal. The causation of those purple whorls had been so self-evident that words were surely unnecessary. I was sixteen when I took my second physics lesson.

I did excel in two things. One was useful: grammar. I may have had problems with physics and poetry, but I made huge strides in learning English and was very good at grammar. Knowing German, and having learnt Russian and Hebrew even if I was fast forgetting them, gave me a basis for understanding grammar that the other girls did not have. My other success was of no importance and happened when the school entered an inter-school handwriting competition and mine won second prize for the school. I did not care and no one else did either. Or perhaps I did not care because no one took any notice of my achievement. Surely any other girl winning a prize for her school would at least have had some acknowledgement, even if only in front of the class? 'Oh, by the way, your handwriting won second prize' was all that the teacher said to me one afternoon as I sat at my desk with no one else listening.

Otherwise, the school made a great fuss about handwriting. Every note, all written work, had to be in standard school writing with standard ink, standard pen holder, and standard nib held at standard angle. Each letter had to be copied from a model sheet to standard size, with standard loops, and always upright. Any sloping was out. It was an unusual way to iron out individuality and I wonder if the girls who went to that institution from eleven to eighteen were marked for life. English public schools tend to have their own ways of diction, but handwriting? There are, of course, national characteristics: American handwriting is distinctive from European and there is quite a difference between English and continental writing and not only in the way '7' is drawn. But this coercion into uniform handwriting was irksome and oppressive and another feature one might have expected in a pre-war German rather than an English school.

The teachers seemed remote apart from one incident with my form mistress, who disliked my untidiness, which has always been monumental. She opened my desk one afternoon, called the class to attention, told them to 'look at this mess!' and asked me: 'Are all Poles like that?' I felt no shame, only raw anger. Uprisings have happened for less.

My mother went to see the headmistress to discuss my feeling of isolation. The headmistress declared, 'I have never had any complaints like this!' and that was that. My mother, with her lack of English, was no match. There is nothing like broken English to sabotage one's dignity and presence. I once heard Thomas Mann speaking over the radio in English, and wished I had never switched it on. His grammar and syntax were faultless but the broadcast reduced him to half the impressive figure he had been. It was not only the accent but the very timbre of the voice – unnaturally high-pitched for a big man – that diminished him. Added to my mother's linguistic handicap was her ignorance of the cultural mores, especially of what went on in English schools. She was helpless to assess whether I had a case or not and she wanted to believe that the school was good for me. Both of us were further disadvantaged by having no contact with the Jewish community, where she might have learnt something about English schools and where I might have met some of the girls from my class.

On the face of it, Henrietta Barnett was not my kind of school and the antipathy was mutual. But I wasn't there for long enough to give it a chance. Daisy stayed at the North London Collegiate school until she was eighteen and was happy enough there. True, her family were members of the local Jewish community, she herself would be uncomplainingly happy anywhere, and perhaps her school was more understanding. But I, with my Jewishness so blurred, must have been very difficult for any school to understand and accept. And I am aware that the standards at my next school weren't a patch on Henrietta Barnett's. The change, even if I was glad of it at the time, had nothing to do with me, but with the war.

# NINETEEN

# A Glorious and Ominous Summer

Between my terms at Haverstock Hill and Henrietta Barnett schools came the glorious and ominous summer of 1939, and with it a holiday that was anything but fun. Daisy had arrived in England a couple of months before me, and she and her mentally subnormal brother had gone straight to a Jewish boarding school in Sussex. The school was near Cuckfield, a name that caused us lots of hilarity because it sounds too much like *kacken*, the German vernacular word for shitting. As the school stayed open in the holidays and my parents were looking for somewhere to send me, we wrote to ask Daisy what the school was like. She wrote back to say it was lovely. Little did we know that all correspondence was censored by the teachers, as were all phone calls. Daisy in any case took the awfulness of the school with infuriating equanimity. It was part of her temperament: everything really was always for the best in the best of all possible worlds. Her letter did the trick and I was condemned to that school. It turned out to be a respite from the extremes of culture shock and the isolation in London, but I loathed it. It was run on totalitarian lines; like Wyk-auf-Föhr, only more so.

Mr and Mrs Cohen were a singularly unpleasant couple, in both character and appearance. Both were short, ugly, with thick lips, heavy eyelids and bulbous noses. He was red-faced, she was pasty. Their regime was supported by their lieutenants: the teachers and the matron. The matron's iron rod was a slipper that must have been stiffened by some metallic substance. It gave me my first stroke of corporal punishment.

Letters were intercepted, but I did manage to get one through to my mother complaining that matron's slipper had bruised the side of my neck. My mother in turn complained to the Cohens. They punished my treachery with yet more coldness and snootiness. Then a male teacher was accused by another parent of being too free with his slaps – a second message had got through the defences. The Cohens took this seriously and lined up the whole school on the lawn. The weather was superb and Mrs Cohen stood by her husband's side wearing a long floral dress. I had never before seen anyone in a long dress. Her husband told the assembled children that his wife's dress was old, but because she was so prudent and careful, it still looked new. 'An example to you all.' Only after this irrelevant piece of sanctimoniousness did he ask if any of us had ever witnessed the accused teacher hitting a child. I had and said so. Mrs Cohen walked down the line, stopped in front of me and asked: 'Aren't you the one who complained about matron?' With that my testimony was disqualified and I was marked out as a vindictive telltale, too eager to get teachers into trouble. Eventually (and how on earth did I manage it – did I make an illicit phone call, did I talk Daisy into helping me?) I contacted my parents again. My mother and her friends the Lederers came down and took me home.

The regime of the school was of course a culture shock in itself. What I and other refugee children and their parents found so outrageous was normal to everyone else. It was no more totalitarian than many English boarding schools but we, the refugees who outnumbered the natives, did not understand that at the time. How could we know that corporal punishment was part of English culture, that the most prestigious schools had far more extreme and complex totalitarian regimes than this little boarding school in Sussex, and that the making of an English gentleman had little to do with gentleness and more with intimidation? Had this school confined itself to taking English children, it would have had no trouble.

Cuckfield was the first time I had to endure corporal punishment, and also the first time I was faced with a bowl of porridge. This punishment was not intentional and I had the choice of adding sugar or salt. Sugar made it sickly, and salt – could food be that disgusting? I bought my first Mars Bar or Milky Way, ate it in one go, and haven't been able to eat one since. Nauseatingly rich. We were taken to a film in which Louis Armstrong sang 'Jeepers, creepers, where did you get those peepers?' I sang it without the faintest idea of what it meant.

Some of the children were born in England, and the nearer it got to September 1939 more and more parents would come and ship them off safer distances from London and imminent war. But most of the children had come as refugees on the *Kindertransport* and their parents were still in Germany waiting for visas which never came. The school fees were paid by a charity and the Cohens let it be known these fees were lower than usual. I never knew what anxieties plagued those children in Cuckfield. There was still a very vague hope that some of the parents might get out in time, and we were all to some extent preoccupied with making the best of not very pleasant circumstances.

As far as the girls were concerned, we became absorbed in other matters. Most of us were about to start menstruating, one or two already had, but that was something I had never heard of. On the train down to Cuckfield, my mother did try to tell me something about it but I had no idea what she meant nor did it sound interesting enough to arouse my curiosity. She appeared absent-minded, and as she talked she looked out of the window at the passing countryside. For a feminist, she was curiously ill at ease when it came to female physiology and sexuality.

Two sisters who had come with the *Kindertransport*, both with enviably lovely long wavy hair, asked me: '*Bist Du schon aufgeklärt?*' I said yes, I had been enlightened. I was sure they were referring to the doctrine of Communism and I was very happy. If one could ask this question of people one did not know, it must mean there was no danger of persecution in this country. Luckily, before I could make a fool of myself, I realised they were not talking politics. These two sisters had been prepared by their mother for their puberty. She knew they would have to face that transition on their own. The agony of having to send your children away knowing that you were unlikely to watch them grow up, that they would be on their own at times of change, joy, pain, barely crossed my childlike mind. And the anxiety of the children did not fully impress and depress me till later. Less than half of me was sensitive to the suppressed anxiety of those two long-haired sisters and others in the same predicament. I did not want to know.

Now it is one of my most searing thoughts. To read about the

*Kindertransport* in *They Came as Children* by Karen Gershon was an ordeal and I wept with each paragraph, and the poems written by the children as they grew up tore at my insides. But I don't read it now. And when I opened *The Policeman Smiled*, another book on the same subject by Barry Turner, I banged it shut never to open it again. I had opened it at the page where a desperate couple hand their baby through the window of a train compartment and beg the adult in charge to look after it, before running off. I want to forget that, just as I want to block out how three years later my little cousin Hélène and her parents were torn apart in Paris by the Nazis. Bang the book shut, blindfold my eyes, cover my ears. But there is still my mind. The attitude of the British government was utterly incomprehensible. They took the children only because they knew exactly what lay ahead, and yet they showed no mercy to the adults and no understanding for the plight of their children.

Before I went to Cuckfield and then when I came back, I began to prepare for grammar school. To get in I had to know enough English to participate in lessons, and be familiar with the English system of weights and measures which, unlike the metric system, is illogical and inconsistent. Nothing could have made me learn the language quicker than daily attendance at a school where no one else spoke German. But equally important were private lessons I had from a teacher who lived in a ground-floor flat in Eton Place. She helped me with grammar, taught me about pounds and ounces, gallons and pints, pounds and shillings and pence, inches, feet and yards, and that if I ran from our flats to Swiss Cottage I would have run one mile. She corrected my pronunciation, which must have been rich with cockney, lent me books about Britain, gave me home-work and encouraged me to join the public library in Antrim Road.

Going to that library gave me a secret and almost sensual pleasure. I can feel it now, and though the library is ten minutes away from where I now live I dare not enter it. I am afraid to break the spell. I don't know what contributed most to this pleasure: that I always went alone, which made this my own experience and separate from my parents'; that the books were quite unlike the books crammed onto the shelves at home; the process of exchanging the tickets for books and then back again; the coloured cardboard tickets themselves with my name carefully written on each; the rows of books from which I could choose without guidance; or the benign and reticent librarians and the calm of the library. It was a sanctuary for my mind and senses. The life I had left behind in Berlin and the life I struggled with now were irrelevant while I was in there and even on my way there and back.

The books I took out, all from the children's section of course, made for slow reading but gradually I understood most of what was going on, and without looking up too many words. I did not bother about Dickens. Oliver Twist had already asked for more in Berlin, and in German. I did not bother about Dr Dolittle because he too had spoken to the animals in a kind of animal German. But I did enter into the adventures of Tom Sawyer and Huckleberry Finn and discovered that kings, like slaves, are known by their Christian names. What never registered, and with my upbringing it should have done, was that America was no more a haven for the disadvantaged than Germany and Britain. I continued to believe America was a promised land. The books enthralled me not for any political or social message I might have gleaned, but for their wit and for the escapades of the two boys and for Tom Sawyer's decision to climb a fence rather than go through the gate, which would have been too easy and straightforward.

I don't know when or how I came across P. G. Wodehouse. It must have been later, but when I did I was hooked. I read one book after the other without having the least idea how these characters fitted into the order of things in Britain. But they must have given me a very peculiar view of the English.

Before my penchant for Wodehouse, I became engrossed in schoolgirl stories. The characters were as exotic to me as Tom Sawyer and his friend. All the stories were set in boarding schools in the rolling English countryside. All made it quite clear what was right and what was wrong. Midnight feasts were against the rules but popular and such fun; getting others into trouble and cheating was unforgivable. So was telling on the cheat, who was bound to be found out in the end anyway. Playing games was most important, and she who excelled at hockey was beautiful, popular and righteous, too. Strangers who lurked outside, especially gypsies,

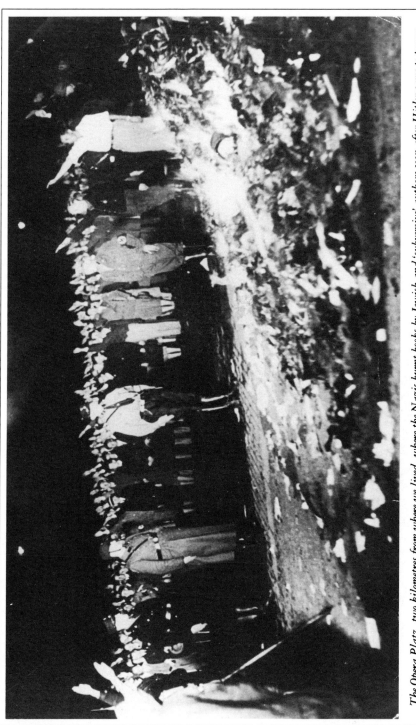

*The Opera Platz, two kilometres from where we lived, where the Nazis burnt books by Jewish and 'subversive' authors soon after Hitler came to power.*

*In the Polish countryside
near Novodno in 1934.*

*In Fanø, Denmark, 1935, with my mother,
who built most of the sandcastle.*

*By the statue of Beethoven*
*in the Tiergarten in 1934.*

*Helga, my blonde friend, who was proud to*
*discover in 1939 that she was a true 'Aryan'.*

*In the Wittenberg Platz with my cousin Hélène in 1936. The KaDeWe,*
*the Harrods of Berlin, is in the background. Hélène died in Auschwitz in 1942.*

*On an outing with Tante Freundlich's class. I am first on the left of the
middle row. Only four out of twenty-five girls survived.*

*Under the swastika flag at a summer camp. I am third from left.*

Der Stürmer, *the viciously anti-Semitic weekly that I regularly saw on the Wittenberg Platz. Nearby, the Salvation Army preached its own message.*

*Solution by fire: the synagogue in Fasanenstrasse, looted and burnt down during the Kristallnacht in 1938. I had been a pupil at the school for four years.*

*Deceptive peace: with my brother André on the Wittenberg Platz
in Berlin shortly before we left for England.*

*New arrivals: with André on his
third birthday shortly after
our arrival in London in 1939.*

*A different kind of politics: electioneering
in Stockton-on-Tees in 1966, with Bill and (from left to
right) Lucy, Juliet and Rachel.*

*The ruined church in Michaelkirch Platz in 1987.*

*Berlin Wall near Adalbertstrasse in February 1990.*

were not to be trusted and spelt danger. In one typical story a Spanish girl had joined the school. She clearly did not fit in, but as she behaved true to the book's view of her national character and made enough mischief to be expelled, all was well again.

I should have been outraged at these morals, but I wasn't. I dreamt of being one of the girls, the most popular, naturally. The books had drawings of the characters: they all looked alike, and I admired the smart uniforms and longed for a Panama hat. In the end, I was to get one. It was the best thing about my next school, a day school without bean feasts, and in which, though neither Spanish nor gypsy, I was the unloved foreigner. I met the real products of the bean feast schools much later. Most of them seem to have married into the Foreign Office.

While I was still at Cuckfield, London was being transformed. Sandbags buffered public buildings, brown sticky-paper tape criss-crossed window panes, barrage balloons floated below the clouds, and people carried gas masks across their shoulders as I had carried my snack box with strawberry sandwiches to school in Berlin. The barrage balloons looked like poor relations of the glamorous Zeppelins, and when I watched one being hauled down I saw they were soft and unmanned imitations. I had first marvelled at Zeppelins when I was a toddler. I have a photograph of me aged two standing at the back of a crowd at Tempelhof, the Berlin airport, watching a Zeppelin taking off. Later, when I watched one and often two Zeppelins cruising low over the houses as I walked along the Bayreutherstrasse, I felt the eeriness of a science-fiction story. These two silvery creatures buzzing and sparkling in the sky above exuded a sinister magic. The plump, grey shapes hovering over London, intended as barricades against German aircraft, did not hum, did not sparkle and had no magic, tied as they were to the ground and regulated by earthbound workmen.

Preparations for blackout made the war seem imminent, but we had already sat through one blackout practice in Berlin in 1938. We had reinforced our curtains with pieces of material – there was no shortage in a tailor's house – had eaten supper by candlelight, and hoped we would be far away from Berlin when the real thing came.

In London there was still peace. Hitler had not yet marched across the Polish border. Then, suddenly in the last week of August, he made a pact with Stalin who loomed on Poland's other side. The Nazi Soviet pact was signed on 23 August, the day before my mother's thirty-ninth birthday. Though the pact shook the faith of many a Communist, it did not shake my mother's. They may have expelled her from the Party, but she did not blame the Party itself, and certainly not Stalin. Like all devout followers of heads of nations, movements or cults, she would not blame her leader. This was far too unnerving and threatening and would cast doubt on her original judgement. It is those around the leader who always get the blame: spouse, lover, priest, entourage, advisors or kitchen cabinet.

My mother kept telling me how very shrewd Stalin was to have made this pact. It was a ruse to lead Hitler, the English and the French into believing Stalin was on Hitler's side. He was such a skilful tactician. But in the end it was Hitler who turned out to be the brilliant tactician, although she never saw it that way. When the British government ratified the Anglo–Polish treaty and pledged to help defend Poland, my mother explained: 'Hitler is getting too close for their own comfort. That's why they now have to stand by Poland!' Cynical but correct.

On 1 September, Hitler's troops marched across the Polish border, accompanied by merciless bombing. The BBC played the dirge-like first movement of Beethoven's Seventh Symphony. On 3 September, even Chamberlain could no longer procrastinate and declared: 'We are now at war with Germany.' It sounded like something out of a film. We were expecting it, but when it came it was no less shocking and unbelievable. I had been imbued with the horrors of war, any war, every war, since childhood but reality made the prospect infinitely more terrifying. England, our refuge, was now the direct target of the regime we had fled. What would happen to our relatives? Our friends in Germany were cut off, too. I was frightened and worried. Had I been my mother or my father, I would not have been able to sleep.

We soon heard how Polish soldiers taken prisoner – and the whole Polish army seemed to have been taken prisoner – were forced to march for hundreds of miles in bare feet. I looked at newsreels. Whose were those feet? Did some belong to Tante Channale's sons? I searched their faces but they were all impressionistic blurs. What dreadful things were in store for my cousins, and my grandparents and Tante Channale and Uncle Leibu? It was a worry I only voiced once. My parents would never discuss it in my presence. It was taboo until the end of the war, when it turned out that our worst fears had been over-optimistic.

That Sunday when Chamberlain faced the facts, I thought of my school friends in Berlin and how frightened they must be. I experienced an aching anxiety and then I suppressed all contemplation of it. When Daisy and I met we never talked about it. We did not know of any of our contemporaries who had come to England. Of the staff, only her uncle had got out. As for my school in Fasanenstrasse, it was not until some years after the war when I ran into Inge Mandelbaum, one of my three surviving classmates, that I knew something of the fate of my old class.

A bizarre escapade a couple of days after war had been declared helped to push my fears into the background. Announcements over the radio and in newspapers had been telling us about intended evacuations, and when from our window we saw that women and children were lining up outside the Haverstock Hill schools my parents believed we had to go too. My mother, my little brother and I walked across the road, lined up, were duly labelled, put on a train and got out at a place called St Albans. We were taken to a semi-detached house on a working-class estate on the fringes of the town. The housewife was appalled at the strange trio that stood on her doorstep: not the Londoners she had expected, which would have been bad enough, but foreigners. She shouted and gestured: 'Wait!' Like most English people – probably other nationalities too – she thought foreigners were deaf. She was, after all, speaking clearly and slowly, and still we could not understand.

We stood in the doorway and watched the landlady roll up the rug, fetch a pile of newspapers and lay them out in a diagonal path that led from the door to the foot of the stairs. It continued up each step and to the door of our tiny room. I don't remember the layout of the house but I cannot forget that line of newspapers, and that we – the dirty foreigners – were not allowed to deviate from that printed path. By the next day she had washed the floor and put down fresh newsprint. Added to this humiliation was the discomfort of the beds. Instead of familiar eiderdowns we were tied down to the sagging mattresses by a blanket that had been ferociously tucked in. Duvets were still as futuristic then in Britain as a walk on the moon. What we did about food I have no idea. Ours was not a case of ingratitude but of incomprehension. It was culture shock made worse by class difference. We thought with longing of Eton Place.

We stuck to the narrow newspaper path for two days. Long enough for me to catch a glimpse of the estate with its identical two-storey houses crossed by untidy roads and patches of grass. A dispiriting semi-urban landscape that I was to see over and over again all over England.

With hindsight I can understand how threatened our working-class landlady must have felt by this strange woman and her children, with their strange clothes and manners, speaking a double-Dutch language and hardly a word of English. She must have seen us as one of the horrors of war, and very polluting. We were to her what pork is to an orthodox Jewish housewife.

My mother and I never spoke about this trip to St Albans. It may have meant nothing more to her than a silly little episode or she may have been too embarrassed to talk about it. After all she, they, everyone, had made a mistake. Had we been part of the Jewish community or the Communist Party, they would have advised us what to do and what not to do and we would never have joined that particular exodus. It had underlined our isolation as aliens who lacked the cushion of comfort and advice from those who had been here for a while. All refugees need a ghetto, at least for the first phase of their immigration. Whether or not my Marxist mother allowed herself such heretical thoughts, both of us were glad to be back in the comparative haven of Eton Place.

While I was at school, my father went to work with the firm which originally gave him the affidavit that helped him to get to England. Messrs Haar was in Great Titchfield Street, the heart of the British rag trade, which was essentially Jewish. His fellow workers were mostly British-born. Their parents had come from Poland and Russia; only a few were refugees from Germany, as were the owners, though they had been in London for some years. The odd man out in the workshop was a black man, the presser, who wielded the very heavy iron always clouded in steam. When this outsider was accused of some misdemeanour, my father was sure he was innocent and that the others were ganging up on him out of prejudice. With some help my father wrote a letter in support of the accused, and he kept his job.

My father made one political contact through Messrs Haar. Hugo Weiss did fashion drawings for the firm and introduced my parents to his brother Victor who like them was very left-wing and very committed. Hugo had taught Victor to draw, and Victor's ambiton was to become a political cartoonist. My parents struck up a friendship with Victor and his wife, and one Sunday teatime we all went up to the Weiss's flat at the top of a block in St John's Wood. The walls were covered with cartoons of film stars. Mrs Weiss was even shorter than her very short husband and a miniature version of the cartoons on the walls: long straight hair curled evenly into a roll at shoulder length, long false eyelashes also curled into a roll. The friendship did not last. Vicky later became the cartoonist of the *Evening Standard* and friend of the powerful and famous. My father said that when he now passed Vicky in the street, Vicky pretended not to see him. My mother said she didn't care, as Vicky's cartoons were now trimming his left-wing beliefs. In the Fifties, Vicky gave a talk at a Fabian weekend school but I did not go up to him afterwards. What do you say to a man who has snubbed your father?

My mother started to learn English with almost as much zeal as she had learnt German. She read newspapers and books and made copious notes in exercise books. She also had some lessons from the schoolteacher who was helping me. Colloquialisms were a special problem for all of us. We used to laugh at a book on whose cover was a cartoon of a man putting his foot in his mouth, his shoulder to the wheel, an ear to the ground, his nose in the air, all at the same time. He did not stiffen his upper lip, keep his eye on someone or pull up his socks until he appeared on an inside page.

Pronunciation we learnt from the BBC but we still got into difficulties, especially with stress and intonation. Until I was in my thirties I called any food that was mouth-watering, a del*ic*acy. No one had ever corrected me. Perhaps they thought it was an affectation.

We may have been laughed at behind our backs, but I never suffered anything like the experience of the late Frank Schon. He was to be knighted by Harold Wilson for services to British industry and then given a peerage, but he had come to Britain as a Jewish refugee from Vienna. This young man found himself in a tube station and did not know where he was. Piccadilly? Hyde Park? Cockfosters? He went up first to one man and then another asking, 'Who am I?' Not a crisis of identity, but a linguistic confusion because 'where' in German is '*wo*'. It would have been ridiculous enough had he asked 'Where am I?'

Until the bombs began to fall in 1940 we never met, and certainly never mixed with, any of the residents of Eton Place whose mother tongue was English, apart from the teacher on the ground floor. We did know one or two other refugees who lived there. One couple with a little girl had a mixed marriage: he was a Jew and she an Aryan so-called who had stuck by him in spite of the Nazi edicts against *Rassenschande*. She was young, tall, blonde and working-class. He was balding, middle-aged and middle-class. One night he was rushed off to hospital with acute sinusitis and came back with a deep scar bisecting his forehead – a ravine far more ghastly than any scar God had sunk into Cain's forehead, and as permanent. After that the marriage faltered and they were divorced. But it was not because she had been repelled by the horrendous scar. It was he who no longer wanted her. In Nazi Germany he may have looked up to her because she was blonde and stereotypically Aryan. In England, away from the adulation of everything blond, and away from overt anti-Semitism, he felt confident enough as a Jew to despise her on grounds of class and intellect.

The people we saw most of were the few old friends who, like us, had been lucky enough to escape. Among them was Jaques Mendelsohn, who got to London at the last minute. He had walked into the office of an organisation in Berlin dealing with refugee travel, and at first they had said he had no hope of getting to Britain or any other country. 'But wait a minute. We have a *Kindertransport* just about to leave and whoever was going to accompany them hasn't turned up. Do you want to take his place? You won't have time to go home.' Jaques had his passport with him and left there and then. He was eighteen. That he had no change of clothes and no toothbrush was irrelevant in August 1939. He simply left a message for his mother.

Jaques was a good-looking young man, which those who didn't know him until he was MP for Penistone cannot believe. He was also extremely clever but spoilt it all by being a *Besserwisser* (someone who always knows best) and a *Wortklauber* (someone who constantly quibbles over words). 'You can't say *natürlich*,' he kept interrupting me, 'there is no such thing as "of course".' My parents criticised him, though not until later, for name-dropping and opportunism: he had trimmed his commitment to the Communist Party in order to get ahead. By then he had got into the London School of Economics, which was evacuated to the even more prestigious fields of Cambridge. After that he flourished in the Education Corps of the British Army of Occupation in Germany, where he taught British troops about world affairs and British politics and converted many of them to socialism. He ended up as Captain Mendelsohn; or was it Mendelson by then?

We had not seen Jaques for a year or so when, not long after the war, he turned up on our doorstep barely recognisable. He was balding, eyebrowless, pasty-skinned and misshapen by flab. He spoke English with a German accent, which I had never noticed as we had always talked in German. He wanted to borrow some money but my father refused; he was still waiting for him to pay back some earlier loans. Jaques, or Jack as he now was, assured my parents he would bear no ill will, but I did not meet him again until many years later when he was an MP and a colleague of Bill's.

Back in 1939 and 1940, Jaques Mendelsohn was always with us on our ideologically selected sightseeing: not the Tower, not Buckingham Palace, but Kew Gardens and St Paul's. In St Paul's we only saw the scientifically constructed Whispering Gallery, but

Kew Gardens had no such restrictions. Its scale was much vaster than the *Botanische Garten* in Berlin and, though it was redolent with echoes of Empire, we allowed ourselves to enjoy it all: the cluster of bluebells, the cedars of Lebanon, the pagoda, the greenhouses, the exotic ducks on the pond.

I don't remember any trip to Highgate cemetery. Maybe the visit to see Karl Marx's grave was too hallowed an occasion to take children. Even if I was old enough, André was not and I was probably left to look after him. I don't think my mother ever indoctrinated André. He was a sweet and nice-looking boy but otherwise I can't remember much about him until he was much older. To have transformed him into such a shadowy figure may have been my way of dealing with my jealousy.

# TWENTY

# Glass Splinters and Christmas Cards

I continued going to Henrietta Barnett School for a while. I wore my Panama hat, played tennis, chafed at the school writing, kept up the muddle in my desk. All this in April and May 1940 while the Germans were spreading through Denmark and into Norway, and overrunning first Holland and then Belgium. They were getting horribly near.

When Churchill replaced Chamberlain, we were glad the man of Munich had got his deserts. Churchill might yet save us all – he at least had his heart in it. My comprehension of English was good enough to appreciate Mr Churchill's calls to arms and courage. I listened to those grave and inspirational broadcasts, and shuddered with emotion but also with fear. 'We shall fight them on the beaches' was fine but implied they would land and succeed in getting through, especially as we had to expect 'blood, toil and tears'. And over the radio from Berlin I heard the Nazi marching song *'Wir fahren gegen Engeland'*: they sounded very determined. Dunkirk at the end of May was indeed heroic and fantastic. Each one of these little boats was a David defying Goliath. But though a triumph, it was a withdrawal and not a victory. What was going to happen to my little cousin cut off in Paris? Weren't they going to catch up with us at any moment?

After Dunkirk, I never doubted for a minute that Hitler would land on the coast of England. And once landed, how could he fail to conquer the whole island? I knew the song that affirmed that Britons never shall be slaves, I heard it over and over again, but it sounded nothing more than just another jingoistic refrain to be whistled in the dark. In any case, Hitler would certainly make the Jews slaves, if not the British – nor would he stop at that.

Part of the contingency preparations for an invasion was the campaign to beware of enemy agents. The British people were warned to distrust strangers with a foreign bearing, strange accents, and those that asked the way. This was surely the most superfluous warning ever. Where could one find an English man or woman who did not distrust strangers? The 'Walls have ears!' cartoons that illustrated this campaign reminded me of malevolent walls in Berlin. And I had been familiar with the warning 'Careless talk costs lives' for a long while.

The impending danger of invasion was discussed on the radio, and in the newspapers, and in more worried tones by my parents and their friends. I said nothing. But I pledged to myself that the moment the Germans landed I would take my life. 'I shall put my head in the gas oven,' I reassured myself. The domestic oven was the only practical method for me, and the only one I did not think too painful. I did not fancy hurling myself down from a great height, and anyway it would be difficult to find this great height. Jumping from a window of our third floor flat would only cripple me. There was no self-pity or dramatisation or hysteria in my decision. It was logical and comforting. I knew I could not face any more Nazi persecution; I knew it would be the end of us – and what kind of end might it be? All the fear I had suppressed while we still lived in Berlin was now acknowledged, and dwarfed any fear that came later as a result of the bombing.

When the immediate danger of a German landing had passed, my parents and their friends mourned the suicide of Ilse, an ex-comrade who had lived not in London but somewhere in the country. 'Die arme Ilse,' they grieved, she was so sure they would land, she could not bear it any longer. I understood perfectly. I don't remember how she took her life but the verdict must have been the usual one for the time: 'Suicide while the balance of mind was disturbed.' Absurd. Her mind was not in the least unbalanced. She was just less patient and more pessimistic than me.

Soon there was another alert. The tide was right, the moon was right, the Germans were expected to invade at any moment. Instead they began the Blitz. A lot of people slept in the Tube stations but the tenants of Eton Place avoided the platforms of Chalk Farm station and slept in the ground-floor corridors of their block. The atmosphere was almost chummy, even with the tenants who were English born and bred. The bombs had brought us together. This friendliness, however, never got beyond the nightly exchanges in the corridor.

Until the United States entered the war, the prospect of a German landing continued to haunt me. In addition, my mother used occasionally to listen to German radio, and extracts of the venomous speeches of their leaders filled me with icy fear. I shiver now when I think of them. I hear Hitler ranting, '*Wir werden ihre Stätte ausradieren!*' and it was no idle boast, he did try to rub out British towns. Much later, when he was trying to vanquish Soviet Russia, he gave his wretched followers another promise and I hear his voice raging and the crescendo as he vows, '*Wir werden Stalingrad berennen und es auch nehmen werden, worauf Sie sich verlassen können!*' (We shall storm Stalingrad and take it, you can be sure of that!) Absurd what echoes are lodged in the lining of my memory, and probably word-perfect too.

But the speech that really crushed me was by Goering. I sat in one of our fat armchairs and sobbed and hugged my knees as I listened to yet another tirade against the Jews, but I do not now recall a single phrase. Possibly he was less of an orator. Possibly my memory has censored the contents. I am surprised the speech threw me into such despair. I would have thought I was more immune by then.

Not all anti-Semitism was disseminated from hundreds of miles away. Early on in the war, as we waited for a bus, it was there right in front of us, glued onto the bus stop. My mother and I read the call to 'Stop this war!' It was a Jewish war. The British people were being duped; they should not allow themselves to be sacrificed for Jews. My mother explained that yes, there were Fascists in England but very few. I never again saw another fly-poster like that. By the time the Blitz began its message would have been high treason.

One bomb attack has lodged in my mind and I think of it every time I see the film *Top Hat* or hear its popular song 'Cheek to Cheek'. Usually the bombing began in the evening, so I went to see this film in the afternoon to be home in good time. It was showing at the Odeon on Haverstock Hill and for once my mother had come with me. André was out to tea. We soon lost ourselves in that most escapist of films, with Fred Astaire and Ginger Rogers at their frothy best. We came out onto Haverstock Hill in high spirits. We had no idea that while we had been caught up with lilting music, feathery clothes and an impossible romance, the Luftwaffe had rushed in with its performance several hours earlier than usual and created havoc. We got home to find my father out of his mind with rage. He had come home in the middle of the raid to find both of us out, having left no message to tell him where we had gone. It was mad and irresponsible of my mother to take me to the cinema in the middle of a raid, he shouted. She shouted back and quickly the row degenerated into the old recriminations. When he accused her of being too friendly with our handsome GP my mother slammed the door of the sitting room. She forgot that it was made of glass and could never shut properly with all that overfed furniture about. The door shattered against the back of a chair and glass splinters showered everything as if we had indeed been hit by a bomb.

The battles inside our home had become fiercer ever since we had moved into Eton Place. My mother had no outlet for her political energies, my father had to work for someone else, both had lost their milieu and both were worried sick about family and friends on the Continent. The fights were also more marked because of the relative calm outside – no storm-troopers in Chalk Farm, or later in Ealing.

Soon after the scene that forever linked *Top Hat* to shattered glass, my parents decided that my mother should take us children to safety. I have always been convinced it was solely for the sake of my baby brother, who had begun to be fretful. The nights were indeed noisy and the atmosphere could get very tense. Furthermore, there were now daytime attacks. I myself was still less worried by the thought of being blown to pieces by a bomb than by the prospect of a Nazi landing.

Our second exodus was private and voluntary, with no queueing up, no labels, no billeting in a council house, and no treading a path of newsprint. We took a train to Oxford. My father had to stay in London, where the ferocity of the bombing had forced him along with everyone else to spend the nights in the Underground.

He escaped to Oxford only at weekends and was more short-tempered than ever. For us, Oxford was a respite from the bombing and from all that was going on in the outside world. It was the least political period of our lives, but filled with problems of family and puberty. And my poor mother was more isolated than at any time in her life.

We were not the only ones seeking asylum from the bombing and Oxford was full to bursting. We arrived during a university vacation and for two short weeks lived in two rooms in North Oxford. I was so sorry to leave that elegant house and area, for rooms in a mean little house in Headington. I am familiar with North Oxford now, and it is still attractive, but it was never more desirable and more unattainable than in 1940. Mrs Costello, who owned the house in Headington, was a plump little busybody who complained about the least noise, even my mother's humming. I couldn't stand my mother's humming either, but then I was her daughter. My mother looked down on our landlady because there was not a single bookshelf in the house and because the only book Mrs Costello had ever read was *Daddy Long Legs*. My mother had never even heard of it, and it sounded neither intellectual nor political.

We rented one and a half rooms. My mother and André slept in the one room where we lived and ate; I slept in the half or box-room. Because the accommodation was too small, especially at weekends when my father came, I was boarded out and came home from school, not to my mother, but to a pleasant, elderly couple in South Oxford. Unlike Mrs Costello, they had shelves with books on, Dornford Yates and Cowboys and Indians stories. There were also some tracts that revealed the truth about the Jews: they were not the same as the Israelites of the Bible, a falsehood spread by the Jews themselves. But the subject never came up with my landlady and landlord, who regarded me as a little Polish girl. I have no idea what if anything we talked about as they watched me eat my supper, which was usually shepherd's pie and apple crumble and very good. It was a friendly but mute relationship. I get a semi-deaf feeling when I think back.

On the whole I liked the tranquility, but I must have been

deeply unhappy because I started to wet my bed. This was probably because my mother had sent me away, kept my brother and saw me only for lunch on Saturdays and Sundays – an arrangement that suited her but made me feel very unwanted. When my hosts told my mother that they could no longer keep me, I was very upset – not even they wanted me. The row that followed when my father came that weekend was more shaming than anything else. We sat in my tiny bedroom where I had committed the misdeeds, and both of them berated me as in Berlin, but now there were no appeals to my Communist principles, only to my nature as a female. A girl has to be more fastidious and cleaner than a boy; something about dirt leading to infections that spread right inside one's body – I think they meant my vagina or womb – and some hints about future generations. My parents, who had pushed aside the Jewish faith, were still obsessed with the polluting power of a woman's body. It would have been bad enough with just my mother warning me, but with my father there too it was acutely embarrassing.

This scene, on top of being evicted by the couple in South Oxford, might have made my bed wetting worse, but it stopped. My mother found another room for me with a cheerful family with small children in Marston. As Marston is very near Headington, I sometimes had supper with my mother and brother, and sometimes with the family. One evening I washed my hair and, as I was combing it through and looked at the comb, a tiny, round animal edged with tiny hairs, wriggled across the teeth of the comb. I was in the living room with the rest of the family and hid my crunchy find and my nausea. The mother offered to comb my hair. I said no, thank you, but she thought I was being shy and brushed my hair with vigour. I sat there in terror and waited for screams of disgust. But I must have caught the only louse that had so far hatched. I slept badly that night as I pictured what was going on in my hair: crunchy fat creatures burrowing in my scalp and nesting in my hair. The next day I discovered that all my family were louse-infected. My father, despite his receding hairline, must have brought the lice back from the shelters where they marched easily from one head to the next. Those underground shelters were rich in material for Henry Moore but also for parasitologists, though I don't know that any of them ever made use of it.

We were careful to keep this guilty secret from Mrs Costello, and locked the door while we washed our hair with a pungent liquid and combed and raked with fine-tooth combs. We harvested a rich crop.

But the worst thing my father brought from London was not the little parasites but his temper. The rows between my mother and father grew in ferocity. My mother had rented a house in Marston, just big enough for all of us. My father's outbursts did not surprise me, but I had never seen my mother so upset. One Sunday evening as he left she was almost out of her mind. Instead of feeling sorry for her and comforting her, I was irritated by her weeping. Why was she making all this noise? I yelled at her to stop. She ran upstairs, sobbing, 'You don't understand', and I didn't. How could I? But I was unnerved. I have no idea what caused these confrontations – money, sex, loneliness, frustration? Perhaps it was because my father had to return to the hell of the Blitz and needed love and humouring and looking after hand and foot, which was something my mother was never prepared to offer.

I had one distressing encounter with my father. He had caught me talking to a group of schoolboys in the nearby park. I was not supposed to talk to boys and I ran away. In my panic I ran into the dead end of an air-raid shelter. I came out and my father gave me a violent clout across my ear. That in turn led to a row with my mother when we got back because we were still Communists and didn't believe in corporal punishment, particularly for nothing more than talking to boys. 'I hit her because she ran away from me, not because she talked to boys!' I did not believe him. But my mother did. 'It was quite wrong of you to have run away from your father!' However, the moment he went back to London, she took my side again.

The incident did not deter me from talking to boys but it had its effects nonetheless. My father had looked foolish as he waited for me at the entrance of the air-raid shelter. Furthermore, he had behaved like the bourgeois paterfamilias we had so despised in Berlin. I began to respect him less but at the same time to be more frightened of his outbursts. He had played right into my mother's hands, since she was always ready to alienate me from him.

I now attended Burlington School, which had been evacuated from Acton in London to share the buildings of Milham Ford school in Marston. Sadly for my future, it was no match for Henrietta Barnett, either academically or socially. The school was streamed and I was put into the 'A' stream. To be in anything else was a hopeless prospect. In the 'B' stream you were left with some self-respect, but you were known to be useless and treated accordingly if you were placed in 'C'. I was very aware of this inequality, but if it worried me I ignored it. In many ways I was happier there. Some of my self-assurance had come back and I was so much more proficient in English. I still had a strong accent, which sounded more like a mixture of Welsh and American than German. I was not shunned by a Jewish faction because there was none. Acton is not a Jewish area and the school's standards would not have been impressive enough for properly ambitious Jewish parents. By then I had learnt to advertise my Polishness rather than my Jewishness. The hot temper for which Poles were fêted was reinforced by the colour of my hair. All the girls knew that 'red-haired people have hot tempers'. I played on both these prejudices and lost my temper more often than I really wanted to.

My foreignness did exclude me from one activity, but it was extra-curricular and had to do with Christmas cards. Christmas cards were new to me. They do not exist in Germany, and I spent hours in the stationery shops looking at snowscapes, robin redbreasts, strange shapes that were puddings with holly on top, and old-fashioned means of transport, as well as Father Christmases and Christian iconography.

With so many postmen in the armed forces, the Post Office called on schoolchildren to help deliver the cards as a patriotic act. It also sounded fun and meant pocket money. A group of us rolled up at the nearest recruiting place, and a genial Post Office official explained our duties and our reward, and took our names. He realised immediately that I was not English, said he was very sorry, but they couldn't take me. 'The Civil Service only employs British people.' He suggested that I should write in and ask if they would make an exception. I walked out and told him – but only in my mind and in German – to stuff his Christmas cards.

I have often thought back to when they wouldn't trust me with their absurd cards: when I launched my Royal Navy ship, when Bill and I received guests in Lancaster House, when we had dinner at Number Ten and at Number Eleven, and various other establishment events. But apart from the episode over Christmas cards, I did not mind being a foreigner and a Pole, though I was more circumspect about my Jewishness. I went to school assembly partly because there was no other Jewish child at first, and I did not want to be singled out. I only ever like to be singled out for admiration – occasionally for rebellion – and no one was going to admire me for being Jewish.

Jews in England were, and possibly still are, only a barely tolerated minority. I knew from my previous school that it was no good being the pathetic Jewish girl persecuted and expelled from another country. I felt quite happy in my role of a temperamental Polish girl because I was not brought up to feel any pride in being Jewish. I was a Jew only because Hitler would have it so. I believed in Internationalism, and so it did not matter what national role I chose to play.

I sensed the undercurrent of anti-Semitism in the school, and when a new girl arrived who did not deny her Jewishness, it surfaced. June was pretty, but not in an Anglo-Saxon way, and she was made fun of because she had very dark, frizzy hair spurting out from two plaits. 'Look at that funny hair,' they giggled, 'she's a Jewess!' And though I could and should have pointed to my straight ginger hair, I didn't. I did not carry my denial to London. When the school returned to its building in West London, there was another Jewish girl in the class called Marion Davies. We became friends. But I still went to assembly instead of staying behind each morning with Marion and a few others from different classes; nor did I stay away from school on Jewish holidays. I could not stay away because my parents would have objected, and I would not have wanted to anyway. I was as friendly with the non-Jews as with Marion.

Sometime around the end of the war, another Jewish girl arrived.

She was German and an orphan whose parents had perished in a concentration camp. I pretended to welcome her, but I resented her. She was popular, she attracted lots of interest and sympathy, and she was without any subterfuge. She played no roles. The particular drama of her circumstances – orphaned by the enemy with the gruesome facts skated over – made it taboo for anyone to show anti-Semitism and for me to show my irritation when she talked about her sufferings. Her circumstances made me feel uncomfortable and probably guilty – guilty that she had suffered and I had escaped, guilty that I resented her. Even the ringleader of the xenophobes, unsuitably named after a flower (Rose, Jasmine, Violet?), resisted taunting this girl.

Quite early on in that school I made it clear, not to the staff but to the other girls, that I was a Communist. I never had anything but pride in that part of my identity, and in view of my upbringing that is no surprise. There was a fellow soul, called Sheila Bennett, who like me had been born a Communist. We both attended assembly – compulsory unless one was a practising Jew – but there were certain songs or verses Sheila and I would not sing. Our pet aversion was 'I pledge to thee my country'. Girls of our religion could not possibly even simulate such blind patriotism. For me it was worse than praising God and mouthing belief in 'Jesus Christ'. Another hymn we banned was 'Onward Christian Soldiers'. We were, after all, pacifists, though our pacifism excluded anything to do with the Soviet Union. Together we sang – not, of course, at assembly – the song of the Red Air Force, whose courage had kept a fifth of the world 'red'! I sang the German words for this song and Sheila hummed the tune, but the *Internationale* was always a bilingual duet. Neither of us knew all the words but we stressed the damned and the *verdammt*.

Eventually, in the Sixth Form, I decided I would no longer participate in any assembly, saw the headmistress Miss Burgess, and told her that I was not Christian but Jewish and that I did not believe in God. This snooty woman put me in my place with a scathing 'I see. You believe in nothing!', and made it sound like 'You are nothing'. I had met my match in arrogance, though she excelled in contempt. My opting out of assembly was quite a step:

no one had done it before and I could not have managed it in a lower form. I was glad and proud of myself, though that icicle of scorn from the headmistress took a long time to thaw out. A splinter lodges still and can hurt like an old war wound.

I got on perfectly well with most of the staff, but not all. The fact that I was not English, and didn't strive hard enough to be like the English, was the main obstacle; being clever was sometimes the saving grace. The art mistress and I did not see eye to eye since I was a Dadaist even then. The maths teacher, with her huge bosom, small head and peremptory manner, disliked me and I disliked her. She was an ostentatious Christian and not keen on anything foreign and non-Christian. I was good at algebra and geometry, but my problems with English measures irritated her. I also irritated the games mistress, who hissed at me in the middle of a netball match with another school, 'Stop making an exhibition of yourself!' As centre-forward, I had scored both of the two goals, my style was flamboyant, and I was showing off, not a suitable member of a British team. After she cautioned me, my game collapsed, we lost the match and the other girls were cross with her.

I now have great sympathy for the German teacher. I kept interrupting and even correcting her. I was bored, I wanted to show off, and as she was a proper German, by which I mean she was not Jewish, she may well have been the target of my revenge as the only representative of the German nation to hand. Poor woman, with her unattractive accent and ungainly figure, she lacked that stereotypical German ability to enforce discipline. In the end she appealed to Miss Burgess and I was, quite rightly, banned from her lessons.

English being my second language continued to help me to excel at grammar but it landed me in difficulties with pronunciation. When, for instance, the class in unison was reading out a passage from Shakespeare, Miss Spencer stopped us and asked who had said 'goaler' instead of 'gaoler'. I put up my hand and she said, 'That's all right, that's different.' It irked me that she was so ready to let me off. As a foreigner, I carried a lot of chips on my shoulder.

# TWENTY-ONE

# What Might Have Happened to Me

By the time we got back to London, sometime in 1942, my mother had been vindicated by Hitler's invasion of Russia, which happened in June 1941. 'You see! I was right about Stalin and the pact!' I had never doubted it and was glad that the Russians and Stalin were now Britain's allies.

We no longer lived on Haverstock Hill but in Ealing, in Hanger Lane, so that I could continue to go to Burlington School. Greystoke Lodge, where we had a flat, is set in grounds that for the duration of the war were turned over to allotments for the residents who in peacetime would not have been seen dead on those consolation plots for the urban poor. My father was overjoyed with the chance to cultivate. He and his forefathers had never tilled the soil before because Jews in Poland and Russia were barred from the land. Here, in Ealing, my father grew radishes, peas, green beans and the occasional useless but pretty sweet pea. Our meat rations were supplemented by lights, or lungs. My mother told the butcher we had a cat, and he sold her this offal that English people only give to their pets and I wished continentals did too. My mother cooked it with rice and I ate as little of it as I could. The paleness and texture of those vesicles were revolting.

We were the only Jews and foreigners in Greystoke Lodge until a Polish couple moved in. They were not Jewish Poles but true Poles – so true that he was a member of the Polish government-in-exile. Nevertheless, we were drawn together by our foreignness, and in the summer we used to sit together on the grass and on deck chairs. Even my father swallowed his anti-Polish phobia and Mr and Mrs Polish government-in-exile seemed to enjoy their conversations, which were lively. They had moved to Ealing to be near the Polish community. For my mother, the move to Ealing had isolated her even more. It removed her from the temptation of the dark eyes of our doctor in Chalk Farm – but also, and this was more serious, from the Left-wing Club in Upper Park Road and the Laterndl cabaret in Finchley Road, both run by and for German-speaking refugees. She did find a non-political group of refugees that met weekly to read and discuss literature, mainly German though some Russian too. Otherwise she had nothing, certainly no outlet for her passion for politics. Jaques Mendelsohn we saw rarely. His visits stopped altogether after my father had refused to lend him yet more money.

Now and again my mother took me to see Russian films in a place like a church hall with uncomfortable folding chairs and a screen that was taken down after each performance. We saw *Lenin in October* and various films about the good life in collective farms. The soundtrack crackled, the screen was covered in the snow of worn-out reels. But it was manna for my mother's political soul and I imbibed it too – from Lenin in that stance where he lifts his hand and eyes towards the horizon, to young men and women working in the fields and singing with love for Russia and each other. The films were uplifting, optimistic and escapist like Hollywood films but less well choreographed and more monotonous. They were in black and white, but it was obvious that the women's plaits were all as blonde as the corn and they could easily have been part of the Aryan cast in a Nazi film. Social realism did not allow one brunette among all those haystacks, a far cry from the early Russian films that had inspired my parents in Weimar Berlin.

The news was full of the sacrifices of Soviet soldiers and civilians and how swaying fields of corn were burnt to ashes by retreating farmers. This scorched earth policy evoked great admiration from the British people. My mother was not in the least surprised that the Soviet people were fighting so hard. 'They have so much to lose, more than any other nation. They remember what it was like before the Revolution. Now they are happy, they are free, they love their country, they love their freedom!' I agreed. I sang '*Denn es gibt kein anderers Land der Erde, wo das Herz so frei dem Menschen schlägt*', the German words of a patriotic Soviet song, and I believed every one of them. To me the Soviet Union really was the country were people felt freer than anywhere else on earth.

When my father was not around, I also sang and listened to songs about the Chattanooga Choochoo and nightingales in Berkeley Square. But the radio was mostly used for following the back and forth of the Russian campaign. I was anxious during the summer months when Hitler began to surge, but luckily the East European winter showed no more respect for him than it had done for Napoleon. When the German troops began to freeze in their tracks with inadequate clothing, I felt no compassion, only *Schadenfreude*, as I thought of my Polish cousins. There were no good Germans for me at that time. My three exceptions – when I thought of them at all – I envisaged freezing to death in a concentration camp, and not on the Russian front. When in December 1941 the United States finally entered the war, the relief was immense. America was unbeatable. But the seasonal see-saw on the Russian front was not over and the Stalingrad campaign in the winter of 1942 was a nerve-racking episode. I never again had that clear resolve to commit suicide but it was not until Hitler was crushed at Stalingrad that I felt safe.

My parents followed the call from Stalin, the British Communist Party and other less extreme left-wing groups for the Allies to start a 'Second Front Now!' They did not paint graffiti on the walls, write letters to *The Times*, or lobby our Member of Parliament – we were much too foreign for any such participation. But they talked about it endlessly and blamed the Western Allies for prevaricating while the Russian people 'are bleeding to death'. At school, Sheila Bennet and I echoed our parents.

On that morning in June 1944 when we heard that the Allies had landed on the coast of northern France, we were euphoric. But it was nearly a year before the war ended. In that year Dresden was firebombed, and London attacked by flying bombs. Belsen and other concentration camps were opened up by the Allies and we began to understand what had happened to our relatives.

The flying bombs arrived a few days after D-Day. They came in planes without pilots and were sinister as well as deadly. They came when our class was taking the General Certificate exams. Halfway through our arithmetic paper, a flying bomb cut out above us, part of the school hall was damaged and I lost my nerve. To my disgrace, I was the only one to have hysterics, which only went to show how unstable we foreigners were. The exam was stopped and everyone was graded according to their term's work. I shall never be certain why I had burst out sobbing. Square roots or bombs? I had been in some difficulty just before the bomb began to hover. I was always nervous whenever one of these malevolent things cut out over Greystoke Lodge, but I had always kept calm before. After the flying bombs came the V bombs or rockets which were even more alarming and heralded as 'Hitler's secret weapon'. This implied hidden powers and awakened an old anxiety in me.

German civilians suffered increased bombing from conventional bombs; these were less sinister but more devastating. When Berlin was bombed, I shut out any pain and pity. 'Serves them right' is all I allowed myself to feel. Twenty years later, I wept. Dresden was blasted and burnt and photographs showed a wilderness of ruins. They told us of the conflagration made worse by the fire storms, and of the huge number of civilian victims, and I thought: 'Good. Less of them. Less of those dreadful and murderous people. The women are no better than the men and the children will only grow up into Nazi horrors.' Paris had fallen by then, and though I am not clear exactly when we knew of the fate of my mother's family in France, nor what had happened in Poland, we knew enough. I am not proud of my reaction to the dreadful fate of Dresden but when I remember the context, I am not too ashamed.

When the war ended in Europe – and I confess that the Far Eastern theatre of war was of indifference to me except when I saw it in American films – we were glad but we did not celebrate. Like the relief felt after surviving a hurricane or an earthquake, our sense of deliverance was tempered by apprehension of how much devastation we would find. Nothing of what was happening to my relatives in Poland had come out during the war. But in 1942 my uncle Charles, who had fled to Perpignan, got news that Regina and Hélène had been taken from Paris to Auschwitz. If he managed to pass this on to my mother, she certainly did not tell me. Their exact fate – the ovens at Auschwitz-Birkenau – was probably not known before the end of the war when my parents also learnt that my two uncles by marriage had come out from concentration camps, alive but damaged, and that all my father's and all my mother's relatives, including those I had met in Lubartov and Warsaw, had vanished. This disappearance was not gleaned from reports but deduced from an absence of any sign of life.

In 1942, Charles knew not only about the deportation of Regina and Hélène, but that Mania and her small son Lucien were being hidden in the middle of France by a French family. My aunt Sonia has told me that before the war started Mania had decided she could no longer tolerate Michel, who was a petty tyrant. She was on the verge of leaving him for a Frenchman – not a Jew – when war broke out and both Michel and her lover were called up and left for the front. When the Germans stepped up their campaign to get rid of all Jews, it was her lover's mother and sister who took the enormous risk of harbouring a Jewish woman and her child while he was away first in the army and then in a prisoner-of-war camp. In the second week of July 1942, Mania received a note from a friend to warn her that the Germans were rounding up all Jews, including women and children. She immediately passed this on to Regina and Paul. At 3 a.m. on 16 July she watched from her window as two Jewish families were pushed into vans by uniformed police. Then they came up to her flat and hammered on her door. 'We know you're there,' they shouted, but she kept quiet and did not open the door. They hammered each day from Tuesday till Saturday. On Sunday, she and Lucien left and went to Joue les Tours near Tours, where her lover's mother and sister lived, and stayed there for two and a half years.

Mania's own account features only neighbours and friends. She would have regarded it as improper to mention anything like a lover to me, her niece. It is from Sonia's account that I infer all might have ended happily had Michel not been put into a concentration camp – a series of camps as it turned out. Dare one say that all might have ended happily if he had not come out? No, one has to say all might have ended more happily if he had not come out a mental and physical wreck and Mania had not been tormented by guilt, a sense of duty, and whatever it was that led her to give up her lover and the chance of happiness.

As soon as he was able to, Michel began to import plastic gloves that looked like leather, and made a lot of money. That was particularly fortuitous, because he had come back from the camps with an obsession for travel, and when he died in 1985 there was hardly a place on earth he and Mania had not visited. This was partly due to a thirst for knowledge for its own sake, but not just that. His quest was not to discover the source of any river, but the source of human iniquity. In his search to understand what had happened to him in the camps, to get a glimpse of what might have been inside his twisted torturers, Michel was eager to see as much of human beings in different environments as he possibly could. In his frenzy for knowledge, he became not only a traveller, but a walking encyclopedia and catalogue of the contents of all major museums of the world. This and the journeys were also an escape from contemplating those very experiences he was trying to understand, or at least an attempt at such an escape. He was never free.

Primo Levi has written about the guilt suffered by everyone who came out of the camps alive. Michel, too, was tormented. I don't know the circumstances of his survival, only that in Paris speculation and accusation spared no one. Stories were told of how Michel had survived and at whose expense. But then the accusers themselves were survivors and therefore not free from guilt. What Michel did almost as soon as he had come back from the camps was to write a letter to my parents. Forgive me, the letter began, but I have to write and tell you about all the things that happened. Everything I saw in the camps. Everything that happened to me. It is so gruesome, so hideous, so painful that I have to tell you about it. Perhaps writing it down will make it feel better for me. It is driving me mad and I cannot keep it to myself.

My parents, who could not bring themselves to tell me Hélène's fate, were relentless when it came to this letter. 'You have to know what went on, it is your duty and for your own good. You are quite old enough.' I was seventeen and they were right, it was certainly my duty. I could not read the letter myself as it was in Yiddish and so they sat down with me and read it out, translating into German whenever necessary. After only a few paragraphs of atrocities, unimaginable if one is not a crazed sadist, all experienced or witnessed by Michel, I begged them to stop. But they would not spare me. 'You only have to listen! What about those who had to endure it!' Such was the scorn and bitterness in their voices that I listened on. I listened as Michel wanders into a room with rows and rows of tables. On each table lies the body of a naked woman. The women have been used for medical experiments carried out without anaesthetic. He touches one body with a buttock cut out. 'I touched her and she quivered. She was still warm.'

I ran out and locked myself into the bathroom. I sobbed and sobbed and in between sobbing bathed my eyes to no effect. To make up for my cowardice, I watched the film of Belsen showing at the local Odeon. I sat in the back row and could hardly believe that those people were my people and that what had happened to them had been scheduled for me. I howled. The usherette asked: 'Are you all right?' 'Yes.' I went home. The truth was that I did not want to know. It may have been my duty, it may have been 'good for me' but I did not even want to think about it. I did not want to dwell on what might have happened to me, on the horrors and the indignities meted out to people like me who had not been lucky enough to catch a train to the Hook of Holland and a boat to Harwich. Apart from the brutality, what upset me then, and alarms me now, is the anonymity. The corpses, whether still alive or already dead, had been eroded of any vestige of identity and individuality. When they were tipped into the mass grave, it was like tipping a month's delivery of coal down a shute.

When shortly after the war my mother took André and me to Paris, I looked forward to it with ambivalence. To see Paris was exciting, but it was Hélène's city. To meet my aunts, uncle, uncles by marriage, and Lucien my cousin, was exciting too, but mixed with the reluctance of being brought face to face with what they had gone through and what they had been spared. And there would be the painful gaps of Hélène and her mother. The force of all this and my own mixed reactions did not hit me till I got to Paris.

We flew from Northolt and were met by Mania and Charles. Charles had escaped from Vichy France by crossing the Pyrenees into Spain. Much as I loathe Franco, it has to be said that Charles and others who sought refuge in Spain were treated well, first in the camps and later when they were all set free. To account for this puzzling behaviour of Franco's a rumour gave Franco a Jewish grandmother.

Charles may have been a Polish Jew but he looked every inch a dashing Frenchman. A sort of Yves Montand who swept me off my feet. He was warm, affectionate and told me how pretty and feminine I was. He bought me a Lancôme lipstick and an exquisite pair of burgundy snakeskin court shoes which I put on the chest of drawers in the hotel bedroom so that I could look at them when I went to bed. He treated me as a niece but also as a pretty young woman. Just a hint of incestuous interest. But underneath that charm and air of insouciance Charles was in torment. He was back in Paris after an absence of four years but it was without his wife, without his sister and without his beloved niece.

Hélène's father, Paul, had come back from the concentration camp and Charles was wild with bitterness against him. As the Germans were nearing Paris, he had urged Paul to pack up and flee, as he and Germaine were doing. 'I begged Paul over and over again to come with us, to take what he could and to leave everything else.' But Paul was obstinate. He had a small child, it wasn't so easy to pack up everything and leave. He decided they should wait and see what happened. 'It won't be so bad,' he comforted himself, to Charles' despair. That morning in July 1942, when Mania rushed to warn her sister and Paul that they were rounding up all Jews including women and children, Paul had yet another excuse. 'I am not well,' he said, 'I can't go anywhere. I have bronchitis.'

Charles never forgave Paul. I am not sure that his sisters did either, but they hid it. Their resentment came out as antipathy towards Paul's new wife. Even I, even now, have a block about her name and it is so unfair. This perfectly nice woman, whose name is in fact Masha, had lost her husband in a concentration camp and only she and her daughter, Jeanette, had survived. Jeanette grew up to establish the fashion house of Chloe and later to buy Ungaro. Hence Paul's life of luxury, because his step-daughter brought him into the firm and treated him generously; she also called her first baby Hélène. When Paul had married my aunt Rivale in Lubartov, my grandmother had deemed him not good enough because he was a plumber.

Shortly after his marriage, Paul invited Michel and Mania to dinner. Mania came into the room, saw Paul's second wife and fainted. My mother's reaction to Rivale's replacement was less dramatic. 'Nothing much to her' was how she demolished and denied her. This was during our visit to Paris when my mother must have met Paul, but I never did. If I had, I might have learnt the truth about Hélène. I do not know what subterfuge my mother and her siblings used to avoid the meeting, nor why I did not make more of a fuss. Everyone colluded in the game of 'We don't know what happened to Hélène', but as I walked along the streets of Paris I wondered about her and thought: 'She knows these places; she has walked along these streets; where is she now?'

When Paul came to London some years later, my mother still did not invite me to meet him although by then I knew the facts about Hélène's death: 'I didn't think you'd be interested,' she said innocently – that feigned innocence that she assumed too often. And why did she never tell me that her parents – Malle and Menasseh, my beloved grandfather with the red beard – had been murdered along with everyone else in the Warsaw ghetto? They had moved to Warsaw before the war to be with Hanna and Leibu. 'They died quite naturally in their bed' was my mother's story to me. It is mad that my parents forced me to listen to atrocities suffered by strangers but kept quiet or fabricated some nonsense about the fate of those I loved.

An extraordinary event that took place in Paris during our visit, was the 'Presse Ball', which was a ball given by and for the Jews. I saw no fine gowns or glittering jewels but it was a ball all the same. It had a band, lots and lots of people, nearly everyone danced and the air was festive. I was astonished and thrilled: 'All those Jews! How marvellous there are still so many Jews left!' The Germans had failed in their extermination. It felt like a crowd of thousands, though there may only have been several hundred. When a man came up and asked me to dance, I refused him because I didn't fancy him. But the moment he walked away, I kicked myself: 'How could I? How awful of me. He was probably in a camp!' But it was too late.

The saddest-looking person in Paris was Malke Zucker, a friend of my mother from Lubartov who like so many Lubartovians had settled in Paris. She cried daily and nightly and her eyes were permanently pink and swollen. She had lost her husband and two sons in the camps. Her daughter had survived; a tiny fragile young woman whose breath always smelled of garlic and who had the most entreating eyes. Did the eyes beg her mother to look at her? To remind her that she was there and needed and loved her mother? It took Malke Zucker only a few years to die of cancer. Her daughter had not been enough to keep her alive.

I may have regretted refusing a stranger a dance, but refuse I did. I may have been sorry for Malke Zucker and her daughter, but I was also irritated by pink eyes and excessive smell of garlic, and grief that showed. I was irritated because I needed to minimise, to downgrade the awfulness of what had happened to them. I looked away. I turned my head. I could not believe I was really Jewish. I did not feel a Jew. Was I a Jew? I didn't look Jewish! Was it all a mistake? Wasn't I liberated from the ties of an ethnic group, a group based on one's birth? I pushed aside the thought that all this dark and unspeakable horror might have happened to me, and very nearly did, time and again. I couldn't believe I was a Jew, I couldn't believe I had escaped.

# TWENTY-TWO

# From Marxist to Non-Jewish Jew

1945 was a national turning point twice over: the war ended and the Labour Government came in. I observed the end of the war with a girl from school who lived above the family's fish and chip shop, whose clothes always smelt of rancid oil and whose father was in the last stages of syphilis. The two of us went to Whitehall, watched Churchill wave to the intoxicated crowds and went home. When the Labour Party came to power, I was with Deirdre, who wouldn't be seen dead in a fish and chip shop. She lived in Greystoke Place, next door to Greystoke Lodge, and was a blonde and blue-eyed Grace Kelly lookalike. The Germans would have adored her colouring: so Aryan. We had spent the day at Roehampton swimming pool and were on our way home, tightly jammed into a crowded tube train. I was hanging onto a leather strap when in the newspapers of passengers lucky to be sitting down I saw the headlines announcing 'Socialists in!' I could hardly believe it. At last I was going to live in a country whose government had politics similar enough to ours! Not the same but similar enough. A pity about Churchill, but those languid Lord Halifax kind of men would be replaced!

Deirdre saw no cause to celebrate. She and her family were conventional Conservatives and feared for their savings, their shares, their standard of living and even their jewels when the Socialists came in. They were also anti-Semitic, but Deirdre granted me exemption from her prejudice by declaring: 'You're all right because you are Polish and in Poland there are so many Jews!' 'All right' as opposed to a Jew from Germany or Britain where our numbers were unimpressively low. Sad irony that by the time of her extraordinary pronouncement there was hardly a Jew left in Poland.

Why did I bother about her? I have no answer except that she was the only girl of my age, though she looked much older, living in the two blocks. In 1945, when both of us were seventeen, I looked about fifteen and she looked in her early twenties. The friendship did not survive. Her physical maturity and worldly wisdom intrigued me but she had no interests and her family were bigots. To them a Jew was a Jew, whether from Belgravia or Poland. Around Hanger Lane there were very few if any Jews, but my parents discovered the Jacobs who lived five minutes away. I don't know how they met, but this friendship brought out their inward-looking back-to-the-shtetl tendencies, though the Jacobs were not from Poland. They were Reform Jews from Germany, bourgeois to their last dinner set and utterly apolitical. I cannot imagine what formed the basis of their friendship – being fellow Jewish refugees in Ealing, I suppose.

Herr Jacob was ugly and withdrawn. Frau Jacob was pretty and sociable but had an offputting obsession about blackheads. She loved squeezing them out and was always on the look-out for them, on herself and on others. My adolescent skin was no roses and cream but had nothing worse than spots and freckles. Only within that puckered scar on my neck lurked the odd blackhead. None was safe from Frau Jacob's fingernails, draped in a white hankerchief as she got to work. Protest was useless.

Their son Albert was my age, a compulsive liar. So was his friend with the anglicised name of Kevin. Our parents pushed us together but we bored one another and Albert and Kevin were an unattractive pair. It sounds like *Fiddler on the Roof* marriage broking, but my father, and unbelievably my mother too, found another Jewish boy with whom to match-make. His parents were refugees from Eastern Europe but otherwise had even less in common with my parents than the Jacobs. A dreary pair whose son was flabby, pasty and large like one of those wretched calves milk-fed till they reach an unnatural size. This trio sometimes came to tea, which was really *Kaffee und Kuchen* and always interminable. The pale boy and I sat in sullen silence and conversation between the adults was marked by uneasy gaps. Away from his parents the boy may well have been a ball of fire.

Apart from my parent's preference for Jewish boys for me, there was another strand of Jewish atavism and one far more damaging to me. It was also mixed up with my mother's growing determination to leave my father, which had nothing to do with Jewishness. She wanted me to have a career that would enable me to provide for her – not for me but for *her* – and her choice of career conformed to that of a Jewish mother.

My parents were so ill-matched that had they been left undisturbed in Germany they would have drifted apart. In England they were chained together as refugees, and the strain of being adrift in exile made them more on edge and even less tolerant of each other. Their quarrels in Berlin had been grim enough, but by the time we got to Ealing the atmosphere was unbearable. My father, who still worked in Great Titchfield Street, was due home from work every evening around seven. The lift shaft was next to our flat and whenever around that time I heard the whirring noise of the lift as it moved slowly up, my heart beat with anxiety as I wondered what the evening would bring. Living with my parents was like living in a minefield.

Their dreadful rows were the only noise to shatter the genteel calm of Greystoke Lodge now that there were no more bombs and rockets. The only way I could ever get them to halt their battle was to yell that I was never ever going to get married. A threat that horrified my father. '*Um Gott*,' he said quietly as he swallowed most of '*Gottes Willen*.' Even my mother, that disciple of Ibsen, was dismayed.

My father, though not happy in this marriage, had no intention of ending it. My mother, however, had made up her mind to leave him. But how? He was well off; he drew a good salary and had made some money on stocks and shares. But according to the law as it stood then, she had no right to any of it. To leave him meant destitution. In Berlin, the Party and friends would have provided help and a refuge for her, and in Weimar Berlin especially the atmosphere would have been more than sympathetic to her plight. In Weimar, Nora would have left her husband and the doll's house. But in England my mother was in difficulties. Her only salvation was me. If I loved her, if I cared what became of her, I would take up a profession that would make enough money to support me, her and my brother. I would not want to see her suffer for ever, would I? True, I was only sixteen, I had only just got the matriculation results, it would take some years, but she could wait.

She had by then succeeded in alienating me from my father, a campaign begun way back in Berlin. So determined was she to prove to me that my father didn't care for me that she used to dig up all sorts of silly stories. According to her, when I was still a baby and they took me in my pram to the park, my father always insisted on eating the apple she had cut into small pieces for me. These tales had their effect, but then my father himself had helped her campaign by being an old-fashioned *Herr des Hauses*, if not over my mother, at least over me and especially in my adolescence and later. His word was law. Friends must be Jewish, lipstick and even powder were for whores only, as was staying out after ten and receiving letters from boys. He intercepted a letter sent by a boy I had met through Daisy and kept it for months. Then he brought it out as proof of my sinfulness.

In the end I studied dentistry, but I have never quite solved the puzzle. Why did I not rebel? Why did I not tell my mother to find her own solution? Why, for six years and more, did I study something for which I had no special talent or interest? I had done no science since that day at Henrietta Barnett School when I watched the permanganate crystals dance to the heat of the bunsen burner. I liked art and history best and wanted to do a degree in history.

You can't do history, my mother said. Your father will never agree. I have spoken to him. It is not practical, he said, what good is a history degree if we are ever refugees again? 'She must be a doctor or a dentist.' My son the lawyer, the doctor, the dentist – he, and she too, were conforming to that stereotypical Jewish stance. In this case, 'my son' was 'my daughter' because my mother could hardly wait another eight or nine years for the son. I have never understood how this attitude deals with the realities of being a refugee. Lawyers who fled to this country from Nazi Germany had to do lowly jobs such as packing up parcels; they were only qualified to practise in Germany. Doctors and dentists had to requalify and pass language tests.

I was in a dilemma. The rule, then as now, stipulates that if your father earns over a certain amount he has to pay part or all of your fees. My father earned more than enough to make him liable for all fees and maintenance and to ensure my continuing dependence and utter misery. It was out of the question for me to go to university and read something against his wishes. He would have let me study art but only as part of a fashion course at the end of which he would take me into the rag trade. I didn't want that and my mother was aghast at the prospect. The thought of her daughter so demeaning herself!

So I started science from scratch and matriculated after a couple of terms of biology and chemistry and physics, and felt sorry for myself and for my mother and wondered, as I do still, why I had never had the guts to talk to my father directly about doing history. But then my mother, that most convincing of advocates, had failed: she assured me he had utterly ruled out a history degree. 'I wouldn't talk to him about it if I were you,' she advised, 'he'll only get livid.' The deterrent worked.

The school and its snooty head had failed me too; as indeed they failed every other pupil. No one ever discussed prospects and degrees and careers with pupils or parents. The school agreed to my mother's request and I started science. Miss Burgess's only comment came at the end of the school report. It was unfortunate, she wrote, that I had decided to do science: 'Silvia has too artistic a temperament.' Not one word about my talent for history or geography, or how I might use that artistic temperament, whatever it meant – red hair, rebellious, undiplomatic, uningratiating and different?

The physics teacher at Burlington School was hopeless and I would never have passed, especially as she was the butt of my delinquent tendencies. It was only a small class but we played up that plain, dowdy and awkward woman without pity. So I went to the North London Polytechnic to get Science 'A' levels and discovered the fascination of science. Towards the end of that year the atmosphere at home was worse than ever. To wait while I found a place at medical or dental school – not easy for a woman at that time – and then to spend another four or five years studying while living at home, was purgatory and I couldn't face it. I began to be more concerned about myself than about my mother. The only course open was to leave home and be financially independent for three years, after which I would qualify as a person separate from my father and be eligible for a grant. I would be a physiotherapist. My uncle Charles wrote to say, don't let her: doctors don't marry physiotherapists! I would be a nurse and get away from it all immediately. I applied to Guy's Hospital and was accepted. And then I had a stroke of bad luck – though I never would have tolerated the strictures of a nursing career.

In Greystoke Lodge there lived the Widdowsons: a dentist with his wife and only son called William. William was a toddler who like to play by the allotments. One day he fell on a piece of wire that was meant to keep away the birds. It lacerated his ear so that the lobe hung on a thread. I washed the blood from his face and neck, and attached the dangling lobe to the ear with a plaster. His parents were forever grateful. Unfortunately, Mr Widdowson's father too was a dentist, an eminent one who had taught at King's College Hospital. My mother told Mr Widdowson about my hopes, or rather her hopes, and he asked his father to pull some strings. That's how I got into King's College Dental School. Not on merit, not on personality, and not because I impressed the interviewers, who looked unapproachable and dour. My foreign accent and the very name 'Szulman', of all impossible names, could hardly have enchanted them. Rugby-playing men of medical families – that is what medical schools wanted, and King's with its Church of England connections favoured those who were also Anglicans. They must have asked, 'Why do you want to do dentistry, Miss Szulman?' and I can't imagine what my answer could have been.

I need not have accepted. The chemistry lecturer at the polytechnic, who also taught at Guy's Medical School, had promised me a place there the following year. It was crazy of me not to have waited for that. I would love to have done medicine. I just couldn't bear the thought of extending my time in Ealing.

I was the only non-British and non-Christian student in the Dental School. Eventually I did discover two Jewish and one Asian student in the Medical School and two years later the Dental School accepted another Jew. As if to boast about it, they chose one with an unmistakable Jewish name and a nose out of a *Der Stürmer* cartoon. The proportion of women to men remained minuscule.

Some of the work I liked, some of it I hated. But I had a wonderful time – enough to drown the sorrow of doing something I did not want to do. Is there anything to match the hilarity and craziness of student life in a hospital? It was a most effective antidote to the atmosphere at home. With hard work and a hectic social life I hardly had a moment to sink into contemplation or feel sorry for myself. Except when I got home to Ealing. And there I found solace in reading Voltaire. Not my mother's serious tracts but *Candide*. That absurd catalogue of disasters used to cheer me up.

The wish to belong to an ethnic or religious group surfaced in my last year at King's and I am not at all sure why. I was not lonely; or rather, not alone. I had lots of friends, mostly among medical students. But I was a Jew, I was foreign, and therefore unique, and I had a marked foreign accent. I was also a woman. And being better-looking, better-dressed and more lively than most of the few women students no doubt helped to transform me into something exotic. I was therefore an oddity and an outsider. But that was nothing new and it was infinitely better than my experience as a freak in the school on Haverstock Hill. Here my very freakishness made me popular.

The only thing that bothered my fellow students was my politics. I was red-hot Labour – the nearest practical alternative to Marxism – in a cold blue sea of Tories; and at a time when the National Health Service was being hawked from medical school to medical school in the face of great hostility. When a civil servant from the relevant department adressed a meeting to explain the new service, the poor man was heckled with contempt by everyone except me. This was my one eccentricity the others simply could not understand but it did not exclude me from friendships. Had my hair been very dark and very frizzy and my nose typically Jewish, it might have been different – or had I been black or brown. The only Asian medical student in the place was shunned. He was the loneliest man I have ever seen. He always sat alone, ate alone and, apart from ward rounds, walked alone. Worse still, when there was a spate of thieving from the cloakroom his fellow students suspected him.

I had girlfriends but I never met their families. It may have been coincidence that they invited me when everyone had gone out. The exception was my friend Julie, whose father was the hospital governor. He himself never showed any bigotry, but his wife and son and daughter-in-law were quite open in their anti-Semitism. Julie's mother looked pained and the younger ones literally looked down their noses. When I introduced Julie to a medical student from Guy's whose name was Hyman, a name only Jewish parents could possibly inflict on a son, Julie's brother and wife pointedly left the room when Hyman and I walked in. The relationship between Julie and Hyman did not last long, but Julie and I stayed friends till she qualified and went to Australia. My mother had tried hard to sabotage this friendship, though not on racist grounds: 'Julie is jealous of you,' she warned me, 'don't trust her.' Echoes of her attempts to turn me against Hélène.

Perhaps my need to look somewhere else for friends and a social life was triggered by the end of my relationship with a medical student. I was still striving for Englishness and the medical student was by accent and style the epitome of a middle-class Englishman. He was also very handsome, the darling of the nurses, and I was flattered by his attention. He was decent, kind but a bit boring and, despite his good looks, left me cold physically. So he sensibly called it a day, and I became rather depressed. Any hint of not being wanted can still shake me like the harshest rejection.

He had replaced another medical student whom I had met in Bournemouth. We were both there with our families for a summer holiday. They were from Manchester but he was a student at Guy's. After a few weeks he told me that his mother had warned him that he could not possibly marry a Jewess. As he seemed to agree with her, that was that as far as I was concerned and not because I wanted to marry him, which I did not. He was blond, good-looking but with a weak face and I suspect he turned out to be a good-for-nothing.

What must have bothered me more than unsatisfactory boyfriends was that I was doing something I did not want to do – and for four long years at that. And then in the background loomed the misery at home. My father had regressed deeper into the ethos of the ghetto, especially in his attitudes to my friends. He was so aggressively hostile to any non-Jewish boy or girl I brought home that I rarely did. My father would sit in the kitchen within earshot of the room where my friends and I were having tea or supper, and he would grumble loudly and angrily the whole time. I never thought that with my Marxist parents I would have to put up with such blatant chauvinism. They seemed to be regressing to *shtetl-*hood, yet they never set foot inside a London synagogue and were still Marxists. I must have been confused, or maybe I am more confused now then I was at the time. My memory is hazy about this period. I felt I was shrivelling further into my protective pupa. Wrong career, wrong home. Wrong country?

It was then that I began to extend my social circle in an unexpected direction. I don't know if I was trying to please my parents, or to rebel, or merely seeking something positive about being Jewish, but I found my way to the under-thirties section of the West London Synagogue. I got there by way of Daisy Meyer, with whom I had never lost touch. The Meyers belonged to the Reform Jewish community and lived in a semi-detached house in Stanmore. The semi was a far cry from that fine establishment on the Heerstrasse but only by being infinitely more modest. Even without a huge garden and without a live-in couple, it had a similar ambiance. Daisy's room was still decked out in flounces and the same dolls lived there, and took a back seat only when she went to do a degree in German at University College, London. Her mannerisms were those she had when she was ten but her corkscrew curls were trimmed into a more grown-up style. She gave the occasional party, which was fun, more so as my disciplinarian father allowed me to stay the night. He no longer scorned my friendship with Daisy: her family were upright and their circle was Jewish.

Through Daisy I met the Newman brothers and Freddie Tuckmann and through Freddie I eventually met Bill. This brought me back to the political world. But that is a large leap forward and seems now to span a gap of several years. In fact it was only months.

At the synagogue club I had met Hugo Gryn. Now he is the rabbi who presides over the West London Synagogue, who braodcasts, and is on a council to further understanding between Jews and Christians. He also liaises with Muslims. Then he was a student. Lively, wiry, with the wisdom of an older man – did he get that at Auschwitz? – and an ironic humour and a smile which he still has. A nice Jewish boy, and intelligent, and how my parents approved! But in spite of her approval, my mother zealously tried to divert him from his rabbinical path. Her zeal had not weakened and anyone who was an actual or potential religious officiant was still an irresistible challenge. But Hugo's faith and determination were stronger than poor Sister Beatrix's in Weimar Berlin.

Hugo used to visit me in Ealing and I used to visit him in his bedsitter which, he reminds me, was in Kilburn. We were good freinds, nothing romantic, nothing sexual. The very idea of my becoming a rabbi's wife had the making of a black comedy. But it was never even an idea – though perhaps one I unconsciously teased my parents with – and we quite soon lost touch and I did not see him again for years. I had all but forgotten his name when my mother brought us together again: Hugo was the officiant at her funeral in the Jewish cemetry in Golders Green. She had joined the West London Reform Synagogue a few years before her death, though not in order to attend. After Poland, neither she nor my father ever entered a synagogue again, not even on the Day of Atonement, yet both lie buried in the Jewish cemetry and the rites were carried out by a rabbi.

They joined simply to qualify for a burial plot and did not listen to the incantation of any rabbi until they were safe inside their coffins. And my mother specified that she was to be buried next to her husband, from who she had been separated for years. She was such an inconsistent woman who, could she have eavesdropped on her funeral oration, would have cheered. She was having it both ways. In that bare little chapel that looks like a waiting room on an out-of-the-way railway station, Hugo Gryn talked to the congregation of my mother's belief, not in God, but in Marx and how she had lent him books on Marxism and hoped to convert him. An unusual funeral address, unbearably moving and utterly right. It almost resurrected her.

Hugo has never forgotten that in one of the books my mother gave him she inscribed Marx's words: 'It is not enough to understand the world, you must work to change it!' She certainly made a lasting impression on him, but finally any triumph was his, not that he would see it that way. As for me and that synagogue, I never joined but I got as far as applying to become a member of the under-thirties club. The faces of the two young men and one young woman who interviewed me were perplexed when I told them that I had never belonged to a synagogue, Orthodox, Reform or Liberal, not in Berlin and not in London, that I had never been to a Rosh Hashanah or Yom Kippur service nor a wedding or a barmitzvah, and that I knew no Hebrew prayer. 'Why do you want to join now?' My reply was only a bit clearer than my reply to 'Why do you want to do dentistry?' but they agreed to make me a member. I never took it up and faded away. My application and interview had put everything into focus and I realised I did not belong. I was a Jew, but as for Judaism I did not believe a word of it – the theology, the values, the morality – all fundamental aspects of the whole organisation and all embedded in a cloying bourgeois matrix. I felt as much an outsider in that milieu as I did in every other, and very much out of tune. I drew comfort from the absence of discrimination, but that in the end was not enough.

Hugo was fine and so were one or two others. But I had nothing in common with most members of the club who lived far from bedsitters in Kilburn but were cossetted in those Bishops Avenue castles now taken over by Arabs. On summer Sundays they gave tennis parties on the courts in their back gardens. Lunches and tea parties and dances happened all year round. I could have revelled in all that were it not for the hosts and guests, who were mostly smug and narrow-minded.

By that time I had other friends whose main focus was neither ethnic nor religious. Through Daisy and through Hugo, I met Freddie Tuckmann, who was more interested in politics. But just before he introduced me to Bill, Daisy introduced me to the Neumanns.

The Neumanns and their cultural setting were very seductive. They gave me an insight into a more enlightened bourgeois life, and I suspect I developed a taste for it then and there. They were German Jews, middle-class and intellectual. The father was a doctor and related to Ernst Neumann who wrote about religion and psychology. They lived in a house in Finchley that was bigger and better than the average suburban villa. Their large rooms were lit by soft table lamps. No run-of-the-mill three-piece suite spoilt their living room, which was mellowed by large, comfortable armchairs. Best of all were the shelves of books that lined the walls right up to the ceiling – not just part of the way. Was this all I had ever really wanted without being aware of it? I never knew where they stood politically, but among their large collection of gramophone records they had *Die Dreigroschenoper* by Brecht and Weill.

People of taste, of quiet wealth, of liberalism as I thought, of intellectual and artistic pursuits, people who would be described as 'civilised'. There was nothing strident about them, nor were they anxious to please or offend their English hosts or anyone else. Their house was such a haven of peace for me; if only my home was like this. If only my parents behaved like cultivated German Jews. If only my father were a doctor.

One thing that drew me to the Neumanns was the younger son. The trouble was that the elder saw me first. Peter was a nice boy but he was not one to make my heart leap, unlike his brother Claus, a bright medical student who was sophisticated and charming. The attraction was mutual but their parents interfered and laid down the near-biblical edict that went something like: thou shalt not dally with the youngest son whilst the elder fancies you. The Neumanns' rigid and illiberal attitude tarnished my glowing view of them, and at the same time I felt uncomfortable in their disapproval. They had enthralled me, but so elegantly and correctly and without seeking to do so. Did they now see me as a scarlet woman out to seduce both their sons and cause strife? As a scarlet woman with red hair, with parents who were atheists and came from Poland, and a father who was a tailor?

In that I misjudged them, but the obvious consequence was that

I saw neither brother except at parties, and then, as my circle of friends changed, not at all. Some months after this drama of restraint in Finchley and Ealing, Claus invited me to lunch at Schmidt's of all places, where before the war Nazis in London used to sup on venison. Claus told me the good news that his parents had changed their mind. It was now all right for us to see each other. 'Claus, I'm going to marry Bill Rodgers.' He took it with a rueful smile.

# TWENTY-THREE

# Loot

Before I met Bill and while I was sorting out my predilections and preferences, my parents had separated, not just once but twice or even three times. The first time came to pass as my mother had planned: almost the very day I qualified and got myself a job as house surgeon at King's, my mother and my brother and I abandoned 21 Greystoke Lodge and my father. We 'did a bunk'. The moment he left for work, we began to pack. We treated him as if he were a wife-batterer, which is unfair, but to have said to him 'Goodbye, we're leaving you' would have caused an awful row and probably physical violence. I cannot see him letting us go with good grace, and the respectable tenants of Greystoke Lodge would have witnessed a sordid spectacle.

While my mother was clearing the cupboards of her belongings, she strayed into his part of the cupboard and came across a packet of condoms. She made me look at them – I had never seen a condom before – and told me what they were then and there. 'They weren't meant for him and me, we don't sleep together any more.' Her face and voice were ugly with rage and I thought, 'Don't tell me, I don't want to know.' But she raged on: 'Now he'll have to give me everything I ask for' (she meant maintenance) 'and I know who she is, too!' She was triumphant by now but I was shaken and wanted to cry. I suppose Oedipus or Electra must have come into this somewhere. And thinking back, I felt much younger than I was, a child of ten or twelve at most.

My mother, André and I moved into a dingy room with shared kitchen and bathroom in a run-down house in West London. The flat belonged to a Jewish refugee couple. The husband had come out of a concentration camp and was now selling second-hand furniture. A simian figure with sallow skin, dark hair on face and arms, flesh bulging over belt and collar, and friendly until he got too familiar and tried to touch me sexually. I have not often had to suffer this sort of intrusion but one incident I remember was years later at the Easter Banquet at the Mansion House when I sat next to an elderly Alderman of the City of London who squeezed my thigh during the first and second course. What a firm grip for such a doddery old gent! I had had to sit next to him the previous year too, when, having heard that I was born in Berlin, he told me: 'I knew Herr Hitler and I liked him'.

Living in the West London house was cramped and seedy but I wasn't there for long. I took the resident house job at King's, which meant living in. To be offered this job was a compliment, and like the blind fool I still was I thought my mother would be proud of me. To my horror, she was furious. How could I abandon her and André to live in these conditions? I was a deserter. I had betrayed her. They were living in misery, and I was preparing to live in style.

She was right. I had a whale of a time – even better and wilder than when I was a student – nor did I suffer much guilt, if any. I had begun to put myself first. I worked ridiculously long hours, which I enjoyed. I got on marvellously well with the resident doctors. Nearly all were men, and Peter, who was older than the rest, became my first lover. He had become a good friend first, and was there when I got a letter from my mother that shattered me.

The letter came from Paris, where she had gone with André to consult Mania, and Sonia who was coming over from Bogota. All three sisters were still nominal Marxists, but Sonia, though the youngest, had acquired considerable status with her sisters because of her wealth. It was she who convened the meeting and, having become thoroughly bourgeois, strongly disapproved of my mother leaving my father. Whatever the outcome, my mother wrote to tell me that everything was my fault. But everything. Her life with my father had been spoilt by me, she had had to leave him because of me, and now she had to go back to him because of me. 'I have no choice,' she said. I was selfish, wicked, a trouble-maker who had no thought for anyone else, who had left her to rot in a dump – and I don't remember what else. I know the letter was worse than anything I can remember and even make up. As I opened it and began to read and take it in, I felt I was being repeatedly stabbed with a long sword. The saint and goddess was demolished for ever.

I sobbed myself into numbness. Peter said the right things to save my reason and to comfort me.

Despite this trauma I continued to enjoy myself. I may have spared my mother a fleeting thought, but there and then I ceased to care about her welfare. An enormous amount of work and a lot of fun left me little time to think. I had the time of my life, and this continued until after Christmas when my term was over. There was nothing like spending Christmas and New Year in a hospital – the nearest one could get to a carnival in Britain at that time.

In January, I moved out of King's into a flat in Knightsbridge, but in the meantime I had arranged to go to medical school and do medicine. Then a message came from Paris saying that as my mother was still there, and André had to go back to school, would I please meet him at Victoria station and look after him. My mother was due back in a week and then André and she were moving back to Greystoke Lodge to resume life with my father. As André walked off the train, I asked him, 'Do you want to go back to Ealing or do you want to come and live with me?' It was a crazy and self-destructive gesture. I am now certain I made it to spite my mother. I regretted it the moment he accepted and have regretted it ever since. It scotched any plans of doing medicine as I now had to earn enough for two. I don't know what sort of doctor I would have made but medicine fascinates me, pathology in particular. Art, together with social anthropology and medicine, decorate the facets of my personal coin, though it has politics scrawled over it, too.

My mother didn't stay with my father for long. When she left, I was to blame for that too. I had enticed André – to do all my dirty chores such as cleaning my shoes – and without André they had no chance of living together in peace. As far as I know my father didn't give her a penny to live on, though her sister Sonia sent her money from Bogota. My mother looked for a job and got one in a school, as a dinner lady. This very continental and smart lady with her strong Polish accent and strong personality got on famously with the other dinner ladies. Even the cook allowed my mother to teach her how not to drown the cabbage in water.

I admired her for taking that job. She could of course have been indulging her working-class sympathies. With those remittances from Bogota she probably had no need to go out to work. She wooed André back to live with her, and I was upset but not really sorry. I was too busy with my own social and private life by then. My mother, though she had read Freud, made it quite clear that she preferred life with her son to life with her husband and would refer to André in the way other women refer to their husbands. Once André agreed to live with her she left my father for good, though they saw each other from time to time. Before that, she had gone back to him and left him at least twice more.

The relationship between her and me also had this back and forth pattern. I never prevented her from seeing my own children. But there were periods when my aversion to her was so powerful that I could not bear to see her myself. I could not understand this aversion. I kept thinking of all the daughters who don't get on with their mothers but nevertheless do their duty and don't sever contact. What I have never been able to face till now was that my own mother was worse than most and that her hostility and envy towards me were grotesque. I did not dare to recognise just how monstrously she behaved when she blamed me for everything that had happened to her — unhappy marriage, unhappy separation, unhappy reconciliation — and when she blackened my character to her sisters and close friends. It is only now that I can look at it and stop feeling guilty about not wanting to see her, and indeed not seeing her.

My aversion towards her was reinforced by an incident that followed the death of my father in 1969. Bill and I had been married for fourteen years by then and had three daughters. Rachel was born in 1957, Lucy in 1960 and Juliet in 1962. We did not see much of my father, though he had proved to be a good grandparent. He had retired, taken up sculpture and found that he had a natural talent for it. He was then in his sixties, and despite his earlier gastric ulcer, the healthiest man I have ever seen. He could run faster for a bus than many a young man, his teeth sparkled and he would have lived to a hundred. But on his way to his sculpture class in early December 1969, a car knocked him down and killed him on a zebra crossing.

I shut myself off from grief. I had to shut out the guilt, too, because a day or so before he died – wasn't it the very day he died? – he had telephoned me. He wanted to see me, he begged to see me, but I refused. It was a time when I could not bear the sight of either him or my mother.

André came to tell me. 'Father is dead.' I shed no tear, I showed no sorrow. I was in slight shock but I did not reveal it. That evening I began to notice an aching hollow just inside my breastbone. The next morning my mother rang to talk about my father's funeral. She was in her one and only moment of remission from atheism and sounded ludicrously sentimental: 'I like to think of him walking in the gardens among the flowers and shrubs, and the birds singing in the trees.' So instead of having him cremated, she was going ahead with the Jewish burial. This was before she learnt that my father had left the bulk of his money to André and not one single penny to her. He had telephoned me some months earlier and asked me to meet him and André to discuss his will, but I had refused. 'A pity,' my mother said later. 'You could have stood up for me!' Something else that was my fault. As his wife, she was due some portion of the estate. But my mother, who was besotted with André, did not contest the will, and he gave her a modest allowance – though not before a scene that should have cured me for ever of any guilt I might have felt towards my mother.

There is a scene in *Zorba the Greek* where the old lady is dying, and even before she is dead the villagers swarm all over her house and loot it. They empty drawers, ransack cupboards, tear curtains from the windows, stuff silver into sacks, pull carpets from the floors. A dreadful scene, and one I witnessed in Ealing. One morning a few days after my father's death, André arrived in Kentish Town where we were living, and grudgingly told me that my father had left me half the contents of the flat. He was on his way there now and if I wanted to come along, I could. I slipped on a coat and found my mother sitting in the car; she was coming too, though nothing in the flat had been left to her. She cursed my father all the way to Ealing. André and I said nothing as she went on and on, filling the car with venom.

We parked in the forecourt of Greystoke Lodge. My mother got out of the car, dragging two enormous empty bags with her. André had some bags too, but I had thought we had only come to look, not to take. Once inside the flat, my mother began to ransack it. She wrenched open the door of a cupboard in the hall: 'Look at all those shoes he bought for himself!' she sneered. She wanted André to take them but they were too small for him. She rushed into the bathroom, grabbed the shaving kit that was made of leather and silver and came from Berlin, and stuffed it into André's bag. Next she tore into the bedroom and decided that the dressing gown, shirts and socks were also too small for André. She carried out sheets and blankets and then went to work on the marital bed, the one with the *Besuchsritze*, my place on Sunday mornings in Berlin. She pulled off the covers and dragged off the part of the mattress that was on her side of the bed. 'I'm taking this back!' and she did. The bed was left lopsided and dishevelled. Her next symbolic act was to open another cupboard in the hall and tear down the paper patterns hanging there. They had been my father's work. She mocked them, she tore then, she tramped on them. As if they were some hated effigy.

She had already packed the silver – cutlery and other objects – into the bags. 'For André,' she explained. My father had left the silver to him and the carpets to me. The dinner set that had silver rims she acquired on the same basis. She was about to requisition the Rosenthal tea set but I insisted on having that for myself. It had no metallic traces on it; she was furious but helpless.

On the small chest in the bedroom stood an empty frame. When I had last seen it, it framed the photograph of my father and me in Berlin, the one where he looks down on me with fond amusement as I scream and scream. It wasn't difficult to guess who had torn the photograph out of its frame. My brother had been in the flat the day before and on his own.

Having caused havoc in the flat, my mother and brother left, dragging their bulging bags behind them. I could not bear to go with them. My mother had behaved like a monster. I also felt qualms about leaving the flat so vandalised. The state of our family had been laid bare and I did not want the world – the solicitor and the removal men – to see it. I felt as wounded as did the innocent flat, and telephoned Bill. Between us we got some order back into the flat. Though nothing could disguise the curious asymmetry of the double bed.

I have no contact with my brother. But in 1993 his daughter Judith visited us. She has come to mean a great deal to me, and not because her hair is deep auburn.

# TWENTY-FOUR

# New Party, Old Love Affair

As for meeting Bill, we met in 1954, one Sunday evening at Freddie Tuckman's. Freddie later became a Conservative MEP but at this time was still a Fabian Socialist. According to the law of love at first sight, we should have met earlier at a Fabian Weekend School near Brighton. It was my first Fabian School but the umpteenth for Bill, who was the Society's General Secretary. Our eyes did not meet across any of the crowded rooms, I did not notice him, he did not notice me. All I remember from that weekend were walks along the Downs and coming in late to the Saturday morning session while Hugh Gaitskell, former Chancellor of the Exchequer, was speaking. He was someone else I did not meet till later.

I had gone to the weekend with a group of former LSE students, all friends of Freddie's. The group was an ethnic mixture of non-religious Christians and Jews and a Hindu called Gandhi. One Sunday, Freddie invited a group of friends to after-dinner tea and cake. I had been invited and so had Bill. Bill very nearly did not come but he had turned down Freddie's invitation twice before and thought he had better turn up. He was very late but in time for a piece of cake made by Freddie's formidable mother, who reigned supreme in her son's life. Freddie boasted that she could diagnose character from handwriting and I was careful she never saw mine. On Sunday evenings her powers were restricted to providing tea and cake, but we were all inspired to play a game of guessing which handwriting belonged to whom. Bill identified my large scrawl, called it dynamic, and I was flattered.

When Bill and I and our three daughters spent a holiday up in the mountains near Lake Garda in 1975, we discovered a tiny lake, a melt water, cold and clear and surrounded by mountain peaks, fine green grass and graceful trees. An idyll which would have inspired Heine, except for one afternoon when a tango cut across the stillness from the only house by the lakeside. Canned music in surroundings like this would normally drive me to frenzy, but the house was a children's home. So instead of tearing my hair out, I sang as much of 'It was all over my jealousy' as I could remember and danced an exaggerated tango with Bill. The girls were amused and enchanted and in the evening asked us how we had met and come to marry.

We told them a Mills and Boon version, thoroughly bowdlerised. It began with how Bill very nearly did not come to Freddie's tea and cake evening and how, when he did, he took a fancy to my handwriting and the way I looked in my new black coat and how I was bowled over by his marvellous eyes. They were the eyes of a poet rather than a politician. We met the following Friday and went to a Chinese restaurant and then a film. It took nearly a year for Bill, less for me, to decide to get married.

We probably didn't tell them about a party that Bill gave and where I first met Shirley Catlin (Williams) and Val Mitchison (Arnold Foster) and how Shirley's very obvious charm had put me off and Val's straightforward and almost rude approach had won me over; I felt more at home with it. I doubt that I told them how Freddie had warned me, when I went to another Fabian weekend shortly after Bill and I had met, that I would be lucky to get a look in. 'There'll be a lot of girls there after Bill!'

It was at the Fabian schools that I first came across all those Social Democrats I had been brought up to despise. But I was very taken with them. They were, especially the men and most were men, people of power and *sympathisch* with it. Freddie told me exactly where each stood in the spectrum of Socialism. When I had been impressed by one of Tony Crosland's lectures, Freddie soon put me right. Crosland is much too right-wing for your tastes, he insisted. He even advocates a reduction in the coal allowances for the old. Freddie had resisted telling me Bill's location in the geometry of Left and Right, but I soon realised that Bill did not worship my red flag. Was it 'despite' this that I fell in love with him, or did it help?

My parents approved of Bill but I didn't see much of either of them; they were separated at the time. My mother admired Bill, even though he was not left-wing; my father was civil to him, even though he was not Jewish. As for what Bill's parents thought of me, when Bill first told them about me and that I was Jewish, they asked whether I had a long nose, and when we met I got on extremely well with them, especially with Bill's father.

To be married to Bill, to have three wonderful daughters – I still cannot believe that such happiness can be mine. For years I used to have the same dream in which Bill and I had come adrift. I always woke up with relief to find him sleeping right next to me. I don't think it's surprising that I wanted to marry Bill. As well as my being attracted and excited by him, he must have suited the part of me that desperately needed to belong but could not bear to be too conventional. Bill was not upper-class, did not wear a public school tie, but he was not an outsider and well on his way to joining the establishment – on its left side. His political allegiance was on the left wing but on the right tip, and therefore moderate. It took me some time to realise that, in some ways, I needed to be moderate. It was the antithesis of my mother.

My immoderate mother was present in my life most of the time till she died in 1979, but not always, because of the many times when I could not bear to see her. On top of my aversion to her, a new problem had arisen. When I was a child, it was her indifference that so hurt me; now it was the uncontrollable envy. When Juliet, our third child, was born and she saw her for the first time, she said, 'Doesn't she have a long nose', and she averted her eyes from the two-day-old baby and murmured something about her own father's long nose. In fact both her father and Juliet have small neat noses. But as Juliet does not have red hair, my mother had to find something else to criticise or invent. This hostility lasted just over a year, and she ignored Juliet's first birthday.

I am sure this had nothing to do with Juliet, but with her envy of me. She herself had given birth to only two children, so I was one up on her. This rivalry sounds absurd, as my mother was hardly the conventional little woman. But what else could it be? And how she envied my closeness to politics. The moment when, early in 1962, the Stockton Labour Party chose Bill as their candidate for the forthcoming by-election, and he rang to tell me, 'It's me! I've got it!' I felt dizzy. Bill would be an MP. I would be the wife of an

MP. I rang my mother; we were in a peaceful patch at the time. 'Ah,' she said, 'that's good.' A pause. 'But he's got to be elected first, hasn't he!' I could imagine what her face looked like: lips pursed and down turned simultaneously, and very cold eyes. My aunt Sonia wrote from Bogota, 'Of course, being a Member of Parliament was always your mother's ambition.'

My mother had, around this time, struck up a friendship with someone who had been a friend of mine, who was my age and pathologically envious of me. The envy was based on the positions of our husbands: mine was rising in the world, hers was moribund. My mother and my ex-friend spent many a malicious hour sipping tea and pulling me to pieces. Before the election, both warned me as often as possible that 'he may not win, you know!' It sounded like wishful thinking.

When Bill was halfway through the election – and it was a particularly tense one, being in the middle of a Liberal revival – my mother, out of the blue, insisted that we pay her back within three days the £300 she had lent us indefinitely. I was able to borrow the money from John Diamond (then a Labour MP, now a Labour peer) always a good friend, and kept my mother's attempt at sabotage from Bill until he had won.

She took pride in Bill as Member of Parliament and as Minister; it was my role she envied. As a feminist she ought to have known better. A political wife is only an appendage. But I think she must have envied me as much for having a good husband as having a political one.

My mother could hardly be described as a good mother, but she became a very good grandmother. She even went so far as to bake cakes for our daughters – marble cakes in the shape of those beautifully moulded rings of *Napfkuchen*. And while she tried to sabotage me during the by-election in Stockton-on-Tees, she occasionally helped our au pair to look after the children. They were, after all, not only my children but also Bill's.

Since I am more of a rebel than a conformist, as well as still being my mother's daughter, my long membership of the Labour Party remains a puzzle. When I joined, the ethos of the Labour Party was well suited to my oscillations between rebellion and conformity. The extreme Left had not yet forced its own tight corset of political correctness on to the Party. Yet I am sure that, had I not married Bill, I would never have joined. Had I not married Bill, I am pretty sure I would have stayed very left-wing, emotionally at any rate.

Bill and I began married life in a modest flat in St John's Wood owned by the Co-op. The driving force of the local Labour party was Kate, the Countess of Lucan. She organised everything from elections to jumble sales. But I remember Kate for other things, for her untidy flat, for the clothes she wore and also, poor Kate, for introducing me to her son, who later became so infamous, while we were standing in the large, messy, dark kitchen in her large flat in Hanover Gate. That flat was the untidiest and dustiest I have ever seen, next to mine, and has endeared Kate to me for ever. Unlike me and other ordinary mortals, she never apologised for the mess. Often when I am on the verge of apologising for the muddle in our house, I stop and think of Kate Lucan. But when it comes to clothes, I can never achieve her confidence. She always wore the same pre-war tweed suit, its skirt dropping at the hem, the jacket coming apart at the shoulder seams. Always and in all weathers the same dried-up old sandals showed up large holes in the heels of her stockings and over her bunions. Her brown functional handbag of ancient leather was crinkled but of far too good a quality ever to crack. It was augmented by a large paper or string shopping bag.

Kate must have started as an Angela Brazil schoolgirl. Her diction was pure Lady Windermere, but the content of her conversation was well to the left of Labour. When I asked Kate to enrol me as a member, she said she quite understood why it had taken me some time to join: 'The party is not really left-wing enough, is it?' My mother met Kate once and the expression on her face showed that she was impressed, overwhelmed even, and uneasy at being so. The lifelong Marxist and egalitarian was not immune to a title. Of course, it wasn't any old title. They were the Lucans of the Charge of the unfortunate Light Brigade, though I don't think my mother was aware of that.

I have a lot of time for the paradoxes of Kate Lucan and her husband Pat, with their noble accents well-matched by their noble intentions. They are welcome incongruities of the People's Party, unlike one or two of the very wealthy Life Peers who lead ostentatious lives, have no holes in their socks, no mess in their flats, and not too many fine intentions.

St John's Wood and Marylebone Labour Party, together with the Fabian Society, was my lesson in local as well as national politics in this country. My first ward meeting was wholly taken up with plans for a forthcoming bazaar. It began with Kate pleading for no more jars of cold cream; she still had a cupboard full from the previous bazaar. One of the other women indignantly defended the jars: the old lady who prepares them was confined to her wheelchair; she who would feel her life was useless if her jars of cream were no longer wanted. We all imagined her suicide and Kate said, 'Of course, we must have lots more cold cream.' We went from cold cream to cream cakes, to jars of jam, to the white elephant stall, to the cake whose weight had to be guessed. Not a word of politics. Could these wards really be the equivalents of the Party cells in Berlin?

But things changed. A strong Campaign for Nuclear Disarmament faction in the local party, led by the Lucans and aided by Ian Mikardo, the left-wing MP for Poplar, wanted to send to conference a resolution in support of that cause. CND was at its height and CND women would start their speeches with 'Speaking as a wife and mother'. I was several months pregnant at the time, and so was my friend and neighbour, Linda. A few days before the critical meeting, I signed her up as a Party member, and then took her with me to the meeting. The Right had begun to copy the tactics of the Left. Linda and I waddled in, sat in prominent places, and eventually I stood up and spoke very briefly against unilateralism. I left the obvious 'Speaking as wife and mother' unsaid; at least I hope I did. I don't think I persuaded anyone, but the resolution was defeated by two votes. Our presence, if not our pregnancies and persuasiveness, had been crucial.

Later in St Pancras, when the extreme Left was on the rise, there was still more politics and very little cold cream. But I only ever attended a couple of ward meetings there in all those years. One was in 1974, when we had got wind that the matter of the

Claycross Councillors was going to be sprung on the meeting, and as the ward was dominated by the Left, I turned up. The martyrdom of the councillors, who had defied the law by refusing to put up rents, was proclaimed with great force and emotion and the ward was called on to pass the resolution in support of the Four, unanimously and without a vote. So I popped up and said: 'I'm very sorry, but I don't really know enough about the circumstances, and I don't see how I could give my support till I do.' This scotched their intended coup of a unanimous voice. One of them said that I was 'politically naive.'

My mother would have been proud of my tactics while disapproving of my politics. Otherwise, these episodes belong less to my life as my mother's daughter than to my life as Bill's wife. In a later episode, when Bill had been a Member of Parliament for four years and was in his second Ministerial job, the two lives got uncomfortably mixed up.

Bill's first Ministerial job was in the Department of Economic Affairs. When he was moved sidewways to the Foreign Office, we were disappointed. It was not really promotion, nor did it bring the rise in salary so badly needed, though it lent some status and some glamour and for me it brought tremendous relief. I had always feared that Bill would never be given a job that carried with it state secrecy implications because of my mother and her Communist connections. Economic Affairs, yes, but Foreign Office or Defence? After the 1966 election and the subsequent reshuffle, when George Brown was made Foreign Secretary and Bill was moved neither up or out of the DEA, my diary reminds me that: 'I suppose I always will have the nagging suspicion that Bill could not be acceptable at the F.O. because of his foreign wife and her Communist background.' Bill thought this was ridiculous and that no one could possible take it seriously. 'You're being very silly,' he insisted and meant it as words of comfort.

When in January 1967 he was transferred sideways to the Foreign Office from Economic Affairs, he was proved right. Some years later, however, Anthony Howard, who had been Washington correspondent of the *Observer* at the time, told me that when the news of Bill's move to the F.O. had come through in Washington, he and some others were surprised because of the very circumstances – with his wife's background – that have always worried me.

The irony of my background and the Foreign Office was compounded some months later when early in 1967 my mother came to lunch. I should have invited her for Christmas, but it would have brought her too much into the bosom of my family and I couldn't face that. It was as much as I could bear to invite her some days later, and even then I inadvertently bought one chop too little. When I opened the door to her, she asked 'Are you cooking fish?' 'No.' 'Smells like fish,' and she wrinkled her nose in distaste. Otherwise she was in superb form and glowed like a young woman in love and ecstasy over her lover. This lover was the Soviet Union.

Her daily and only newspaper was the *Daily Telegraph* but that was quite misleading. Her faith in Communism and Marxism had never been shaken despite the occasional doubt over the Soviet Union – and she had, after all, been excommunicated from the Party. But now, and I have no idea how it occurred, the period of estrangement was over, she had regained her faith in the Soviet Union and they in her. A reunion of old lovers. She was a frequent guest at the Soviet Embassy, who knew exactly whose mother-in-law she was. At a recent party they had shown her a letter from Bill's private office declining an invitation because he had a previous engagement. 'That's a convenient excuse,' she had thought, but was later 'reassured' because when she got home, there he was on her television screen.

With Khruschev gone and Brezhnev and Kosygin in charge, everything in the USSR was paradise again and, like a young girl who can't stop talking about the man she has a crush on, she couldn't keep off the subject. My mother, always lively except when she was sulking, was so intoxicated by her regained love and faith that she exploded, sparkled and bubbled over. Her voice was a whole crescendo louder even than usual, her neck was suffused with red, her eyes commanded, her hands and fingers underlined each point, not with the graceful movements of a Continental lady, but with the firm gestures of a politician well used to speaking in public. It was the old fervour that roused them in Berlin in the 1920s and 1930s. She had been given back her reason for being.

She insisted – not that we had asked her – that she was still not a member of the Communist Party. How then had she come to be invited to the Embassy? 'I belong to . . .' – and she could not get right the initials of whatever organisation it was, and which propagated Anglo-Soviet cultural relations and perhaps Marxism, too. She mentioned a building somewhere near Tottenham Court Road, with a library of 10,000 books – on culture, on Marxism? – and where they frequently held meetings. Some meetings were so large, they had to hire a hall. She was delighted with the enormous volume of cultural exchange. As one of their translators and interpreters, she was kept very busy. They payed her, but uneasily I wondered why? There must have been heaps of people with a truer command of English. She enthused about the Russians she had met and with whom she had exchanged gifts and addresses. All the time she spoke, and she spoke all through lunch and afterwards, her accent was noticeably more Russian than her more usual Polish. But as she recounted a particular meeting with two Soviet women, she lapsed into German. What struck me then was that the three women apparently addressed each other in the familiar second person singular reserved for family, close friends – and Party comrades. She kept stressing, rather defensively, that she was not a Party member. But I was alarmed by her involvement at a time when Bill was a Minister at the Foreign Office.

I wonder if at this time, when my mother and the Soviet Union got back together again, a former friend of my mother had also relented. This friend was an active and respected member of the Co-operative movement. Her devoted following believed her to be wholly committed to the movement but she was in fact a card-carrying, ardent member of the Communist Party. The friendship had been important to my mother, whose contact with other Communists was all too rare. But when her friend heard that I had married Bill Rodgers, she ended all contact with my poor mother. 'I cannot trust you any more!' she told her.

# TWENTY-FIVE

# Nothing After Death

My mother died on 24 November 1979 of cancer of the stomach. I am still surprised at the exemplary daughter I became from the moment I knew she was terminally ill. I took her to her hospital appointments, I visited her daily, I provided her with food and meals. I saw her more in two weeks than I had done in twenty years, not I think out of guilt, but perhaps out of some long-suppressed love or need. I certainly did my duty, which she took for granted, and for once it came easy to me. I no longer had to fight my aversion to her, probably because I knew the relationship was coming to an end, but also because she had sloughed off those parts of her persona that I found so intolerable. She seemed a different person, and almost without realising it I stopped being wary of her.

She was still decisive but she no longer had to be right about everything. She conversed without making speeches. She was still in control but only over her own affairs, no one else's. The command she kept over her papers and accounts, how she ordained who was to be told of her imminent death and who was to be informed afterwards, was impressive. She was relaxed and calm and knew exactly how to phase the progress of her illness. She ordered a day nurse three weeks before her death, and added a night nurse for the last week. It was as if she were in touch with whoever was in charge of her fate, which in her case couldn't have been God.

Sonia's daily phone calls from Bogota – Sonia treats transatlantic calls as if they are local calls – pleased but irritated my mother because Sonia would pretend that she was going to recover. 'She keeps on about going on holiday together next year!' she would tell me with an ironic glance.

My mother faced death with equanimity, and with no more emotion and far less fuss than if she were going on a trip round the world. Talking about her past life was what gave her most pleasure. We took her a cassette recorder, but she found it difficult to use on her own and preferred to talk to her grandchildren or Bill with the machine recording in the background. These conversations reminded her what a full life she had had, and were an insurance of her immortality, which mattered despite her atheism.

I was careful never to be present when she talked about the past and I never asked her a single question about past events, past hurts, past misunderstandings. I regret it now, but at the time the only mother I could bear to be with was the mother who was dying with her old persona already buried. A few days before she died, when she was hovering on the edge, she told me with utter certainty that 'there is nothing after death. Nothing.' I felt devastated and immensely sad. I still cannot understand why, especially as any definite idea of an after-life terrifies me.

I saw her for the last time on 23 November. She was no longer conscious, but as I looked at her a slight spasm of exasperation crossed her face. 'She had just passed water,' the nurse explained. My mother had been aware enough to wince at that last loss of control and dignity. I went home but couldn't sleep and telephoned in the very early hours of the morning. 'She went twenty minutes ago,' the nurse said. I drove to Willesden, looked at her, went to the appropriate office, signed the appropriate forms, rang Mania in Paris. I was in a cold state and everything felt unreal. This peculiar concussion continued the next day when Bill and I went to my mother's solicitor, who told me that my friend Rabbi Gryn was going to conduct the funeral. I said, 'I don't know any rabbi', and then I realised who it was.

I did not weep one tear until the funeral. There, in that tiny chapel in the Jewish cemetry in Golders Green, which looks more like a British Rail waiting room in a little used country station, Rachel, Lucy, Juliet and I wept uncontrollably. But Mania's weeping was the most passionate and heart-rendering. It was as if she hadn't wept in years and was now weeping for all the people she had loved and lost and all the horrors they had suffered and all that might have been. Hugo tried to comfort her. Then my mother's coffin was wheeled to the grave on that traditional meek wooden bier that stems from Roman times. A Jew's death, when it isn't horrific, is humble, unlike a Christian's.

I almost came to regret that the funeral service and the little wooden cart were the only traditions left over from my mother's *shtetl* past. As I found myself sitting day after day on a cushion on the floor of our living room and mourning the mother I had and the mother I never had and now never would have, I understood the comforts of the *shiva* when the bereaved stay at home for seven days and are visited by friends and relatives. I was sitting there, but without the visitors who would have come with gifts of food and talked about the dead.

My cousin Lucien is a psychoanalyst of an unconvential sort. He told me about one patient who, after several sessions that had focused mainly on his long dead father, went with Lucien to the cemetery where the man's father lay buried. 'You are dead, you are dead, you are dead,' incanted the son to the tomb. 'And he is now free of his father,' claimed Lucien. I have never said this to the tomb of my mother, in which she lies next to my father. It would take more than this to free me of her.

My mother died after she had proved such a good grandmother to our three daughters, after some years of supplementing her income by taking in lodgers – blacks only on principle – after my brother had gone with his family to South Africa to be a radiologist at the Groote Schnur hospital, after Charles had died in New York, still not on speaking terms with her. She died years after I had dropped dentistry and taken up art, and after I had decided to take two years off from art and my studio to read Social Anthropology at the LSE. When I extended the two years and started a doctoral thesis at Oxford, she was dying.

She died during Callaghan's government, while Bill was in the Cabinet and after she had conceded to him that there may be circumstances when it would be all right to be a Social Democrat. Not that she ever became one. She remained a Marxist fundamentalist and even critised the Jews who tried to leave the Soviet Union.

She was still alive when I went back to Berlin for the first time, taking the comforters and shock absorbers of Bill's life with me. My mother offered me no addresses of old comrades to look up but told me she had asked Jack Mendelson whether he had met any on his visits to Berlin. 'I couldn't make out whether he had or whether he hadn't. He behaved very strangely and didn't want to talk about it.' She was vexed and hurt that, like her friend from the Co-operative movement, he no longer trusted her. She herself never set foot in either Poland or Germany again. But before she died, she visited the land of her dreams, the Soviet Union. I can't recall that she talked much about it.

She died before Mrs Thatcher took office. I cannot imagine what she would have thought of her. They were opposites in politics but so close in character – blinkered, confident, domineering, compelling, captivating. When one described herself as resolute and the other as absolute, the epithets were interchangeable. I'm told that my attitude is a psychological commonplace: if you don't see Mrs Thatcher as your nanny, you see her as your mother.

She died while the Labour Party was turning sharp Left and fists were raised and intimidation ripe at meetings and Party conferences – as they had been in Weimar Berlin. We avoided asking her what she thought of it all. She died well before I left the Labour Party and so I couldn't tell her that it felt like leaving Germany, Berlin – the place where I had felt at home – all over again. And what a pity she was not there to watch the foundation of the SDP, the Social Democratic Party, founded by the 'Gang of Four' of which Bill was one. I would have enjoyed fighting with her over that. I feel cheated. Though who knows? It is just conceivable that she might have applauded the new Party, even if only for its courage.

She died before I got my doctorate and began teaching on United States military bases for the University of Maryland, before I promoted my left-wing views of social issues and before I tasted that exhilaration of 'enlightening' an audience on which my mother had flourished in Berlin. My daughters and their friends may well have been camping outside Greenham Common while I crossed their picket lines, and taught, among other topics, the rudiments of Marx and Engels. When I talked about Opium of the People, alienation at work and exploitation, my squaddie students nodded. But they knew better when I came to Marx's view of the unimportance of ethnic boundaries. Many of them were black or Hispanic.

My mother died before the Berlin Wall and the Communist regimes in Eastern Europe, including the Soviet Union, came tumbling down. And thank God she did. I was glad that she wasn't there to see how bad things had been and were; how poisoned the land and water; how wretched the people; how betrayed; how corrupt Hoeneker, among others. I am glad she wasn't there to see the defacing and demolishing of Lenin's monuments. Her life's work wasted? So much risked and sacrificed for an illusion, a long lie? My poor mother, and I wept for her. It also occurred to me that my life might have been easier had she not followed this creed. But she would always have needed the tight frame of a dogma into which to fit her life and, with it, mine. Nevertheless, when I went out in the evenings, I pinned a badge of Lenin to my velvet or silk lapels. She had brought the badge back from Moscow and I wore it as a sign of pity for and empathy with my mother, if not solidarity. It seemed to take the place of the black armband no longer worn by relatives of a deceased. Was I marking the ideological death of Lenin as well as that of my mother? Was it in memoriam of my childhood? I admit I enjoyed the surprise and comments the badge evoked.

# TWENTY-SIX

# Still on Edge

Do other immigrants, refugees, exiles, ex-patriots find their every moment so criss-crossed with their otherness? After all, most people are marginal at some time or other. And every woman is born a marginal – though some may not see it that way – and every Jew certainly is. So why do I make such a meal of it, a meal that I often rather enjoy?

Perhaps my problem is that my otherness is free-floating. It has no one root but an anchor that can be put down anywhere and as easily dislodged. I am not clearly a Jew, a German, a Berliner, a Pole, or British. The only sharp identity I was born to – that of a Communist – has been transformed. Perhaps a social identity is particularly important for me because my private identity is somewhat flimsy and needs a protective shield. Of course, I blame my mother for this flimsiness; I was never anywhere near the centre of her world, but kept well on the periphery. By marrying Bill I missed out on not only becoming a card-carrying Communist and fist-waving revolutionary, but on consolidating one of my free-floating identities – that of a Jew. Had I married a Jew, I might have become a Jewish wife. I might have lit candles and cooked fish every Friday night, gone to synagogue if not every week then twice a year, arranged a *seder* every Passover. But is that realistic? Could I have done it? When during the Six Day War, or the Yom Kippur War, I was moved to go to synagogue, I felt out of place even though it was a very untraditional synagogue in a Victorian house in Knightsbridge. When I opted to fast on one Yom Kippur when Israel was again in danger, I discovered I had fasted on the wrong day. When I went to a Friday evening service in Hugo Gryn's progressive synagogue, I sat there thinking 'what am I doing here?' and I shrunk as I felt all eyes on me as people recognised me as an impostor.

My Jewishness is purely secular, kept going out of loyalty and affection to my dead relatives and my teacher Tante Freundlich, and fuelled by anti-Semitism. In that wise folktale, where the sun and the wind vie with each other to remove the coat of the young man as he goes walking, it is the sun that makes him remove his coat. The wind, the harder it blows, makes him draw it all the tighter round him. If the wind is anti-Semitism, that coat is my Jewishness, though it is not so easy to cast off.

As for my national identity, marrying Bill gave me yet more right to a British passport – I already had one because my father had been naturalised after the war. That passport, until Prince Philip married Princess Elizabeth, qualified my Britishness with the words 'British by naturalisation'. I like having a British passport, qualified or not, and like a child with its first watch often hold it so that other people queuing at passport controls can see it. But I always remember the 'British by naturalisation' and never feel completely sure of it. In my more irrational moments, I fear they could take it away from me and then, like my father, I will be stateless.

Nor do I have any other firm national identity. I am not German. I am not Polish. For Germans, blood and semen are thicker than earth, territory and culture, and as I was not conceived by German parents I was not given citizenship despite being born on German soil. On top of that, the Germans saw me unequivocally as a Jew and a Pole, an *Untermensch* twice over, and so they threw me out. My own feelings towards Germany, Germans and the German language further muddle things up. They were clear when I married – I hated them and my children missed out because I would not teach them German. But my hostility is eroded, though my feelings are still in flux. My confusion – love, nostalgia, pain, resentment and fury – takes me by the throat whenever I am in Berlin. When the Wall collapsed I was in pain and turmoil. I could cope with Berlin and Germany divided, that is, when they were not in the shape and state they were in my childhood. I wonder if I felt it served them right? Now it is whole and I am once more plagued with a sense of longing, loss, missing out, having been pushed out. Plus the recognition that I may be a Berliner but I have nothing and no one there. When I explained to my German friend Liesl, who has lived in Britain for over thirty years, why I would not go to Berlin with her to celebrate unification, she said: 'But you're not German anyway.' I hated her.

Some years ago, when a German woman old enough to have been a Nazi asked me what language comes to my mind when I am alarmed, I lied and said 'English'. I still say *'Gottes Willen'* when I am alarmed, but other words are slipping away and I now cling in some panic to what I remember of my first language. I attend the Goethe Institute and I am retrieving more and more. When I speak German I feel and behave, not completely different, but more lively and with a different and deeper understanding. One of the teachers did not recognise that German was my mother tongue, and it made me immensely sad. As if, for the first time, I had experienced the extent of my loss.

But I still have an allergy to some aspects of Germanness and it extends to German Jews. This allergy surprised me at an unexpected time and place. When in 1963, Bill as a Member of Parliament was invited to Israel by the Israeli government, they changed his first-class ticket for two in tourist class and welcomed us both. I visited Tante Freundlich in Jerusalem in a house in Abba Hilka Street that had belonged to an Arab family who had fled in 1948. I hadn't seen her since I was seven. We sat in her dark living room and she opened a well-thumbed file. She took out a letter of love and pain signed by all the pupils she had abandoned when she left for Israel, as well as individual drawings and letters from each of us. Mine was a picture I have always remembered drawing: deer in a snow landscape and not my best. The bulk of the pictures, letters and signatures were from girls long since dead.

Tante Freundlich looked the same and was every bit as warm and wonderful as I had remembered. Yet when Bill went back to London and she invited me to stay, I could not bear to accept for more than one night. What put me off was the Germanic claustrophobia of her home and the stereotypical Germanness of her husband. He was a very nice man but his pedantic voice, pronounce-ments and advice depressed me.

As for being Polish – I am not. I wasn't born there; I don't speak the language and in any case we all know that a Polish Jew is not the same as a Pole. But what about my relatives? And I certainly feel torn to emotional pieces at the very thought of Poland.

If marrying Bill did not fix my nationality, it fixed my allegiance to a political party. I felt at home in the Labour Party, and later, when I had to leave, it was like leaving Germany all over again. What had been home had become hostile and totalitarian. I wept, which I did not do when I left Germany.

As for my being a feminist, Bill, when he married me, thought he was marrying an independent woman. I am in fact a failed feminist. But the flaws in my feminism as laid down by my mother were not revealed till later when I was more interested in Bill's career and seduced by being on familiar terms with other politicians. This wasn't a complete waste of time because it was fascinating but it was foolish. I should of course have concentrated on sticking to a career, one career – and I don't mean dentistry. But I have chopped and changed: art, archaeology, anthropology. The moment I think I am succeeding – the moment I am in danger of belonging – I change.

In all this, is there not a symbolic parallel with my feelings about my home and my mother? Do I feel I never belonged to my mother? My marked ambivalence towards her, and hers towards me, were revealed after my marriage and after I had children. My dependence on her, my fury at this dependence, my wish to be loved by her, my hatred of her and her unmotherly feelings towards me – all those were laid bare. How she envied me my good marriage, and my political involvement.

The trouble is that this involvement is principally through marriage. It is not that I don't enjoy talking politics to politicians and others; I come to life when I do, and the nearer it gets to plotting the better. And I am pleased by my minuscule role in the State Opening of Parliament, and my major role in the launch of a Royal Navy ship, and I do appreciate the surrealism of these grand events. But I wish I could allow myself unadulterated joy. Why can't I just get a kick out of saying to myself that this little refugee girl, daughter of a Polish Jewish tailor, is now sitting among Cabinet Ministers, Peers of the Realm, Admirals of the Fleet, having dinner at Number 10, but it seems I can't and not only because I am not sufficiently impressed.

Why am I compelled to make it quite clear that I do not belong? After a NATO dinner at Greenwich, I was standing next to the head of the Dutch Armed Services as the band of the Royal Marines prepared to 'Beat the Retreat', that mysterious ritual. I had told him how I came to be in England and he was intrigued and sympathetic. They started to Beat the Retreat, we were both very moved and he said: 'You and I have a lot to thank the British for.'

While we waited for the Queen to open Parliament, I told the Peer's wife next to me about my origins – I went right back to Lubartov this time – possibly because she herself was Belgian and anti-German. But she seemed alarmed, even though I had said nothing about my Red Flag waving mother.

Possibly, the view from the centre makes the margins stand out more. At a very Establishment dinner – it was to celebrate Roy Jenkins' Order of Merit – Keith Thomas, President of Corpus Christi College, teased me for describing myself as 'marginal'. 'Look around you,' he advised, 'you're part of the Establishment.' But the Viscountess Runciman, who as Ruth Ellman had Jewish parents and was born in South Africa, completely agreed with me. The nearer she got to the centre, the more marginal she felt.

'What am I doing here?' is what I ask myself at the State Opening, in a synagogue, and at a Party conference. Sartre warned that 'if you go into exile, you lose your place in the world'. Is that how it is with me? Or is it that I have too many other possible places and too many possible careers and never really opt for just one?

But one point of the anchor has almost metamorphosed into a root which ties me to this country, a metamorphosis purely due to Bill and our children. Rather like Ruth in the Bible: where they are, there is my place. And yet, when Bill and I sit on a hillside in Berkshire on a summer afternoon and are enraptured by the panorama unrolled before us, I envy him that he can think what I can't think: 'this is my land.'